Infertility and Patriarchy

Infertility and Patriarchy

The Cultural Politics of Gender
and Family Life in Egypt

Marcia C. Inhorn

University of Pennsylvania Press

Philadelphia

Library of Congress Cataloging-in-Publication Data
Inhorn, Marcia Claire, 1957–
    Infertility and patriarchy : the cultural politics of gender and family life in Egypt /
by Marcia C. Inhorn.
        p.   cm.
    Includes bibliographical references and index.
ISBN 0-8122-3235-6 (alk. paper). — ISBN 0-8122-1424-2 (alk. paper)
    1. Fertility, Human—Social aspects—Egypt.   2. Childlessness—Social aspects—Egypt.
3. Patriarchy—Egypt.   4. Sex role—Egypt.   5. Women—Egypt—History.   I. Title.
HB1071.7.A3155   1996
304.6'32'0962—dc20   95-31951
                                                                                         CIP

For Kirk and Carl, my *usra*

Contents

Acknowledgments

I am extremely grateful to all of those who have contributed in both direct and indirect ways to the publication of this book. First and foremost among them are the Egyptian women—and especially those with children missing from their lives—who opened their hearts and homes to me and thus made this study possible. Without their candor, tirelessness, and willingness to answer questions that were occasionally painful, often personal, and usually emotionally loaded, the fieldwork upon which this book is based would not have succeeded as it did. My fond gratitude to these heroic women, whom I miss as I write this book but whose memories I carry with me, is immense.

I am also grateful to those individuals in Egypt who facilitated logistical aspects of this study. These include my research assistants, Shayma' Hassouna, Rosie Kouzoukian, Hassanat Naguib, and Azza Hosam Shaker, and my many colleagues at the University of Alexandria's Shatby Hospital, particularly Drs. Hassan Aly, Soad Farid, Mohammed Mehanna, and Mohamad Rizk, who facilitated access to the hospital's patient population. In addition, the administrative and bureaucratic assistance provided by the staff of the Binational Fulbright Commission in Cairo—and especially its director, Ann Radwan—proved invaluable during my fifteen-month tenure in Egypt.

My intellectual debts to teachers and colleagues, several of whom have directly shaped the character of this manuscript, are many. I want to thank especially Joan Ablon, Frederick Dunn, and Nelson Graburn, who have all played key roles in the development of this book and in my development as an anthropologist. I also want to thank Gay Becker, Peter Brown, Mia Fuller (whose photographs are displayed herein), Ira Lapidus, Sandra Lane, Catharine McClellan, my gifted editor Patricia Smith, and the book's anonymous reviewers for their encouragement and excellent guidance along the way.

I am also grateful to the organizations that generously funded this research. These include the National Science Foundation (Doctoral Dissertation Research Improvement Grant #BNS-8814435); the Fulbright Institute of International Education; and the U.S. Department of Education's Fulbright-Hays Doctoral Dissertation Research Abroad Grant Program. Post-fieldwork support for manuscript preparation was provided through the Soroptimist International Founder Region Fellowship Program. Additionally, I am grateful to three institutions, the University of California at Berkeley, the University of Arizona, and Emory University, which have provided me with professional "homes" during the period of manuscript preparation.

Finally, my life during the period of fieldwork and the writing of this book has been enriched by many friends, family members, and colleagues who visited me in the field, continue to provide intellectual camaraderie, and have generally taken an interest in my subject. I owe special thanks to my parents, Shirley and Stanley Inhorn, who provided me with living examples of productive, contributing people; to my childhood friend, Kristina Austin Nicholls, who has been my sounding board and confidante for twenty-five years; and to my husband, Kirk Hooks, who is my loving soul mate and the devoted father of our precious infant son, Carl.

*   *   *

Some of the ideas presented in this book have been developed in different ways in my earlier book, *Quest for Conception: Gender, Infertility, and Egyptian Medical Traditions* (University of Pennsylvania Press, Philadelphia, 1994).

Notes on Transliteration

Because my research was carried out in colloquial Egyptian Arabic, I have attempted to transliterate words according to colloquial pronunciation, while generally following the transliteration system for vowels and consonants found in *The Hans Wehr Dictionary of Modern Written Arabic* (edited by J. M. Cowan, 1976). Thus, while most Arabic words in the text have been transliterated according to the *Wehr* system, words that differ in colloquial Egyptian Arabic are transliterated according to that pronunciation. Most important, in Alexandrian Egyptian colloquial, "j" becomes a hard "g," and most "q" sounds are not vocalized and are represented by an apostrophe. The Arabic letter *hamza*, a glottal stop, is also represented by an apostrophe ('), while the letter *'ayn* is represented by an inverted, superscripted comma ('). As in the *Wehr* dictionary, stressed Arabic consonants are indicated by a dot below the letter and long vowels by a line above. However, I have not followed *Wehr* in that I spell out "kh," "sh," and "dh."

I have used Arabic plurals (e.g., *usrāt*) rather than adding a nonitalicized "s" as is often practiced (e.g., *usras*). Place names and names of individuals are not necessarily written as pronounced, but rather as commonly transliterated by Egyptians themselves.

For simplicity's sake, I have made no attempt to transliterate all words of cultural significance, but only those that have particular bearing upon the themes presented in this book. A glossary of these terms is provided at the back of the volume.

1. Infertility and Patriarchy

> Wealth and offspring are the adornments of earthly life.
> —Qur'an 18:46

Money and children, the divinely extolled allurements of worldly life, are seemingly beyond reach for thousands of Egyptian women—the former by virtue of urban poverty and the latter by virtue of infertility, the inability to conceive a child. Yet, for these infertile women, it is less poverty than the absence of children—and, by extension, motherhood—which is felt, suffered, mourned, and feared each and every day of their lives. In a society where the patriarchal fertility mandate is emphatic, the social and psychological consequences of "missing motherhood"—of being a woman unable to deliver a child for her husband, family, affines, community, faith, nation, and, not inconsequentially, herself—are nothing if not profound.

It is these consequences as lived by childless Egyptian women that constitute the subject of this book. As will be seen in the stories of Egyptian women that will follow, infertility may be accompanied by, *inter alia*, emotional duress, self-doubt and alienation, ostracism and harassment by kin and neighbors, the twin threats of polygynous remarriage or divorce on the part of husbands, and, in some marriages, violence of an emotional and physical nature. Of all of the types of persons that one could be in Egypt, there are very few less desirable social identities than that of the poor infertile woman—or *Umm Il-Ghāyyib*, "Mother of the Missing One," as Egyptians are apt to call her—giving this particular identity all of the classic features of a stigma. In his seminal essay on this subject, Erving Goffman (1963:3) defined a stigma as "an attribute that makes [her] different from others in the category of persons available for [her] to be, and of a less desirable kind—in the extreme, a person who is quite thoroughly bad, or dangerous, or weak. [She] is thus reduced in our minds from a whole and usual person to a tainted, discounted one. Such an attribute is a stigma, especially when its discrediting effect is very extensive."

The stigma of infertility—and the consequent, pervasive fear of infertility among women, upon whom the blame for barrenness is usually placed—is, however, but one axis of stigmatization in poor Egyptian women's lives. Here, I will argue that by virtue of their triple social stigmata—femaleness, poorness, and barrenness—poor infertile Egyptian women stand in a particularly devalued and disempowered position in a society that, by all definitions, can only be seen as patriarchal. Although Goffman's original analysis of stigma was not explicitly concerned with issues of gender or class relations, more recent studies of women and deviance have emphasized the significance of power resources and women's continuing social, economic, political, and legal subordination in patriarchal societies, including those of the West (Schur 1984). As will be apparent in the women's stories in this book, an often abysmal lack of social power plagues these women's lives and limits their options for effective resistance and self-determination. Furthermore, children are a source of power that infertile women cannot claim, and this serves to devalue them significantly in many cases. Simply stated, to understand why infertility can tarnish so seriously Egyptian women's social identity, intimate relations, and quality of life, it is necessary first to locate the discussion of infertility and stigma within the broader context of Middle Eastern patriarchy and gender politics, then explore the issues of religious and class membership as they articulate with these themes.

Middle Eastern Patriarchy

The term "patriarchy" is polysemous, with a multiplicity of meanings dependent upon scholarly venue. Many feminist scholars, for whom the concept of patriarchy serves as a theoretical metonym (Appadurai cited in Abu-Lughod 1989), adopt a liberal definition of the term, viewing it broadly as "gender oppression" (of females by males) or as "male domination/female subordination." Especially among radical feminists, whose view of patriarchy is often criticized as being totalizing, monolithic, unrealistic, and too abstract (Jaggar 1983; Kandiyoti 1988), it is "*the* patriarchal system," a universal system rooted in economic, legal, and political structures, as well as social and cultural institutions, that oppresses women, through the assertion of male power, dominance, hierarchy, and competition (Tong 1989:3).

At the other extreme are so-called strict definitions of patriarchy, including traditional anthropological and sociological ones (harking back to Max Weber), which situate gender oppression exclusively within the family. There, male patriarchs, or father figures, exert considerable control over family decision making and the lives of both women and junior males in the household. Thus, as described by Turner:

> A patriarchal relationship is one in which the male head of household domi-
> nates the members of the house whether these are male, female, adult or juve-
> nile. This patriarchal structure is legitimized by legal, political and religious
> norms which give the adult male a virtual monopoly over the subordinate
> groups within the traditional household. In such a system, the wife ceases to
> be a legal personality on marriage, and divorce is typically proscribed as a sys-
> tem for the dissolution of marriage. (Turner 1987:97)

In the literature on the Middle East, definitions of patriarchy reach both ends of the spectrum—as well as many sites in between[1]—and are sometimes accompanied by a troubling, conceptual conflation of the meanings of patriarchy as father dominance and gender oppression. Yet, it is clear in the works of feminist scholars who have theorized Middle Eastern patriarchy based on the actual study of women's lives in the past or present that patriarchy qua gender oppression is seated in the domestic realm and family life. Namely, traditional Arab family structure is patrilineal, patrilocally extended (three-generation), patriarchal, pyramidally hierarchical, and preferrably endogamous (Kandiyoti 1988, 1991; Moghadam 1993; Barakat 1985); the socialization into patriarchal role taking among males and females occurs within the family at an early age (Hatem 1987b; Joseph 1993, 1994); and support for patriarchy is often derived from retrogressive Muslim personal status laws that shape family life and are institutionalized by the contemporary neopatriarchal nation-state (Hatem 1986a; Sharabi 1988). Throughout the Middle East, female subordination is intimately tied to the dynamics of family life, as well as to a more generalized patriarchal familialism. Thus, for this region of the world, definitions of patriarchy as gender oppression and patriarchy as oppression within the family require synthesis.

For the purposes of this discussion, it is useful to merge the liberal and strict definitions of patriarchy by referring to it as follows: Patriarchy is characterized by relations of power and authority of males over females, which are (1) learned through gender socialization within the family, where males wield power through the socially defined institution of fatherhood; (2) manifested in both inter- and intragender interactions within the family and in other interpersonal milieus; (3) legitimized through deeply engrained, pervasive ideologies of inherent male superiority; and (4) institutionalized on many societal levels (legal, political, economic, educational, religious, and so on). Therefore, according to this definition of patriarchy, women's subordination is first experienced—sometimes subtly, sometimes profoundly—within the family, which serves as a template for the reproduction of patriarchal relations in other realms of social life.

The reproduction of patriarchy within the Middle Eastern family has been especially well detailed by two Middle Eastern gender theorists, Deniz Kandiyoti and Suad Joseph, who approach the subject from somewhat divergent perspectives. Their insights provoke relevant questions about the specificity of Middle Eastern patriarchy as seated in the family and the particular historical and ethnographic manifestations of patriarchy in this region. For the purposes of this discussion, their work does much to illumine the context in which infertile women experience the pressures of patriarchy and thus is described here initially in some detail.

Classic Patriarchy and the Patriarchal Bargain

Kandiyoti (1988; 1991), a feminist historian, is interested in the system that she calls "classic patriarchy," as found in the "patriarchal belt" (Caldwell 1978) extending from North Africa through the Muslim Middle East (including Turkey, Pakistan, and Iran), and into southern and eastern Asia (specifically India and China). According to Kandiyoti (1991), the key to the reproduction of classic patriarchy lies in the operations of the patrilineal, patrilocally extended household, which is commonly associated with the reproduction of the peasantry in agrarian societies. In such households, the senior male has authority over everyone else, including younger men. For women in such households, the implications in terms of control and subordination are marked and appear to cut across cultural and religious boundaries (e.g., Hinduism, Confucianism, and Islam) in the patriarchal belt.

Under classic patriarchy, young girls are married into households headed by their husband's father. There, they are subordinate not only to all the men, but also to the more senior women, especially their mothers-in-law. Often having no claim on their father's patrimony, young brides enter their husbands' households as effectively dispossessed individuals who can establish their place in the patriliny only through childbearing (especially by producing male offspring). However, as Kandiyoti explains:

> A woman's life cycle in the patrilocally extended family is such that the deprivation and hardship she may experience as a young bride are eventually

superseded by the control and authority she will have over her own daughters-in-law. The powerful postmenopausal matriarch thus is the other side of the coin of this form of patriarchy. The cyclical nature of women's power and their anticipation of inheriting the authority of senior women encourages a thorough internalization of this form of patriarchy by the women themselves. Subordination to men is offset by the control older women have over younger women. Women have access to the only type of labor power they can control, and to old-age security, however, through their married sons. Since sons are a woman's most critical resource, ensuring their life-long loyalty is an enduring preoccupation. Older women have a vested interest in the suppression of romantic love between youngsters to keep the conjugal bond secondary and to claim their sons' primary allegiance. Young women have an interest in circumventing and possibly evading their mother-in-law's control. There are culturally specific examples of how this struggle works to the detriment of the heterosexual bond, but there are striking similarities in the overall pattern. (Kandiyoti 1991:33)

The class or caste impact on classic patriarchy produces additional complexities, according to Kandiyoti. Among the wealthier strata, the withdrawal of women from nondomestic work is frequently a mark of status institutionalized in seclusion and exclusion practices, including veiling. For the women of the poorer strata, this cultural ideal can rarely be observed, but the ideology of seclusion and dependence on men still exercises a powerful influence that severely restricts the range of options available to them. Kandiyoti argues that, ultimately, women's access to resources is mediated through the family. Thus, in situations where the observance of restrictive practices is a crucial element in the reproduction of family status, women will resist breaking the rules, even if observing them produces economic hardship for themselves and their families.

Kandiyoti further argues that, in order to avoid overt rule breaking while improving their own situations, women under classic patriarchy engage in so-called "patriarchal bargaining," or various strategies to maximize security and optimize life options within a set of concrete constraints. According to Kandiyoti, a patriarchal bargain indicates the existence of rules and scripts regulating gender relations, to which both genders accommodate and acquiesce, yet which may nonetheless be contested, redefined, and renegotiated. In more concrete terms, patriarchal bargaining occurs when women adopt interpersonal strategies that maximize their security, often through the manipulation of the affections of sons and husbands. Ultimately, however, these individual power tactics do little to alter the structurally unfavorable terms of the overall patriarchal script. Indeed, through such interpersonal strategizing, which may pit one woman against another, women actively collude in the reproduction of patriarchy, or their own subordination.

According to Kandiyoti, different forms of patriarchy present women with distinct "rules of the game," with varying potential for active or passive resistance in the face of oppression. These patriarchal bargains not only inform women's rational choices, but also exert a powerful influence in shaping the more unconscious aspects of women's gendered subjectivity, since they permeate the context of their early socialization, as well as their adult cultural milieu. Hence, patriarchal bargains help to determine the nature of gender ideology and the reproduction of patriarchy in different historical and cultural contexts.

Although this system of classic patriarchy described by Kandiyoti represents an ideal type, instantiation of its basic features is abundantly apparent in the ethnographic literature on the Middle East, including the case of urban Egypt to be described here. As we shall see in Chapter 4, young brides, whether or not they are physically present in their fathers-in-law's households (neolocal residence is increasingly the rule), are often dominated by their affines, especially the women of the husband's family. This is especially the case when children are not forthcoming following marriage. A woman who cannot produce heirs (especially male heirs) to her husband's patrimony is deemed "useless" by the husband's patrilineage, which desires offspring for the purposes of social reproduction. Young women who find themselves in this difficult position are often subject to covert and overt abuses by their affines, who may attempt to tear their marriages asunder through appeals to husbands' loyalties and best interests. Infertile women who succeed in stabilizing this tumultuous situation and preventing repudiation by their husbands often do so through strategies of conjugal accommodation, or, to use Kandiyoti's term, "patriarchal bargaining" with their mates. Women of the Egyptian urban underclass tend to be entirely economically reliant on their husbands vis-à-vis an ideology that views nondomestic female wage labor as degrading and shameful (and, hence, a last resort). Therefore, poor infertile women view marital accommodation—even when it demeans them in various ways—as the most prudent strategy in a situation offering few viable options for resistance.

Patriarchal Connectivity

Whereas Kandiyoti is interested in the ways in which women learn to operate within a system of constraints posed by classic patriarchy, Joseph (1993; 1994) is interested in problematizing the internal psychosocial dynamics of Arab family life to understand how patriarchy is reproduced within the family, as well as the implications of such reproduction for individual men and women.

Noting the multiplicity of uses of the term patriarchy, Joseph (1993: 452) defines it as "the privileging of males and seniors and the mobilization of kinship structures, morality, and idioms to legitimate and institutional-ize gendered and aged domination." However, Joseph's primary concern is with the interaction between patriarchy and "connectivity," a psychologi-cal term coined by Catherine Keller (1986) to denote relationships in which a person's boundaries are relatively fluid, so that persons feel a part of significant others. According to Joseph, socialization within Arab families places a premium on connectivity, or the intensive bonding of individuals through love, involvement, and commitment. In the context of traditional Arab family structure, connectivity serves to reinforce patriarchy, or gen-dered and aged domination, because individuals who feel themselves to be connectively related in this way may find it natural to assume the roles of dominator/dominated in a patriarchal but loving schema. As Joseph ex-plains it:

> Patriarchy entails cultural constructs and structural relations that privilege the initiative of males and elders in directing the lives of others. Connectivity entails cultural constructs and structural relations in which persons invite, re-quire, and initiate involvement with others in shaping the self. In patriarchal societies, then, connectivity can support patriarchal power by crafting selves responding to, requiring, and socialized to initiate involvement with others in shaping the self; and patriarchy can help to reproduce connectivity by craft-ing males and seniors prepared to direct the lives of females and juniors, and females and juniors prepared to respond to the direction of males and seniors. (Joseph 1993:453)

The implications of patriarchal connectivity for gender relations within the Arab family are interesting, as evident in Joseph's (1994) own ethnographic analysis of brother-sister relationships in a working-class neighborhood in Beirut, Lebanon. By virtue of patriarchal connectivity, the family patriarch, or senior male, sees his wife, sisters, junior siblings, and children as extensions of himself, whose lives he is free to enter, shape, and direct. Thus, the patriarch typically speaks for his family members, makes important decisions about their lives, and reads and expects to be read by them. The role assumed by father figures in directing the lives of family members is modeled by sons, whose first "practice" in such forms of domination comes in interactions with sisters, especially younger ones. Yet, it is important to bear in mind that such men in patriarchal connective systems are also raised with diffuse boundaries, responding to and requiring the involvement of others. Although they are likely to have more relationships in which they see and act toward others as extensions of themselves, it is these significant others, particularly their family members, upon whom they depend for a sense of completion.

Furthermore, patriarchal connectivity does not preclude the possibility of women assuming such dominant positions. Because women's power tends to increase as they proceed through the life cycle, women, primarily older women, can and do take power in Arab patriarchal systems, often drawing upon connective claims to their children to accomplish desired ends. Yet, the presence of strong women in Arab societies does not mean that these societies are not predominantly patriarchal. As Joseph sees it, patriarchy is culturally sanctioned by Arab societies at large and is reinforced by state institutions, ideologies, and processes.

Joseph notes, however, that connectivity exists independently of patriarchy and probably occurs in most cultures in which individuation, autonomy, and separation are not valued or supported. In such cultures, perhaps especially in the Arab world, family members are generally deeply involved with each other, expecting mutual love, exerting considerable influence over each others' lives, prioritizing family solidarity, and encouraging subordination of members' needs to collective interests. Persons are thus embedded in familial relational matrices that shape their deepest sense of self and serve as a source of security when the external social, economic, and political situation is uncertain. Furthermore, as noted by Joseph, patriarchy seated in these conditions of love, nurturance, and commitment may be much more difficult to unseat than patriarchy in which love and nurturance are less supported.

As with Kandiyoti's work, Joseph's analysis of patriarchal connectivity is quite germane to the discussion of infertility and patriarchy. As we shall see in Chapter 4, life for young couples in urban Egypt is a family-intensive affair, with natal family members, especially aging parents, expecting a continuing role in directing the lives of their married children and making claims on their time and loyalty. When the young couple establishes a family of their own, often in a new residence, the connectivity they feel to natal family members may lead to structural tensions. While attempting to meet the financial and nurturance needs of their own children, they may still feel the need to fulfill obligations (including financial ones) to their aging parents, as well as to married and unmarried siblings.

However, I would argue that patriarchal connectivity is particularly manifest—in frequently unexpected ways—when children are *not* forthcoming in a marriage. When this happens, natal family members, typically senior members of the husband's family, intensively activate connective claims to their son. They may direct him—sometimes in an overt and coercive fashion—to divorce his infertile wife or to replace her through polygyny with a fertile cowife. According to Egyptian women, men who are "weak" are unable to withstand this family pressure, and may initiate the process of finding a new wife with the help of their mothers and sisters. Yet, despite widely held expectations of marital demise, many husbands do not exercise this option, choosing instead to stay with their infertile wives and to nurture conjugal relationships characterized by love, involvement, and commitment. I would argue that the socialization into connectivity that occurs in the Egyptian family of origin may carry over in unexpectedly positive ways when individuals marry but fail to produce a family of procreation. If, in patriarchal connective systems, connection with others is required for a sense of completion, and children, who are one's primary ego extensions, are missing from the union, then connective relationships are often developed, nurtured, and sustained in infertile marriages between husbands and wives, who, by virtue of their mutual socialization, rather easily and immediately "connect" with one another, needing the other for the completion of their relational selves. The strength of this connection, which is usually characterized by intensive feelings of love, often proves refractory to attempts by natal family members to intervene in ways deleterious to the marriage. Although a variety of factors to be detailed in Chapter 3 serve to promote such connubial connectivity, suffice it to say here that infertile marriages among the urban Egyptian poor are often bastions of loving connectivity—much to the amazement and occasional displeasure of husbands' family members, whose own connective claims are effectively superseded.

Yet, it is important to point out that infertile couples would choose to have children, for themselves and their families, if they could. The desire for children is a near cultural universal among Egyptian couples, and perhaps especially among the urban poor, for reasons to be described in Chapter 6. As suggested by Joseph, one of the primary reasons for having children is connective completion of the self, given that children serve as primary ego extensions for both Egyptian fathers and mothers, who view their children as their "memory" in life and after death. But, as we shall see, children "complete" Egyptian women in other ways as well—as full females and as full women, the two being only partially coterminous.

Namely, a woman without children feels, and is viewed as, less than a normal female—a "pseudo-male," who is more masculine than feminine by virtue of her uncooperative reproductive organs. In addition to her ambiguous sexual identity, the infertile woman's gender identity is marred, for, without claims to motherhood, she can never be viewed as a complete woman, who has fulfilled her God-given adult role in life. Thus, infertility is a serious blemish on a woman's social identity (Goffman 1963)—a failure of a woman to achieve "norms of being" widely held among a pronatalist Egyptian populace. The implications of identity failure for the social construction of gender is a theme to which we will turn in the next chapter.

PATRIARCHY, POWER, AND RESISTANCE

In addition to the prima facie importance of Kandiyoti's and Joseph's aforementioned arguments concerning the dynamics and reproduction of patriarchy, their analyses point to a number of other important issues regarding the cultural and historical specificity of patriarchy in the Middle East. One of the most salient has to do with the issue of power and specifically women's power.

As with the term "patriarchy," the term "power" is variously defined by scholars or, as is often the case in the gender literature, is left undefined under the assumption that the fundamental meaning of the term is known and shared by all. Many feminist anthropologists, drawing upon Weberian notions, use the term "power" to mean, either implicitly or explicitly, "the ability to make someone do what they do not wish to do, to act effectively on persons and things, to take decisions which are not of right allocated to the actor's role or to the actor as an individual" (Moore 1988:210). Thus, power as a general term incorporates a number of concepts, including force, legitimacy, and authority. "Authority" is defined more simply as "the right to make a particular decision or follow a particular course of action, and to command obedience" (Moore 1988:210). Whether power is exercised through influence or force, it is inherently subject to competitive pressures. Authority, on the other hand, entails a hierarchical chain of command and control (Rosaldo 1974). The important point is that power and authority are not synonymous; the use of one term does not necessarily imply the other. For example, even though women in a given society may have political power by virtue of the right to vote, they may lack any real authority in exercising that power. On the other hand, as much cross-cultural research has shown, even though women may have neither the right nor the duty to make decisions (i.e., they lack authority), they often have power through demonstrable influence on the decisions that are made (Rosaldo 1974). Although Rosaldo did not use the term "patriarchy" (nor, for that matter, "resistance") when she wrote the following passage, she provided a classic exposition of the difference between power and authority under patriarchy, which she deemed universal:

> Everywhere, from those societies we might want to call most egalitarian to those in which sexual stratification is most marked, men are the locus of cultural value. Some area of activity is always seen as exclusively or predominantly male, and therefore overwhelmingly and morally important. This observation has its corollary in the fact that everywhere men have some *authority* over women, that they have a culturally legitimated right to her subordination and compliance. At the same time, of course, women themselves are far from helpless, and whether or not their influence is acknowledged, they exert important pressures on the social life of the group. In other words, in various circumstances male authority might be mitigated, and, perhaps rendered almost trivial, by the fact that women (through gossiping or yelling, playing sons against brothers, running the business, or refusing to cook) may have a good deal of informal influence and *power*. While acknowledging male authority, women may direct it to their own interests, and in terms of actual choices and decisions, of who influences whom and how, the power exercised by women may have considerable and systematic effect. (Rosaldo 1974:20–21)

Feminist scholars of the Middle East who have theorized power have emphasized the aforementioned factor of women's *influence*—what is sometimes called women's "informal" (MacLeod 1991) or "unassigned" powers (Rassam 1987). Drawing upon the work of Dennis Wrong (n.d.), Cynthia Nelson, in a seminal essay on "Public and Private Politics: Women in the Middle Eastern World" (1974), recommended rethinking notions of "power" as an embodied quality institutionalized in types of social structures and instead recognizing it as a particular type of social relation, *as reciprocity of influence*. Instead of Middle Eastern men always assuming power over women, as earlier, male-biased ethnographies seemed to imply, Nelson argued for the concept of a "negotiated order," an ongoing dialectical process of social life in which *both* men and women were involved in a reciprocity of influence vis-à-vis each other. If power were to be defined as such, she claimed, then the relevant question for the study of Middle Eastern women would become: In what ways and in what spheres of activity can and do women influence men to achieve their own objectives? Drawing upon ethnographic literature from throughout the Middle East, Nelson showed that women can and do exercise a greater degree of power in various spheres of social life—for example, through the structural linking of kin and religious and supernatural control—than had previously been appreciated. Yet, because male ethnographers did not have access to many women-centered aspects of social life, they had focused almost exclusively on the public, official, visible spheres of social life—the public political arena, where men have official power—to the exclusion of women's informal spheres of influence, or the world of unofficial, private politics (Bourdieu 1977; Harding 1986; Jones 1988; Nelson 1974).

Nelson's call to study the domains of women's power in the Middle East struck a resonant chord with feminist ethnographers. Since the mid-1970s, anthropologists and other ethnographically minded social scientists have documented the many ways in which women assume power in an otherwise patriarchal milieu through influencing the lives and decision making of significant others, including their menfolk. As noted by ethnographers, the household is probably the primary site of power for most Middle Eastern women. The significant influence and even direct power that women assume over domestic matters is manifest in actual decision-making authority and control over household resources, children's education, and marriage negotiations (Hoodfar 1988; Smock and Youssef 1977). Additionally, in their own homes, women have power as wives and mothers. Fertility, the ability to bear men's children for them, is perhaps women's most significant form of power over men (Early 1993).

As noted by Boddy (1989:121) in reference to rural Sudanese women: "Women give men the ultimate source of their supremacy in bearing them descendants. The one powerful bargaining card that women have, both individually and collectively, is their fertility. But since fertility (like husbands or *zayran* [spirits]) is neither predictable nor always controllable, it is in essence a wild card, and may be of no help at all."

If fertility is recognized as perhaps *the* most potent (if uncontrollable) source of women's power, then infertility, which serves to strip women of this power, can only be seen as unusually threatening. Not only does infertility pose a threat to women—whose fundamental value in the eyes of their husbands, relatives, communities, and themselves may be closely bound to their reproductive abilities—infertility threatens men as well, for it effectively nullifies proof of their virility and masculine procreativity, as well as their ability to perpetuate the patrilineage, its name, and its patrimony. Furthermore, infertility may be particularly threatening to both women and men under conditions of classic patriarchy, where the patriarchal fertility mandate valorizing both motherhood and fatherhood as personal imperatives is felt especially strongly. Under this mandate, all women are expected to marry and become mothers. Motherhood is believed to be the most important role for women and the perceived essence of a woman's identity. And, for men, the institution of fatherhood is at the ideological core of classic patriarchy. Fatherhood alone allows men to reproduce the particular relations of family life that are crucial to the reproduction of patriarchy itself.

That infertility is feared on multiple levels—the source of real danger —should become apparent in the chapters that follow. Because infertility undermines women's domestic and nondomestic relations, it represents a potent threat to their social and economic security. Given its disruptive power over women's lives, infertility provides a unique lens through which crucial issues of kinship and family life, gender relations and sexuality, cosmology and religion can be examined. Infertility also affords the examination of negative or paradoxical forms of attributed power. Namely, because infertile Egyptian women are perceived as dangerous to others by virtue of their uncontrollable envy, they are feared by Egyptians for the ways in which they jeopardize the well-being of those around them. Their perceived dangerousness may in and of itself constitute a source of power (Rosaldo 1974), although few infertile Egyptian women view themselves in this way.

Furthermore, infertility, especially when it is widespread, poses a political threat, in that it challenges the social reproduction of the body politic.[2] Thus, even when the state attempts to control fertility among a reluctant populace, infertility is rarely viewed as a tenable option. In societies such as that of Egypt, which is plagued by burgeoning population growth, it is children, not the state, who provides vital welfare assistance to their aging parents. In short, the state is less burdened when an adequate supply of new citizens assumes responsibility for its elderly citizens. As noted by Moghadam:

> The joint household system and intergenerational wealth flows that are characteristic of patriarchal structures provide welfare and security for individuals. This, of course, is incumbent upon an adequate supply of household members, especially sons. The material consequences of reproductive failure are disastrous. . . . It is especially dire for women, who attain status and old-age security through their sons. In all cases, the persistence of patriarchy relieves the state of the responsibility to provide welfare to citizens. (Moghadam 1993:113)

Given the multiple threats posed by the condition, women who are infertile in Egypt go to great lengths to overcome their childlessness. This quest for conception—or the "search for children," as Egyptian women themselves call it—is typified by relentless attempts by women to be cured of their infertility through both indigenous "ethnogynecological" and Western-based "biogynecological" therapies (Inhorn 1994). This therapeutic search constitutes one of the primary ways in which Egyptian women attempt to resist their infertile status and accompanying loss of social power; engagement in the therapeutic process itself implies movement toward therapeutic resolution. (Unfortunately, however, infertility "cures" are often not forthcoming, for numerous reasons described in Inhorn [1994].)

As suggested earlier, the other primary means by which infertile women attempt to resist their particular subordination *as* infertile women is through the creation of insuperable marital bonds, to be described in Chapter 3. The negotiation of viable relationships with husbands serves to mitigate tensions inherent in other social relations, including those with female affines, who are usually among the key sources of infertile Egyptian women's subordination.

Despite growing attention in the Middle Eastern literature to women's informal power, it must also be made clear that women in many parts of the Middle East continue to be staunch supporters of traditions and social relations that constrain and limit women's lives, including the lives of the infertile (Kandiyoti 1988, 1991; MacLeod 1991). As they advance through the life cycle, Middle Eastern women may "buy into" patriarchy, often using their accumulating social power to subordinate their own sex (Bowen and Early 1993). In so doing, they serve only to reinforce further the foundations of patriarchy, the perpetuation of which has both heterosocial (intergender) and homosocial (intragender) aspects (Hatem 1986b).

Arlene MacLeod (1991), a feminist political scientist, argues that this kind of complicity and accommodation by women needs further examination in light of the idea of women's informal powers. Drawing upon Antonio Gramsci's (1971) concept of hegemony, MacLeod reexamines the ongoing struggle of women, as subordinate actors, to contest and try to expand the boundaries of their experience while also consenting to and accepting their situation. She states:

> Power, in other words, involves a relationship in which women, even as the subordinate players, take an active role. Women may appear as passive victims, unable to muster any opposition to the forces allied against them; or as consenting partners, acquiescent and apparently satisfied with their deferent role;

or even as active participants, supporting and sustaining their own inequality; yet women also, when the times are ripe, seize the opportunity to participate in an ongoing series of negotiations, manipulations, and strategies directed toward gaining control and opportunity. Whenever changing circumstances open a political space for the possible renegotiation of existing relations, this contradictory process of hegemonic politics is at work. (MacLeod 1991:19)

MacLeod draws our attention to both hegemonic consent and counterhegemonic resistance—the ways in which women both assist in and protest their subordination under patriarchy. Her analysis of the new veiling by Cairo's lower-middle-class women tells a great deal about the dialectic of consent and resistance—of women acquiescing to an essentializing discourse about the imperative of women's modesty through veiling and the proper role of women as wives and mothers, while using veiling to protest the abominations of the public workplace and to advance the position of women who have been encouraged by education and economic necessity to enter the tedious, dehumanizing, poorly remunerating wage labor market. MacLeod views lower-middle-class urban Egyptian women as active yet ambivalent actors, who wish to accommodate as well as resist their subordination in a changing patriarchal setting. For these women, veiling becomes a "weapon of the weak" (Scott 1985), one of the oppositional practices of everyday life common among the subordinate members of a society (de Certeau 1984).

In a study of resistance among a rather different group of Egyptian women, Bedouins of the Awlad 'Ali tribe, Lila Abu-Lughod (1990) argues that anthropological and historical studies of everyday resistance tend to romanticize it and fail to adequately examine resistance as a diagnostic of power. Michel Foucault's (1978:95–96) assertion that "where there is power, there is resistance" forces us, according to Abu-Lughod, to question our understanding of power as always essentially repressive. Furthermore, power relations take many forms, have many aspects, and interweave. "And by presupposing some sort of hierarchy of significant and insignificant forms of power, we may be blocking ourselves from exploring the ways in which these forms may actually be working simultaneously, in concert or at cross-purposes" (Abu-Lughod 1990:48).

The "hierarchizing" of power is especially apparent in studies of "formal" versus "informal" gender power, which, Abu-Lughod argues, is one of the more difficult forms of power to analyze. Although a large body of Middle Eastern literature has located sources of women's informal power, and a growing number of studies (especially on Middle Eastern feminism) [3] attempt to cite areas of resistance to restrictions in women's lives, few studies adequately examine the relationship of resistance to power, tending to focus as they do on explaining *either* women's power or women's resistance.

As I will attempt to show in the chapters that follow, women's power and women's resistance are inextricably linked. Infertile women, with the help of other women close to them, find various ways of resisting not only male power (e.g., men's power to repudiate them or replace them with a fertile cowife), but also the subordinating power ploys of other women (especially mothers-in-law and neighbors), whose overt strategies of marginalization can be nothing short of cruel. Thus, many poor infertile Egyptian women are everyday resisters, engaged in an ongoing struggle to overcome the stigmatization wrought by their childlessness. However, although infertile Egyptian women are resistant, their individual efforts cannot be counted as truly counterhegemonic, for the infertile constitute no fundamental group in Egyptian society and hence lack a collective voice as subalterns. This lack of collective organization is reflected in the absence of a national infertility self-help association in Egypt (such as RESOLVE in the United States) or, for that matter, a nationally coordinated policy or program to help the infertile seek medical redress of their condition (Inhorn 1994). Thus, as it now stands, infertile Egyptian women struggle on their own, although, as we shall see, their common plight is shared by many.

It is also important to bear in mind that although infertile women are resisters, they are not always successful in their resistance. As we shall see in Chapter 3, some women *are* repudiated by their husbands, despite their best efforts to appease their spouses and become cured of their infertility. Some women *are* humiliated and degraded by their affines, despite their concerted attempts to "manage" these social relations. And some women continue to be suspected by their neighbors as casting the evil eye, despite their kindnesses to these neighbors and their children. Thus, as important as it is to identify areas in which women successfully assume power and resist constraints, it is also imperative to recognize that, in relative terms, women may lack significant social power, even on an informal level, and they sometimes fail miserably to resist others' assertions of power over them. Without the capacity to muster real social, economic, or legal-political resources, some women remain confined to the margins of social life, unable to overcome their multiple sources of oppression.

Frankly, for most infertile Egyptian women, life is a sad affair.

Although some women are successful in achieving peace of mind and peace in their marriages—and these positive gains will certainly be emphasized in the chapters that follow—for many women, life is marred by emotional and sometimes physical abuse that is difficult to fend off. Furthermore, few poor urban infertile women are in any position to challenge the oppressive, patriarchal norm that makes motherhood a female mandate. Uneducated, illiterate, and unequipped for anything but manual labor, these women are not prepared for other options besides motherhood, nor are most willing to challenge the cultural norm that disallows women's independent living. In other words, these are not women on "the cutting edge"; their lives *as lived* do *not* tend to challenge many of the traditional assumptions about Middle Eastern patriarchy or suggest that Egyptian women are achieving emancipation from it. Although poor urban Egyptian women often see themselves as oppressed—speaking of themselves in a poetic discourse as "broken-winged"—the notion of a feminist political struggle against patriarchy is certainly alien to most. Put another way, not all Middle Eastern women, even the most degraded, are protofeminists, as is too often assumed in the feminist literature.

Patriarchy and Gender Politics in Practice

This is not to suggest, however, that poor urban Egyptian women are not political actors. If "politics" can be understood as the ways in which power is structured and enacted in everyday activities, and the definition of politics can be extended, therefore, to include the personal realm and issues of concern to women, then the "domestic politics" of Egyptian women's everyday lives must be seen as the stuff of real politics, and the local social arrangements within which both gender and reproductive relations are embedded in Egypt must be viewed as inherently political (Abu-Lughod 1989; Ginsburg and Rapp 1991; Moore 1988).

Unfortunately, much of the literature on Middle Eastern women and patriarchy is plagued by a continuing idealist bias that directs attention away from the political realities of women's everyday lives and toward "ideal" evidence, especially the Islamic scriptures and the writings of Muslim jurists and theologians (Hatem 1993; Keddie 1979; Nelson 1991). What is missing from these more abstract discussions is the examination of women's personal lives in patriarchal Arab societies, or the *lived experience* of patriarchy by the women—and men—who are social actors within these systems. Such "everyday life studies," based on a "culture in praxis" approach derivative of Bourdieu (1977), de Certeau (1984), and LeFebvre

(1971), are just beginning to emerge from the Middle East (e.g., Abu-Lughod 1993; Bowen and Early 1993). These scholars focus on the ordinary lives and struggles of real people rather than abstract theories of social action, and they tend to view women as major players in the politics of domestic life.

Indeed, for most poor urban Egyptian women, gender politics—the whole field of struggle between the social interests constituted within gender relations (Connell 1990), involving contestations and negotiations of power between men and women and among women themselves—comprise a crucial part of their everyday existence. Yet, relatively little is known about what Foucault (1977) would call the "microphysics" of power negotiations in Egyptian gender relations. Namely, what do Egyptian men and women think of each other on both a general and interpersonal level? How do these views affect their actual social relations? Is it true, as Boddy (1989) has argued for Sudan, that women who wield power must do so implicitly, leaving the appearance of power to men? And, is it true that men and women inhabit different social worlds with different views of reality, or do their arenas of social action and fields of reality overlap; if so, to what extent (Abu-Lughod 1989; Harding 1986; Rosen 1978)?

Furthermore, if gender politics is to be more broadly defined to include the interplays of power *among* women and among men rather than just *between* them, then how do women view other women and men other men? Do men, especially younger men, view themselves as constrained by a patriarchal social system (Joseph 1986), and does this affect their attitudes toward and treatment of other men as well as women? Similarly, do women under a patriarchal system view themselves as needing to cooperate or to compete with other women, especially senior women, for access to power resources? Are there situations in which Egyptian women find themselves at cross-purposes with other women, and does this mean that they become "enemies" in debates surrounding issues of propriety, morality, and the redefinition of women's roles?

As I will argue, the answers to such questions are to be found in the lives of infertile Egyptian women, who face unofficial political dilemmas on multiple social structural levels. Indeed, one of the main goals of this book is to amplify the scholarly examination of social power in the Middle East by revealing the politics of gender as they affect the lives of poor infertile Egyptian women. Among the inherently political relations to be explored are those involving infertile women and their husbands, parents, parents-in-law, sisters-in-law, siblings, nieces and nephews, and female neighbors. As we shall see, some, but not all, of these relations are characterized by a dialectic of open hostility and tension. This is especially true of relations involving other women, which, for reasons that can only be traced back to patriarchy, tend to be fraught with difficulty for infertile women. An understanding of all of these relationships—inter- and intragender—as they are played out in the urban Egyptian context is necessary to understand the power of the infertile status itself to shape poor women's lives.

In the discussion of gender politics that will follow, it is important to bear in mind that the overarching gender asymmetries found in Egyptian society are never absolute, especially as they are experienced in the realm of personal relations. Rather, in the lives of individual infertile Egyptian women, the distribution of social power is dynamic and shifting, and gender relations are less given than made, unmade, and remade through personal strategies involving the negotiation of reality (Rosen 1978). In other words, gender politics among the Egyptian urban poor have a distinctly fluid quality about them, in that social power is gained and lost by women and by men as everyday social relations are enacted. Furthermore, poor urban infertile Egyptian women do not constitute a monolithic group in terms of their access to power resources. Some women, for reasons that are shared or idiosyncratic, are more successful than others as political actors, navigating the "treacherous patriarchal shoals in Egyptian society" (Badran 1994:222) to create lives and relations for themselves that are satisfying on multiple levels. The reasons for their success, as well as for others' failure, are issues to which we will attend.

Patriarchy and Ideology

It is impossible to understand issues of gender and power in Egypt or elsewhere without reference to ideology, or the way in which ideas serve to structure relations of power and inequality (Abu-Lughod 1989; MacLeod 1991). The concept of ideology has suffered from as much definitional imprecision as the concepts of patriarchy and power. Early Marxist notions of ideology indexed "false consciousness," a distortion or manipulation of reality by the ruling class, reflecting relations of inequality in a society's economic base (Barrett 1988). However, later neo-Marxist revisions of the term, especially by Gramsci (1971) and Louis Althusser (1971), freed the concept of ideology from its epiphenomenal relationship to the economic structure, and expanded its definition to encompass the idea of "articulating principles" that organize beliefs, behaviors, and social relations and influence the lived experiences and meaning making of thinking subjects.

Today, most scholars, including those of the Middle East, draw upon revised notions of ideology to explore the relationship between systems of cultural meaning and social life *as practiced* (Bourdieu 1977; Yanagisako and Collier 1987). For example, MacLeod (1991:75), in examining competing ideologies within the subculture of lower-middle-class Cairo, sees ideology as "the world view or the commonsense set of assumptions that people employ to think about their lives. It is the framework or paradigm within which attitudes and actions are shaped, decisions made, and questions raised . . . an overarching arena for both thought and behavior, a discourse that shapes the way people tend to think about and act on opportunities for change."

As reflected in this passage, feminist scholarship has moved away from notions of ideology as either epiphenomenal to the material realities of women's lives, or determinative of on-the-ground gender relations and specific forms of women's oppression. Instead, the "embedded nature of gender," both as a material, social institution existing in a set of practices and as a set of ideologies reflected in cultural meaning systems, has been recognized (di Leonardo 1991; Yanagasiko and Collier 1987). Furthermore, the relationship between ideology and practice has been construed as dialectical; ideologies are no longer seen as rationalizations of on-the-ground social realities, nor are these social realities the simple actualization of cultural ideals or rules of practice. As Bourdieu (1977:17) has argued, talk of rules can be fallacious in societies where most practices, including those seemingly most ritualized, "can be abandoned to the orchestrated improvisation of common dispositions."

For example, although Islam represents a potent ideological system, with extremely well articulated rules for living, it would be a mistake to assume that all Muslims, including Egyptian Muslim women, practice their lives in accordance with that set of rules, or that improvisation in religious practice does not occur on a regular basis, necessitating reinterpretations of the meanings of those rules. The same can be said of many other areas of social life, where the practices of everyday living may diverge considerably from behavioral ideals, serving to modify those ideals in a gradual fashion. As we shall see through numerous examples in the chapters that follow, the cultural ideologies that prescribe certain standards of living for poor urban Egyptian men and women are often unachievable in practice, because of economic hardship or the realities of a changing urban milieu. Over time, individuals not only come to expect a different standard of social practice, but actually behave in ways that may diverge considerably from the official rules of propriety. The ideologies supporting such practices, too, may begin to change, as behavioral standards simply shift beyond previous recognition. This shifting dialectic between such ideals and the on-the-ground realities and indeterminacies of Egyptian women's lives will be a recurring theme in the chapters that follow.

For many poor infertile Egyptian women, such shifts in ideology and practice—especially regarding what it means to be a "couple" and a "family"—have had salutary effects on their lives. In other areas, however, repressive ideological dictates still hold sway, despite transformations in these standards occurring in other parts of Egyptian society. To take but one example, although Egyptian women from the upper, middle, and even lower-middle classes have begun to enter the nondomestic wage labor force in significant numbers, a still pervasive ideology of female seclusion is felt in practice as poor married women are barred by their husbands from working outside their homes, except in cases of dire need. For poor infertile women, such domestic seclusion is often felt by women themselves to be extremely detrimental to their lives, sinking them into depressions that stem largely from their isolation and loneliness. Yet, few poor infertile women seriously question the clearly patriarchal mandate that makes men "breadwinners" and women idle "housewives" and may, in fact, defend this ideal for a variety of practical reasons.

In other words, cultural ideologies, including the official prescriptions of Islam, may be extremely powerful in shaping the arena of practical social relations, including those between husbands and wives. In patriarchal societies, it is clear that the reproduction of patriarchy itself depends upon support from ideologies valorizing the attributes of males and devalorizing those associated with females. Indeed, patriarchal gender relations in Egyptian society and elsewhere could not be sustained were it not for the existence of pervasive and powerful ideologies of inherent male superiority in one or more fundamental realms of human existence. These "male ideologies" (Strathern 1987) or "male dogmas" (Nader 1989) may or may not represent the dominant ideology in a given society and may or may not represent women's point of view or experience. Nevertheless, such ideologies in patriarchal societies allow men to define themselves as having something that women (by anatomy or nature) do not and cannot have (Gilmore 1987), and, as such, they may underlie and serve to justify men's subordination of women.

In Egypt, one of the most powerful patriarchal ideologies of this nature, which has widespread acceptance among the urban Egyptian poor, has to do with the superior procreative powers of men. Namely, men's patriarchal power, on both a general societal and familial level, is viewed by most members of the Egyptian urban underclass as only "natural," given that men—not women—are seen as procreators, the makers of fetuses. In this "monogenetic" reproductive scenario—monogenetic in the sense that only one parent, the father, is seen as contributing to the genetic substance of the offspring (Delaney 1991)—men are thought to create preformed fetuses through the process of spermatogenesis. These fetuses are carried by their "worms," as sperm are called among the urban Egyptian poor, to women's waiting wombs during the ejaculatory moment of sexual intercourse.

Although I have described this monogenetic theory of procreation in some detail elsewhere (Inhorn 1994), suffice it to say that this theory severely marginalizes women in the reproductive process. According to three popular variants of this theory, women's bodies are viewed as either (1) catching and then carrying these male-created fetuses in their wombs, (2) supplying menstrual blood, a problematically polluting substance, for the growth or cushioning of these fetuses, or (3) producing eggs, which mix with the male sperm during conception (i.e., the "modern" medical version of procreation, which is only gradually supplanting indigenous beliefs), but which are viewed as less vital than men's sperm to fetal development. In all three variants, women's role in reproduction is seen as less than that of men. Women are acknowledged for their ability to gestate and then give birth to babies, but the ability to give life, to actually create the children that women expel from their bodies, is an inherently male capacity. Ultimately, then, it is fathers—and not mothers—to whom children owe their own lives.

This distinction between men as life-givers and women as mere birthers has been extremely well articulated by anthropologist Carol Delaney (1991), the first scholar to examine the implications of monogenesis in the Middle East in her study of procreative folk theories among rural Anatolian Turks. As Delaney explains:

> In the village I studied, the theory of procreation is what I have called "monogenetic" because, as we shall see, it is the male who is imagined as the creative, engendering person, in which character he is symbolically allied with God. In this view of procreation, it is men who give life; women merely give birth. Giving life and giving birth are not synonymous. This subtle but extremely important distinction has been overlooked by social scientists as well as feminists; as a result, there has been a great deal of confusion about the rela-

tions between reproduction and women's inferior status, especially when the former is viewed as the cause of the latter. It may not be procreation that is devalued but only women's culturally perceived role in the process. (Delaney 1991:26–27)

She continues,

Because of the structural and symbolic alliance established between men and God, men partake of this power; as a result, their dominance seems natural and given in the order of things. This association is part of the power behind these patriarchal systems, for it is the glorification, not just of the male, but of the male as "father." That, to me, is what patriarchy is all about. The widespread use of the term "patriarchy" to refer to other systems of male dominance seems intellectually sloppy, for the term "father" derives its meaning from an entire system of beliefs about procreation that are not universal. (Delaney 1991:35)

Delaney points to a number of important issues. First, beliefs about procreation are definitely *not* universal, as is too often assumed by Westerners and even anthropologists. For reasons cogently outlined by Delaney, anthropologists early on stopped asking meaningful questions about how informants themselves conceive of conception, largely because of ethnocentric Western assumptions about the universality of "duogenetic" theories of procreation. However, as mounting ethnographic evidence has shown, not all people theorize conception in a duogenetic framework— that is, as an act entailing an egalitarian, substantive contribution from both a male and female partner (Jordan 1987; Valsiner 1989). This is certainly true of the Middle East, where ethnographers from Iran (Good 1980) to Morocco (Crapanzano 1973; Greenwood 1981) have pointed to procreative models in which men are seen as contributing more to conception than women. Yet, the implications of such "Middle Eastern monogenesis" for gender relations, kinship reckoning, family planning, and a host of other domains of social life are barely understood, given the lack of theorizing in this area.

Second, the bias that women, and not men, are universally perceived as "closer" to human reproduction has thoroughly pervaded gender studies, where it has been argued, most notably by Sherry Ortner (1974), that women are universally subordinate because their "natural procreative functions specific to women alone" place them in the inferior, unculturized realm of "nature" (Ortner 1974:73). However, this assumption that women bear the greater burden and responsibility for human reproduction appears to be "more a metaphorical extension of our emphasis on the fact that women *bear* children than a conclusion based on systematic comparison of the contribution of men and women to human reproduction" (Yanagisako and Collier 1987:33). In Egypt as in Turkey, it is not women's ability to bear children that makes them inferior to men by aligning them with nature, but rather their natural *inability* to procreate at all, making their role in the process of reproduction much less vital than that of their male counterparts.

Given this patriarchal procreative scenario, it is truly ironic that Egyptian *women*, the purportedly unprocreative partners, are typically blamed for reproductive failures of all kinds (Inhorn 1994). Just as men are seen as giving life, women are seen as taking life away, by virtue of wombs that fail to facilitate the most important act of male creation. That Egyptian women are most often held accountable for infertility can only be understood as the expression of a thoroughly patriarchal ontology (Inhorn 1994). To wit, men cannot be blamed for failures of procreation, unless, because of impotence or premature ejaculation, they are unable to pass their worm-enveloped children into women's wombs. In other words, barring male sexual inadequacy, men cannot fail reproductively so long as their bodies are the least bit spermatogenic. On the contrary, women's bodies are viewed as being plagued by numerous problems that bar the facilitation of conception or result in an unsuitable gestational "home" for the child that a man "brings" in his ejaculate.[4] This is why every act of sexual intercourse does not result in pregnancy. This is also why Egyptian women are seen as suffering from a whole host of infertility conditions, described in detail elsewhere (Inhorn 1994). Although men are now known by Egyptians of all classes to suffer from "weak worms" (i.e., sperm and semen problems), and this possibility is often discussed when a couple is childless, poor urban Egyptians tend to be less willing to accept male infertility as the absolute cause of any given case. In other words, even when men are acknowledged as having "worm problems," their problems are seen as more amenable to treatment than the intractable infertility problems thought to be associated with women's reproductive organs.

In the realm of infertility in Egypt, the persistence of women-blaming, the concomitant glorification of men as fathers and potential fathers, and the patriarchal backlash that infertile women suffer for denying men their children cannot be overstated. Even women who have been given a clean bill of health by numerous physicians continue to be condemned as infertile by affines, neighbors, and even husbands and continue to search for therapies under the assumption that there *must* be something wrong with them. In fact, the internalization of blame on the part of poor urban Egyptian women is often quite remarkable and will be explored in greater detail in the following chapter.

Delaney argues that the glorification of men *as fathers*—particularly evident in the monogenetic procreative scenarios found in the Middle East—"is what patriarchy is all about" (Delaney 1991:35), and, as previously noted, she criticizes more liberal feminist definitions of patriarchy qua gender oppression as being "intellectually sloppy" (Delaney 1991:35). In my view, however, rejecting the liberal definition of patriarchy is like throwing the baby out with the bathwater; for, in the Middle East at least, one cannot speak of patriarchy without referring to the crucial link between widespread female subordination and the dominance of fathers in family life. In other words and to repeat an earlier theme, generalized patriarchy in Middle Eastern gender relations is seated in familial patriarchy; the generalized valorization of father figures of all types, be they teachers, religious leaders, politicians, or God himself (Barakat 1985), is seated in the glorification of men as fathers to their children; and such glorification of fathers is supported by monogenetic procreative ideologies giving men exclusive life-giving powers.

Delaney sees the crucial symbolic link as the one between men and God as life-givers. In the cosmologies of all three of the major monotheistic religions to have arisen in the Middle East (Judaism, Christianity, and Islam), the universe and all earthly life are ultimately created by a male God, his creative powers being symbolically allied with the monogenetic procreative powers of earthly males. Although Delaney is particularly interested in the ways in which Islam upholds this view, I (Inhorn 1994) and several Middle Eastern historians (e.g., Ahmed 1989; Musallam 1983) have argued that Islam may be less supportive of this monogenetic theory of procreation than Delaney suggests. In Egypt at least, theories of male procreation predate Islam by several millennia, receiving support in pharaonic mythology, later pre-Islamic Hellenic medical philosophies, and, ultimately, in various "preformation models" introduced into Egypt with the postcolonial hegemonic incursion of premodern Western medicine. Although this history is described at some length elsewhere (Inhorn 1994), suffice it to say here that, in Egypt at least, a long history of monogenetic theorizing is not specifically linked to Islam per se but rather to a host of other patriarchal philosophical traditions that achieved hegemony throughout the centuries.

PATRIARCHY AND ISLAM

This is not to say, however, that Islam is not patriarchal, ideologically or practically speaking. Many feminist scholars have pointed to Muslim personal status laws as one of the most glaring examples of the nexus between patriarchal ideology and practice in the Middle East, where Islam is the predominant religion (Badran 1993; Coulson and Hinchcliffe 1978; Hatem 1986a; Smock and Youssef 1977; White 1978).

Through its scriptures (the Qur'an and hadith) and legal code (*sharī'a*), Islam institutionalizes legal restrictions and gendered inequalities in inheritance, marriage, divorce, child custody, and the ability of women to serve as witnesses (White 1978). Although interpretations of the legal code vary slightly according to the four schools of Islamic law, the law in all its variants generally reflects the patriarchal and patrilineal nature of a society in which women, whether as daughters, wives, or mothers, occupy an inferior position (Coulson and Hinchcliffe 1978).

Perhaps the most egregious example of patriarchy under Islamic family law concerns the matter of polygyny, or the marriage of a man to more than one wife simultaneously. Traditional Sunni Islamic law permits a man to have up to four wives at any given time and does not require him to obtain permission of the court or of his current wife before contracting an additional marriage. Although the Qur'an stresses that a man must be able to treat his wives equally if he is to marry more than one, the law regards this as a matter of personal conscience and therefore does not attempt to legislate equality (Coulson and Hinchcliffe 1978).

Furthermore, under Islamic law, men have the unfettered power to repudiate their wives at will, whether or not the wife is blameworthy. Although it is considered morally reprehensible for a husband to divorce his wife without good cause, the law again regards this as a matter of personal conscience and therefore does not require a man to seek permission for the divorce in a court of law (Coulson and Hinchcliffe 1978). Rather, Sunni Islam recognizes two types of husband-initiated divorce by repudiation, or *talāq*. In the first type, the husband may either pronounce a single formula of divorce ("I divorce thee"), which will become effective when the wife has completed her *'idda* (the legally prescribed waiting period of three menstrual cycles or, if she is pregnant, until she has delivered the child), or he may pronounce three oaths of divorce in three consecutive months. Under this type of divorce, the husband gives himself a chance to reconsider his decision, and intermediaries may be able to reconcile the couple. Thus, this form of divorce accords well with principles of Islamic morality. However, under the second type of divorce—*ṭalāq al-bidʿa*, or divorce of innovation—the husband pronounces three divorce formulas at the same time, thus immediately and irrevocably dissolving the marital union. Unless a man's wife consummates a marriage with another man and this marriage, too, is legally terminated, the husband cannot remarry the wife he divorced in this way. Although this form is regarded as sinful, it is still legally binding and is, unfortunately, more commonly employed than the first type (Coulson and Hinchcliffe 1978).

With either type of divorce, the wife is entitled to claim any unpaid portion of the *mahr*, or bridewealth, although she may have to bring a civil suit in order to recover it. Her right to maintenance, however, continues only during the *ʿidda* period; she has no right to apply for alimony in either a lump sum or as periodic payments (Coulson and Hinchcliffe 1978).

In most Muslim countries, legal reforms enacted by governments during the past century have attempted to mitigate some of the more glaring inequities in these Muslim marriage and divorce laws while still following the general guidelines set forth by the Islamic *sharīʿa* (Coulson and Hinchcliffe 1978; White 1978). In the case of Egypt, codification of the Muslim personal status laws by the state began in the 1920s, with minor reforms enacted twice since 1979. Overall, the Egyptian legal code as it has been fashioned by at least three different political regimes over the past seventy years diverges only slightly from the traditional Islamic legal code (of the Hanafi school), leaving patriarchal gender relations effectively intact and patriarchs "in maximum private control in the family," according to feminist political scientist Mervat Hatem (1986a:26).

Specifically, the 1920 divorce and financial support law attempted to specify the situations under which a woman might be justified in seeking a divorce from her husband. However, the 1920 "reforms" were limited, for the law severely restricted women's right to divorce to extreme cases of lack of male economic support (e.g., desertion, disappearance, imprisonment) or to serious male illness (Hatem 1986a). Although the law stipulated that a husband's failure to support a wife constituted immediate grounds for divorce, women were not allowed to divorce if the poverty of the husband could be proven (effectively legitimating the condition of women whose husbands were simply poor providers). Under this law, a wife was also allowed to file for divorce if the husband suffered from an irreversible fault, such as madness, leprosy, or impotence, whether or not it developed before or after marriage. Again, the law focused on extreme cases of illness of an irreversible nature. And, in all cases, women seeking divorce were to come before a court of law administered by a male judge. Although a 1929 law expanded women's right to divorce based on the concept of "harm" (i.e., that which contributes to marital discord and makes smooth marital relations impossible), the 1929 law left the determination of harm up to these male judges, whose decisions were apt to reflect prevailing patriarchal standards (Hatem 1986a).

On the other hand, the 1920 divorce and financial support law officially validated divorce as a male prerogative, providing no limitations on the warrant for male exercise of that right. Whereas only certain women were allowed to seek divorce in a formal court of law, all men were allowed to divorce their wives by uttering the formula of divorce in the privacy of their own homes. Even with the rise to power of socialist president Gamal Abdel Nasser in the early 1950s, the Egyptian personal status laws governing divorce remained unchanged. The 1962 National Charter, Nasser's blueprint for socialist transformation in Egypt, endorsed equality for women in voting, education, and employment, but did nothing to modify the gender inequities in divorce institutionalized by the personal status laws of the 1920s (Hatem 1986a).

Not until the late 1970s, under the presidency of Anwar Sadat, were further amendments in the law made. Although Sadat declared a "war on polygamy" in 1972, the 1979 personal status amendments signed into law by Sadat were actually limited in their scope, due largely to pressures from Islamist groups in the country. Namely, the 1979 amendments: (1) required legal notification of the first wife that her husband had divorced her or taken a second wife; (2) considered the husband's decision to take a second wife to be a source of harm to the first wife and therefore offered her a choice between staying married to her husband or obtaining a divorce within one year of the polygynous remarriage; (3) allowed a divorced mother to keep the apartment in which she had lived while she was married until the end of the period of maternal child custody; and (4) prevented married women who were refused divorce by the court from being forced by police to return to their legal household.

As Hatem (1986a) argues, the 1979 amendments did little toward achieving gender equity in marriage and divorce rights. Although Muslim men maintained the automatic right to divorce their wives, Muslim women could only ask for divorce in cases of lack of support, severe illness, and now polygyny. Furthermore, if a woman was denied a divorce, she could be forced by law to "the house of obedience"—namely, going back to the husband's household. As Hatem (1986a:37) states, "The law left this concept of coercive matrimony intact, deleting only the formal use of the police to force a woman to return to her husband's household."

Although women's real gains were relatively minimal with the passage of the 1979 personal status laws, male and religious opposition to the laws led to their repeal in 1985 on the grounds that they were passed by presidential decree and presented to the Egyptian Assembly as a *fait accompli*. Later in the same year, due largely to pressures exerted by elite Egyptian women's organizations, the laws were passed again, but with some revisions detrimental to women. For example, whereas the 1979 law stated explicitly that "taking a second wife is considered a source of harm for the first wife" that justifies her filing for divorce within a year of the polygynous marriage, under the 1985 law "a wife whose husband takes a second wife may file for divorce if she suffers from material or nonmaterial harm that makes smooth marital relations within that particular class difficult" (Hatem 1986a). As with earlier determinations of "harm," male judges would decide whether harm had been done and how definitions of harm might vary from one social class to the next. Hatem concludes:

> The history of the last sixty-five years of the current Egyptian patriarchal system shows that it has relied on the potentially contradictory tendencies of increasing the public integration of women while maintaining the gender asymmetry within the patriarchal family in the name of nationalism. . . . The result is the very anomalous situation of women, who, even though they have gained more public rights (to education, work, and political participation), still confront serious forms of gender inequality in the family. (Hatem 1986a:39)

These forms of gender inequality are particularly pronounced in the lives of infertile Egyptian women, who, as will be shown in Chapter 3, live in fear that their husbands will divorce them or take a second wife. Because the 1985 Egyptian personal status laws have remained intact over the past decade under the regime of President Hosni Mubarak, husbands still monopolize the right to repudiate their wives outside a court of law or take a second wife arbitrarily. In cases in which wives have failed to provide offspring for their husbands, husbands who might otherwise frown on either divorce or polygyny may feel justified—and are often encouraged—to exercise these options due to the perceived male right, even obligation, to produce progeny. Many husbands of infertile women choose not to divorce or polygynously remarry, whereas frequently husbands of fertile women with children exercise these options with little consideration for their families. Nonetheless, it is infertile women who are deemed and who deem themselves particularly vulnerable to retrogressive personal status laws, because their "defect" makes their replacement seem quite reasonable.

When a husband is infertile, on the other hand, a wife rarely exercises her option to divorce him in a court of law. With the advent of semen analysis in Egypt, male infertility, along with infertility-producing impotence, is now seen as one of the "serious male illnesses" that might make a woman's request for divorce legitimate in the eyes of a judge and her community. Nevertheless, among the urban Egyptian poor, community standards still deem a woman's request for a divorce immodest and even shameful— no matter the gravity of her marital complaint. Hence, many Egyptian women are effectively prevented from exercising their limited legal rights to divorce, of which they may be extremely poorly apprised. Furthermore, women tend to pride themselves on their superior humanity, especially evident in the treatment of infertile husbands. Whereas a man may use his wife's infertility as an excuse to humiliate, repudiate, or replace her with a fertile cowife, a woman usually protects and pampers her infertile husband, being grateful for her marriage and the likelihood of its increased security.

It is extremely important to emphasize in this discussion of Egyptian personal status laws that these laws are derived from Islamic jurisprudence but are codified by the Egyptian state. The Egyptian state provides a classic example of what Middle Eastern historian Hisham Sharabi (1988) has called "neopatriarchy," a type of "modernized" patriarchy. Sharabi argues that neopatriarchal Arab societies such as Egypt are "schizophrenic," in that beneath the modern appearance is a latent patriarchal reality. Like Middle Eastern gender theorists, Sharabi maintains that the Arab patriarchal family, characterized by relations of paternal authority, dominance, and dependency, is the core building block of a more generalized patriarchy seen in other societal institutions, including the workings of the state. Thus, it should come as no surprise that the Egyptian state promotes modernity in some of the more visible realms of social life, such as women's education, work, voting rights, and participation in moderate feminist organizations, but prefers traditionalism in the private structure of the patriarchal family (Badran 1993). In a sense, then, the Egyptian state plays the role of "general patriarch" (Connell 1990), leaving each Egyptian family with an "individual patriarch" who is free to exercise his Islamically ordained right to ruin his wife's marriage.

The rise of the state in the Middle East may, in fact, be responsible for the very evolution of the patriarchal family, characterized by a pattern of female subordination (Lerner 1986; Ortner 1978). Sherry Ortner (1978), for one, calls the rise of the state "the great divide" in the evolution of male-female relations.

> Indeed here for the first time the term patriarchy becomes applicable, because the structure involves the absolute authority of the father or other senior male over everyone in the household—all junior males and all females. And now women are for the first time brought under direct and systematic control, first by their natal families, and then by their husbands and their affinal kin. Among elites, one has the image of women being rounded up in great numbers and confined in harems and analogous arrangements elsewhere. (Ortner 1978:25–26)

According to Ortner, such a pattern, characterized by idealization of female chastity, an ideology of protection, control, and seclusion of women, and the accountability of husbands/fathers for their family unit vis-à-vis the state, would have developed in one area of the ancient old world and then spread to other early states through trade and other mechanisms of diffusion. Ortner argues that this pattern can still be found in a "broad band" stretching from the circum-Mediterranean area, across the Middle East and southwest Asia, across India, and into China—that is, in the belt of classic patriarchy (Kandiyoti 1991).

If, as Ortner and others have argued, this patriarchal belt still exists, then it becomes clear that this pattern of female subordination does not correspond with any particular religious type, but instead can be found among most of the major world religions, including, minimally, Hinduism, Confucianism, Judaism, and Christianity. Although much comment has been made in both scholarly and lay forums about the particularly emphatic nature of patriarchy under Islam, Islam is not necessarily more patriarchal than these other major world religions, including the other monotheistic religions of the Middle East. As argued by both Kandiyoti (1991) and Moghadam (1993), patriarchy should not be conflated with Islam simply by virtue of geographical coexistence. Like Judaism and Christianity before it, Islam came into being in a patriarchal society, where patrilateral endogamy, the practice of marrying within the tribal lineage, set the shape for the oppression of women in patrilineal society long before the rise of Islam (Tillion 1983). Thus, Islam's patriarchal tendencies correspond to a pre-Islamic situation where women's needs were different from those of the present day and the patrilineal-patrilocal complex described by Kandiyoti (1991) was already in place.

Furthermore, despite its inequitable personal status laws, Islam is not necessarily more determinative or constraining of women's lives than these other religions are (Joseph 1986). Although much comment has been made in the Orientalist and ethnocentric Western feminist literature about the inherently oppressive nature of Islam as the major source of control over women's lives in the Muslim world,[5] gender oppression experienced by Middle Eastern women may have much less to do with Islamic ideology and practice per se than with social, cultural, and political-economic conditions that are often class-based and that cross the boundaries of religious sect. Nonetheless, what is true is that a resurgence of patriarchal gender oppression in many parts of the Middle East can clearly be tied to the rise of Islamism, or what is often referred to as "Islamic fundamentalism" (Marshall 1984; Sharabi 1988). Contemporary Islamist discourse in countries such as Egypt extols the virtues of traditional gender segregation and essentializes women as daughters, wives, and mothers (Badran 1994; Haddad 1980; Moghadam 1994; Rugh 1984).

As noted by Badran (1994:208): "In the current popular Islamist discourse in Egypt there is an essentializing of culture, an allocation to women of timeless attributes. The Muslim woman is first and foremost, if not only, a good daughter, wife and mother, ideally spending her life in the home ministering to her family. This is an ageless model for women exhorted by Islamist men and, to a lesser degree, by Islamist women."

The implications of such Islamist gender typification for infertile Middle Eastern women who are unable to fulfill the wife-mother role have yet to be fully realized, but are likely to be ominous, as we shall see. Yet, for the poor urban Egyptian women who are the subject of this book, Islamism as a social movement has affected their quotidian existence relatively little, for Islamist patriarchal scripts as described above are not the major source, if any, of their subordination. Indeed, Islamism—especially as manifested in the "re-dressing" of women through various forms of extensive veiling—is something new, alien, and mystifying to them, the source of not a little bemusement and a great deal of pragmatic skepticism.

This is not to say that poor urban Egyptian women are unaffected by traditional Islamic ideology. As described in the following chapter, Islamic scriptural passages valorizing women as homemakers, men as breadwinners, and children as the love and gift of God are known even by poor, religiously illiterate women, who view themselves as "good Muslims" and thus attempt to uphold these scriptural ideals. For many of these women, furthermore, religious faith is what enables them to make sense of their difficult life situations and to have hope that God has prescribed a better future with children in store. The various forms of class and gender oppression experienced by these women are often rationalized by reference to God's divine plan, the wisdom of which human beings cannot question.

In summary, Islam, and especially modern extremist versions of it, plays a role in the perpetuation of patriarchy in the Middle East. But, Islam *is not* patriarchy, nor is Islam particularly patriarchal when compared to other major world religions. Decoupling patriarchy from Islam is necessary so as to better understand both the indigenous, pre-Islamic roots of patriarchy in the Middle East, as well as the other potent sources of Middle Eastern women's oppression that are not religiously based.

PATRIARCHY AND CLASS

For many women in the Middle East, the inequalities wrought by a hierarchical class system interact with those wrought by patriarchy to create a double burden of oppression constricting women's lives and opportunities. Yet, the nexus of class and patriarchy in the Middle East and elsewhere is relatively poorly understood. While Marxist feminists have adopted a materialist perspective to understand women's exploitation under capitalism, especially as workers and unpaid domestic laborers, and feminist scholars of other persuasions have adopted a cultural idealist perspective to understand women's oppression under variable sex/gender systems, relatively few scholars have modeled the multiple and overlapping sources of women's oppression, which, in addition to gender and class, may include religion, race, ethnicity, nationality, or other markers of identity, including one's status as a parent. Not only do women's experiences differ, perhaps significantly, across these multiple dimensions (Tong 1989), but the sources of women's oppression cannot be assumed to be merely additive in their effects. As Moore (1988) notes, gender everywhere is experienced through the specific mediations of history, class, race, colonialism, and neo-imperialism. In other words, women are not simply a single oppressed group by virtue of their difference from men; rather, the differences *between* women based on geographic, class, and other foci of inequality may be quite pronounced and may serve to radically separate women from each other in societies where such inequalities are operative.

The need to recognize these multiple sources of women's oppression —and particularly the crucial dynamic between patriarchy and class stratification under capitalism—has been noted by a number of scholars of the Middle East (Gendzier 1981; Hatem 1986a, 1987a; Joseph 1993; MacLeod 1991; Moghadam 1993). However, the concept of "class" in the Middle

East is a problematic issue—perhaps more so than the concept of patri-archy. Namely, the Middle East has often been represented as an area of the world so fundamentally different from the capitalist West that one cannot speak of classes, making class analysis seem irrelevant (Bill 1972).

This view has resulted in a theoretical lacuna that has profoundly affected Middle Eastern gender studies. For example, despite the recent profusion of studies on women and work under changing capitalist con-ditions,[6] class analysis per se is lacking, and certain segments of the female population, particularly urban upper-class women, are relatively overrepre-sented in recent studies (Abdel Kader 1987; Keddie 1979). As Keddie (1979:235) sums up the situation, "The application of class analysis of ide-ologies and movements on more than a crude simplistic level is rare for the Middle East and virtually nonexistent in the study of attitudes toward women and of women's activities."

Yet, there *are* classes in the Middle East, including in Egypt. If "class" can be understood in the Marxist sense as determined by employment—specifically one's position in relationship to ownership or control of the means of production—then it is quite clear that a number of different classes have traditionally existed in the Middle East (Bill 1972; Moghadam 1993). These classes have had differential access to political power and the state, power often being a more important dimension of stratification than wealth in the Middle East (Bill 1972). Furthermore, class location has pro-foundly shaped cultural practices, life-styles, ideologies, and even relations of reproduction in the Middle East (Moghadam 1993); for example, mem-bers of the upper classes in the Middle East may have more in common with members of the upper classes in other countries than with the lower-class members of their own societies, about whose lives they may know very little (Bowen and Early 1993; Rugh 1982).

Although Middle Eastern classes have been variously described,[7] soci-ologist Saad Eddin Ibrahim (1982) has provided the most useful descrip-tion of the class divisions present in urban Egypt. Using the components of income, occupation, education, and durable goods (life-style), he distin-guishes between six class strata in Cairo, providing population estimates for each stratum as follows: (1) the lowest stratum—the destitute (11.2 per-cent); (2) the low stratum—the poor (10.3 percent); (3) the low-middle stratum—the borderline (26.5 percent); (4) the middle stratum—the up-wardly mobile (36.1 percent); (5) the upper-middle stratum—the secure (15.3 percent); and (6) the upper stratum—the rich (1.0 percent). Although this class division may not apply exactly to other urban

Egyptian centers and may have changed slightly over the past decade, it remains a most useful indicator of the socioeconomic hierarchy persisting in Egyptian society, where income, occupation, education, and life-style are all major components of one's perceived class position. This division also points to the high level of poverty in Cairo and probably other major Egyptian cities as well. According to Ibrahim's estimates, nearly half of all families live in the lower end of the class hierarchy, although the majority of these are not truly destitute. Ibrahim distinguishes between the three lowest sectors of the class division by noting the following differences: (1) The *destitute* are families living well below the poverty line, who are supported by a single, unskilled, illiterate breadwinner, live in a one-room apartment, and own very little in the way of durable household goods; (2) the *poor* are families living immediately below the poverty line, who are usually supported by a semiliterate, semiskilled or clerical worker, live in a one- or two-room apartment, and can afford to leave their children in school, perhaps even send one or more to college, although they may own relatively little in the way of durable goods; and (3) the *lower-middle-class borderline* are families living on the upper edge of poverty, who are supported by a skilled or clerical worker, live in a two-room apartment, and may own a number of household appliances, such as a television, refrigerator, and a stove. Although many of these lower-middle-class families are upwardly mobile and identify with the middle class in their values and aspirations, their incomes are barely above the poverty line and thus prevent them from achieving many of their goals and expectations. Nonetheless, the lower-middle class are careful to distinguish themselves from the urban poor, whom they view stereotypically as ignorant, uneducated, uncivilized peasants. This is especially true of lower-middle-class women, who, by virtue of their increasing education and work opportunities, see the gap between themselves and the illiterate, uneducated, unskilled women of the lower and lowest classes as quite wide (MacLeod 1991).[8]

It is extremely important to note that, instead of achieving upward mobility, more and more urban Egyptian families may be sinking into all three lower sectors of the class hierarchy for reasons beyond their control. Perhaps most important, continuing rapid urbanization, fueled by both natural population increase and the seemingly relentless rural-to-urban migration of mostly poor peasants, has taxed urban economies and infrastructures beyond their capacity and has contributed to rampant inflation, particularly in housing prices, in the major cities. As of 1991, approximately 46.7 percent of the total Egyptian population of 52.4 million was urban

(Obermeyer 1992), with more than half of these urbanites living in two cities—namely, Cairo, the largest city in the Middle East and the fifteenth largest in the world, and Alexandria, Egypt's second largest metropolis. Population densities averaging 40,000 persons per square kilometer and exceeding 100,000 per square kilometer in some of Cairo's older districts are indicative of the severity of urban housing shortages and subsequent overcrowding in buildings that are often structurally unsound (Omran and Roudi 1993; Schiffer 1988). An estimated 23 percent of Cairo's population is composed of slumdwellers and squatters, whose homes typically lack clean drinking water, waste disposal facilities, and electricity and are located at a distance from paved roads and transportation lines (Omran and Roudi 1993; Weeks 1988). Because these marginal city dwellers are largely of rural backgrounds, cities such as Cairo and Alexandria have become increasingly "ruralized," with some peri-urban neighborhoods nearly indistinguishable from rural towns and villages (Ahmed 1992; S. Ibrahim 1985).

Moreover, because urbanization has outstripped both population and economic growth in Egypt, the economies of these megacities cannot absorb all the new residents seeking employment. Currently, Egypt has a surplus of working-age adults because young people, both men and women, are entering the labor force faster than the Egyptian economy can create jobs. As a result, the per capita gross national product in Egypt declined from $690 to $620 per year in the four-year interval from 1987 to 1991. To avoid unemployment and to support their families, many urban Egyptian men have chosen "underemployment" in marginal service jobs or glutted government bureaucracies, while thousands of others have become labor migrants in the petro-rich countries of the Gulf, Libya, and before the Gulf War, Iraq. Indeed, Egypt, with the largest population in the Middle East but with relatively small oil reserves, has been the major sending country—supplying approximately 60 percent of the foreign Arab labor (mostly in construction, services, and manufacturing) for the richer countries of the Middle East (LaTowsky 1984; Omran and Roudi 1993). In the mid-1980s, Egyptians working in Iraq sent home an estimated $2 to $3 billion per year, with an additional $800 million to $1 billion coming from Egyptian professionals living in Kuwait (Omran and Roudi 1993). However, the Gulf War sent thousands of Egyptian men, including half of the 1.5 million working in Iraq, home to Egypt, resulting in a major decline in remittances and an additional glut of male workers seeking employment in urban Egyptian centers. This return migration, coupled with $4-billion annual losses in the Egyptian tourist industry following murders of foreign tourists by Islamic extremist groups, has sent the Egyptian economy into a further downward spiral.

As a result of these multiple pressures, urban poverty rates in Egypt continue to rise, sometimes at rates higher than rural areas, and the gap between rich and poor continues to grow (Kennedy 1991; Omran and Roudi 1993). With the limited availability of affordable housing, poor urban Egyptian families of as many as a dozen people may occupy small, dark "apartments" consisting of only one or two cramped rooms, with the cement or mud floors used for everything from sleeping to cooking to the raising of small animals. Because many apartments lack plumbing, multiple families within one apartment building may share inadequate water supplies and bathroom facilities. And, because of the frank shortage of space in most households, domestic activities, such as food preparation and cooking, bathing of children, and eating, tend to spill out into communal passageways, serving to blur any distinction between "public" and "private" space (Nadim 1985).

It is women, rather than men, who face the major burden of living under such conditions of urban poverty. Although lower-class men experience various forms of oppression as laborers in urban working environments that are often unhealthful and sometimes dehumanizing (Inhorn and Buss 1994), relatively little of their daily existence is spent in the bleak quarters of poor households, where women, most of whom do not work outside the home, struggle to meet their families' most basic subsistence needs on their husbands' limited earnings. Struggles with husbands over money are common, since husbands may or may not turn their salaries over to their wives and are notorious for spending what little money they earn on themselves (e.g., "pocket money" for cigarettes and coffee, tea, and meals taken outside the home) rather than on household needs. As Homa Hoodfar (1988) describes the situation among poor families in Cairo, women are the losers in a changing balance of power between husbands and wives. Because women have lost their traditional productive skills in the urban environment and because they lack access to income except through the poorly paid informal sector, women have become more dependent on their husbands as major cash earners, whereas men have become less dependent on their wives for services that they now can purchase outside the home. As Hoodfar states:

> The new social changes have failed to provide corresponding cash-earning opportunities for women of the lower social strata, who are handicapped by

widespread illiteracy coupled with a lack of formal education, saleable skills, and any sizeable capital. Other important constraints are the crippling cultural practices and values that allow a woman to engage in independent cash-earning activities only if her husband fails to provide for the family. This failure is so socially discrediting for both the husband and the wife that only the most desperate family will admit it. In addition, the social necessity of obtaining the husband or male guardian's permission to work for an income, together with sex segregation, keep women in a disadvantaged position.

The changing socioeconomic conditions in urban Egypt have intensified the inequalities between lower-income husbands and wives. . . . All the women in my sample, although readily accepting the ideology of man the breadwinner, thought it necessary under the existing social order for a woman to have an income of her own to help provide a better life for her children and herself and to make her more of an equal partner in the eyes of her husband. (Hoodfar 1988:142)

As we shall see in the following chapter, this patriarchal ideology of "man the breadwinner, woman the homemaker" constrains infertile as well as fertile Egyptian women with children. Despite their freedom from child-rearing responsibilities and their dire needs for money to support their costly therapeutic quests, most poor infertile women continue to be disallowed by their husbands from working outside the home, either as factory workers or domestics. Not only would such work reflect poorly on a husband's ability to support himself and his wife, but it would also expose a woman to the indignities and degradations of manual labor in a typically mixed-sex milieu. Consequently, poor infertile women spend their days at home, but without the joys and responsibilities of motherhood to fill their empty hours. The psychosocial consequences of such forced solitude can be quite profound, especially given the neighborly ostracism that many infertile women experience. Yet, given the strength of the cultural norm barring women from work after marriage, poor infertile women are in a strongly disadvantaged position in terms of resisting this norm, and many of them frankly accept it as a laudable ideal.

In work as in many other important areas of social life, poor urban Egyptian women, both fertile and infertile, experience the pressures of patriarchy more intensely than women of the higher classes. Patriarchy exists in an inverse relationship with class in urban Egypt: The higher the class position of a woman, the less likely she is to be constrained by patriarchal ideologies and practices that serve to limit her life options; and, conversely, the lower the class position of a woman, the more likely she is to experience gender oppression as manifested in, *inter alia*, lack of educational and work opportunities, restricted mobility, early arranged marriage to a man she does not know, marital inequities and insecurities of various kinds including increased fear of repudiation, domination by affines who may live in the same household, social control by female kin and neighbors through gossiping and other forms of informational exchange, and, most important to this discussion, increased expectations of immediate and continued childbearing. In other words, although Egyptian women of all classes may experience various forms of patriarchal oppression, this oppression is intensified at the bottom of the socioeconomic ladder, where class oppression in the form of real economic struggle magnifies the problems of patriarchy in many cases. By virtue of the poverty they are forced to assume with their husbands, poor women are more likely to share living accommodations with kin who may subordinate them, to be victimized by angry, frustrated husbands who are unable to provide adequate support, to be prevented from obtaining the skills, education, and employment that might help to facilitate their economic mobility, and to be expected to achieve fulfillment from motherhood alone.

With respect to this last point, although Egyptian women of all classes are expected to become mothers, often abandoning their jobs permanently following the birth of their first child, motherhood expectations are exaggerated among the urban poor, who view motherhood as less a role than as a woman's primary identity. Because poor urban women have been stripped of the productive roles still held by women in the rural economy, they have been forced, in a sense, to focus exclusively on their *re*productive roles. The impact of the loss of poor urban Egyptian women's contributions to domestic production on the evolution of a unitary, even obsessive focus on reproduction and mothering cannot be underestimated. Not only does it help to explain poor urban women's fertility behavior (Inhorn 1996), but it also suggests why the experience of infertility among poor urban women is so significantly determined by the absence of legitimate roles other than mothering. Indeed, poor infertile women, who as a group are unschooled, illiterate, and unskilled, see themselves as being at a great disadvantage in relation to the educated women of the middle and upper classes. Such educated women, they argue, are able to marry "enlightened" husbands, support themselves and fill their empty hours through work, and achieve independence should infertility end their marriages. Poor women, on the other hand, are economically dependent on their husbands, who often lack enlightenment (their "brains are locked"), and thus they see the magnitude of their own infertility problems and resultant insecurity as being much greater than that of the women of the higher classes.

Furthermore, the desire for children and the consequent level of child-bearing among the Egyptian urban poor are in many ways tied to (if not directly determined by) membership in the rapidly growing urban under-class. Although pronatalism, or child desire, among the urban poor will be analyzed in some detail in Chapter 6, suffice it to say here that children become one's primary capital in the urban environment—less a means of production through future labor returns than a form of symbolic capital and perpetuity after death. With widespread anomie and alienation in the urban environment, the Egyptian poor look to their children as compensation for all that is lacking in their own lives of hardship and despair. Moreover, one's children may provide the sole memorial to relatively short and bitter lives spent on this earth.

Thus, studying the particularly difficult life situations of the urban Egyptian poor and the childless among them would seem to have special merit. Not only can an understanding of the infertility experience in a poor country such as Egypt shed significant light on issues of *fertility* and why impoverished people desire and need children (Inhorn 1994), but understanding the infertility experience can reveal a great deal about the nature of human suffering, particularly in the absence of physical pain. Investigating such suffering—as well as other forms of human misery—is an essential (although unsettling) enterprise, especially if such problems are to be overcome. Exploring the suffering of infertility as experienced by a group of poor urban Egyptian women is only one small step in that direction. However, understanding the subjectivities of such "women on the margins," including on the margins of Middle Eastern social life, is an enterprise whose time has definitely arrived.

PATRIARCHY AND WOMEN'S SUBJECTIVITY
If we focus on the margins of society in our studies of Middle Eastern women, "the ideological structures and cultural attitudes surrounding and defining women's roles acquire a clarity and starkness." So argues Judith Tucker (1985:10), a feminist historian who has drawn attention to some of the most subaltern segments of Egyptian society in her study of nineteenth-century lower-class women, particularly prostitutes and slaves. Yet, Tucker is but one of a growing number of feminist scholars who have chosen to focus their studies on Middle Eastern women on the social

periphery—women who, by virtue of their class position, relative power-lessness, social obscurity, illicit activities, or official dismissal, have led lives unknown even to other members of their own societies. This is as true of the poor infertile women whose lives are to be described in this book, as it is of the women prostitutes and slaves (Tucker 1985), traditional midwives and spiritist healers (Inhorn 1994), Cairene *baladī* women (Early 1993), and Bedouin women of the Western Desert (Abu-Lughod 1986; 1993) whose stories and struggles have been represented in other recent Egyptian eth-nographies and social histories.

Following some provocative critiques of scholarly complicity in either ignoring, misrepresenting, or "muting" the voices of the weak, powerless, and oppressed (Ardener 1975; Spivak 1988), Middle Eastern feminist schol-ars have recently pointed to the need to give voice to such individuals and groups—to let women subjects speak for themselves (instead of scholars speaking for them), thereby revealing their consciousnesses and subjectivi-ties under various forms of oppression (Abdel Kader 1987; Abu-Lughod 1989; MacLeod 1991; Mernissi 1989; Morsy et al. 1991; Nelson 1991; Sulli-van and Ismael 1991a). In methodological terms, this has meant a move-ment away from standard source materials (e.g., the Islamic scriptures, theological treatises, censuses) to various forms of historical and ethno-graphic research in which the researcher remains empathetically engaged in the lives of real, speaking subjects. The result has been most interesting and has included recent works rich in various forms of ethnographic life-storytelling (e.g., Abu-Lughod 1993; Early 1993; Friedl 1989), as well as discourse-oriented narratives and dialogical interviewing about women's lives (e.g., Abu-Lughod 1986; Early 1982, 1985; Mernissi 1989).

What has been revealed, in part, is that women's own reflexive dis-course differs substantially from the pervasive male discourse found in earlier male-biased ethnographies, contemporary Islamist pronounce-ments, and other "official" representations of women's lives. Indeed, women's subjective views of men and of themselves as women, includ-ing their beliefs about maleness and femaleness, may diverge substantially from those of men, making the need for careful, nuanced ethnography about women's belief systems quite obvious (Dwyer 1978a). Furthermore, such new approaches have yielded a number of other important insights about Middle Eastern women. For one, individual women's lives are often rich in complexity and may differ substantially from those of other women, including those sharing supposed similarities in life circumstances (Abu-Lughod 1989; Abdel Kader 1987; Acker 1986; Inhorn 1994). Furthermore, Middle Eastern women are not the stereotypically silent, pitiable, downtrodden souls represented in Western discourse (Nader 1989); their strength, courage, fortitude, and dignity, even in the face of significant odds, are often abundantly apparent in works in which women subjects are given the opportunity to talk about their own lives.

In addition, when women are allowed to speak and tell stories, themes such as "honor and shame," which have obsessed generations of Middle Eastern scholars, may be obviously overshadowed by other moral principles (Gilmore 1987). Because analysis of the experiential level has too often been overlooked in the literature on Middle Eastern women's lives —in favor of textual, symbolic interpretive, structural functionalist, and historical materialist analyses, to name but a few—certain subjects have been privileged at the expense of others.[9] Thus, in the Middle Eastern literature on women, the preoccupation with the discourse on "honor and shame" is widespread, given the titillating association of these concepts with women's sexuality and comportment. Yet, interestingly enough, actual knowledge of Middle Eastern women's sexuality—including beliefs and practices—is lacking (Keddie 1979; Eickelman 1989), as is an understanding of the importance of other morally based concepts, such as piety, pride, and compassion, in women's lives.

To wit, among Egyptians, women are adamant that infertility has "nothing to do with honor and shame," although it certainly affects personal pride and dignity. According to poor urban Egyptian women, honor infractions are behaviorally induced; the source of shame always resides in behavioral violations, particularly in the realm of sexuality. Infertility, on the other hand, has nothing to do with immodest behavior, and thus does not reflect on a woman's honor, which remains unmarred. Rather, infertility is viewed as "out of one's hands," or beyond one's control. The nonvolitional nature of infertility may, in fact, generate sympathy among others, although infertile women are still viewed with suspicion given their perceived "incompleteness" and their purported ability to cause harm to others by way of envy.

That we know "too much" about certain limited themes in Middle Eastern women's lives, such as honor and shame, and much too little about many other realms of women's existence, such as the experience of infertility, is a problem requiring remedy (Abu-Lughod 1989; Ahmed 1992; Sullivan and Ismael 1991a). As Leila Ahmed (1992:248) puts it: "The sum of what is currently known about women and gender in Arab societies— the many and different Arab societies and cultures that there are—is miniscule. The areas of women's lives and the informal structures they inhabit that are still unexplored are vast." However, in critiquing the Western feminist discourse on Arab Muslim women, Ahmed calls for self-reflexivity in portraying Middle Eastern women's lives and cautions against focusing only on the worst practices and forms of oppression (e.g., the "harem," purdah, polygyny and temporary marriage, and female circumcision).

The need for reflexivity and nuanced portrayals of women's lives is especially true if one considers the profound social transformations affecting women often for the better but sometimes for the worse throughout the Middle East. Such potentially positive changes include: the erosion of the patriarchal extended family and traditional kinship systems, particularly in urban areas through the process of residential nuclearization (Barakat 1985; Joseph 1994; Moghadam 1993; Rassam 1987; Sharabi 1988); the entrance of vast numbers of women (usually of specific classes) into educational facilities and workplaces (Moghadam 1993; Rassam 1987); reform of Muslim family law, including in some Middle Eastern states the abolition of male repudiation and polygyny, secularization of inheritance law, and, in the most extreme case, replacement of all religious law with a civil code (as in the case of Turkey) (Moghadam 1993; White 1978); and the rise of potentially revolutionary women's movements throughout this region (Sharabi 1988). Indeed, as Valentine Moghadam (1993) and others have pointed out, the very foundations of patriarchy are being undermined through such transformations, with implications for women's lives that have yet to be fully realized or understood.

On the other hand, not all social transformations occurring in the Middle East are potentially liberating for women. Nuclearization of the family, with its potential for democratization of the conjugal relationship, may paradoxically lead to a shifting balance of power in favor of husbands (Hoodfar 1988). This is especially the case in urban areas where men have become proletarianized workers and women the consumers of men's earnings. Moreover, the breakdown of the traditional patriarchal extended family, especially in urban areas, has been deemed one of the most important causes of the "reaction" of Islamism in the Middle East (Moghadam 1994), which reinstates classic patriarchal conditions in ways that have not been realized for centuries.

Given these escalating but countervailing pressures, the need to study Middle Eastern women's lives under specific, historically contextualized, class-based and culturally localized conditions is greater than ever. Just as it is false to speak of "Middle Eastern" or "Arab" or "Muslim" women in monolithic terms, so is it false to speak of a unitary "Middle Eastern" or "Arab" or "Muslim" patriarchy that oppresses them. Middle Eastern patriarchy, too, must be historicized, localized, and "class"-ified if women's lives and subjectivities under it are to be fully understood (Hatem 1986a, 1986b, 1987a; Kandiyoti 1991).

In this book, I attempt to represent the lives of poor infertile Egyptian women as ones deeply affected by a changing patriarchal system in a highly class-stratified urban setting. Unlike so many other recent ethnographies of women's lives in Egypt (Early 1993; MacLeod 1991; Rugh 1984; Watson 1992; Wikan 1980), this book focuses not on Cairo, but on Alexandria, Egypt's second largest city (of three to five million inhabitants, depending upon the estimate) and the country's major Mediterranean seaport. Despite Alexandria's glorious history as the beautiful, cosmopolitan hub of the ancient Hellenic world (Inhorn 1994), the city today is a sprawling, increasingly polluted, newly industrializing center that continues to draw thousands of job-seeking poor peasants from the Nile Delta region and Upper Egypt, as well as summer crowds of affluent Cairenes, who vacation in the villas and hotels stretching for miles along Alexandria's Mediterranean shoreline.

The women who form the collective voice of this book are members of Alexandria's growing legions of urban poor. When I met these women during the period of October 1988 to December 1989, some were truly destitute, a few had achieved lower-middle-class status, but the vast majority were simply poor—able to meet their daily subsistence needs but struggling to afford much else.

Meeting these women was greatly facilitated by the location of my ethnographic fieldwork, which was based at the University of Alexandria's Shatby Hospital. As a large, public teaching hospital, "Shatby" (as the hospital is usually referred to) caters primarily to lower-class women from the Alexandria vicinity and its provincial outskirts, who use the facility for both primary and tertiary care. In addition to the large number of deliveries that take place at Shatby each day, the hospital provides contraceptive services, a walk-in outpatient clinic for minor gynecological complaints and prenatal care, inpatient services for gynecological surgeries and cesarean deliveries, and an outpatient infertility clinic. As a public teaching hospital, most services are offered at a nominal charge.

Because of the nature of Shatby's patient population, I was able to meet both infertile women attending the hospital's infertility clinic, as well as fertile women coming to Shatby for childbirth, contraception, and a host of other reproductive services. During the course of my fieldwork, I interviewed and often befriended one hundred of these infertile women, as well as ninety fertile women, whose views of infertility were important to gather for comparative purposes. Although I conducted all semistructured interviews within the confines of the hospital, I was invited to many women's homes in the poor neighborhoods of Alexandria and, in a few cases, the provincial cities outside Alexandria. There, I conducted the less formal aspects of my fieldwork, including talking to husbands, healers, neighbors, and kin, and generally observing and participating in family and community life.

Although a detailed discussion of my fieldwork experience and methodology and a profile of my infertile informants can be found in *Quest for Conception: Gender, Infertility, and Egyptian Medical Traditions* (Inhorn 1994), it is important to mention a number of points here. First, the infertile women who became my informants were all seeking treatment for infertility and seeking that treatment at a hospital. Obviously, not all Egyptian women seek biomedical treatment for infertility (although I would wager a guess that most do), and those who do so may seek treatment in a variety of nonhospital settings (Inhorn 1994). Presumably, infertile Egyptian women who end up seeking treatment at a hospital may represent more difficult, intractable cases of infertility. Thus, these women may not be representative of the wider population of infertile women, who may become pregnant spontaneously or with minimal interventions by private physicians or traditional healers.

Second, I suspect that the significant proportions of cousin and "love" marriages encountered among infertile women in this study may reflect the fact that husbands who are related to their wives or who married them "for love" are more likely to "stick by them" and see to it that they receive the most comprehensive, up-to-date care (Inhorn 1994). In other words, proportionally, the women in my study may have had more successful marriages than would normally be encountered among infertile Egyptian couples. This issue of marital success versus failure will be taken up at length in Chapter 3.

Third, it is important to note that, despite the location of my fieldwork in Alexandria, many of my informants hailed originally from other regions of Egypt (Inhorn 1994). Ethnically, they represented all four of the major groups in Egypt, as indigenously defined (i.e., Lower Egyptian, Upper Egyptian, Nubian, Bedouin). Thus, in a sense, women of the entire nation of Egypt were included in this study, and, from the standpoint of infertility, their problems and responses often crossed ethnic boundaries, suggesting that the infertility experience involves common features in Egypt.

Fourth, the fact that I dealt almost exclusively with women, as opposed to men, was both intentional and an artifact of the fieldwork process itself (Inhorn 1994). On the one hand, I intended to produce a study that was gynecocentric, given my feminist interests in women's issues in general and women's health issues in particular. In designing this research, I was extremely cognizant of the fact that in Egypt—as in most of the world, including the West—infertility tends to be viewed as a woman's problem, rather than as a man's or a couple's problem. In settings around the world, this view is reinforced through the infertility care-seeking process, in which women's bodies—and not men's—undergo often inordinate amounts of biotechnological intervention (Inhorn 1994). In Egypt, not only are women the primary targets of therapeutic manipulation—whether or not the infertility problem is located in the woman's body—but infertility treatment is rarely undertaken by "couples," given the fact that, on the "official" social structural, ideological, and linguistic levels, "couples" do not exist in Egypt. (Both the "official" and "unofficial" aspects of this issue will be explored in greater depth in Chapter 3.) In the research setting, I discovered that husbands only occasionally accompanied their wives to the hospital for infertility treatment and usually only on days in which their semen was needed for analysis or artificial insemination. Furthermore, because most Egyptian men work during hospital or clinic hours, they either are unable or refuse to participate in their wives' infertility diagnosis and management. As a result, I had much better access to women than to men. Although I eventually met many husbands—some of whom acknowledged their own infertility and most of whom were quite open with and friendly toward me—these interactions with men in my informants' homes were limited to what I would characterize as "formal hospitality." My level of understanding of men's lives, including those of my informants' husbands, was superficial compared to my eventual knowledge of women's lives, both infertile and fertile (Inhorn 1994). Thus, it is extremely important to state at the outset that I came to know much more about Egyptian *husbands*, as seen through the eyes of Egyptian wives, than about Egyptian *men* in either a general sense or individually. In other words, this is a book about Egyptian women and, to a lesser extent, about Egyptian husbands viewed from a feminine perspective. As the postmodern feminist Luce Irigaray (1985) has argued, the only woman we know is the "masculine feminine," the woman as man sees her (in literature, philosophy, scholarship, and so on). Here, I attempt not only to explore the "feminine masculine," or perceptions of Egyptian men from the woman's point of view, but also the "feminine feminine," or women's views of themselves and other women.

I attempt to represent the lives of these women not only in their individuality, but as ones deeply enmeshed in the relationships of marriage, kinship, and neighborliness. Because their lives share common features, I will concentrate on crosscutting themes. Nevertheless, these women's individual stories contain unique complexities. In addition, they are usually poignant—some extremely so. In an attempt to represent both the commonalities and contrasts of women's experiences, I will draw upon individual life stories throughout this book, and I will also use segments of women's narratives in an attempt to give voice to their realities. Although I intend to make clear the profound tragedy of infertility for most of these women, I also intend to represent the dignity, resourcefulness, and courage with which they face the emotional and practical dilemmas of their infertile lives.

Furthermore, in representing gender relations and the political negotiations they entail, I intend to focus on the lived experiences of women and their "local moral worlds of suffering" (Kleinman 1992). Although the literature on Middle Eastern women and gender is rapidly proliferating, I find myself disturbed by a continuing idealist bias, based on official ideologies of gender. Instead of examining women's lives *as lived* and the everyday enactment of gender relations between women themselves and between women and men, many authors, including anthropologists, tend to rely on less direct sources of evidence—be they texts, historical documents, media accounts, stories, poems, diaries, or formal interviews—as the basis of their conclusions about women's and men's lives in the Middle East. Although these sources of information are important in their own right, I believe that they can never substitute for the insights gained through phenomenologically oriented, experiential participation in women's lives and empathic, in-depth interviewing of women themselves. Furthermore, to understand the complexities of the gender relations among and between the sexes, one must come to understand how men and women *actually relate*, which is perhaps best accomplished through systematic but sympathetic entrance into the cultural worlds of others (di Leonardo 1991), vis-à-vis participant observation and in-depth discussion with social actors.

Having attempted such a methodological approach, what I offer here is an analysis that is neither symbolic interpretive nor historical materialist, but phenomenological and social interactionist in perspective. I am interested in situating infertile Egyptian women at the center of a web of practical relationships, with husbands nearest the center and community members nearest the periphery. Thus, I have organized the chapters of this book in concentric circles of social action, beginning with the key players, women themselves, and ending with the children who form a desired but imagined part of their existence.

In Chapter 2, "Missing Motherhood," I focus on the infertile women of this study, whose lives are marred by isolation and questions of identity. In particular, I am interested in the cultural specificity of the social construction of gender and motherhood among the Egyptian urban poor. What does it mean to be a "female," a "woman," and a "mother"? Are these sources of identity and social role connected? Although infertile women perceive their own lives as diverging considerably from widely accepted identity norms, they are often grief-stricken over this divergence, given their beliefs in the inherent rightness of motherhood and all it entails. Because infertile women are "missing motherhood," they see their lives as paling in comparison to those of other women, especially given the domestic seclusion and loneliness that are a daily part of infertile women's existences. As we shall see, such isolation is tied to the cultural privileging of motherhood itself, which is bolstered by the patriarchal ideologies of Islam and by recent capitalist transformations that have metamorphosed poor urban women into housewives. For infertile women, the psychosocial implications of the valorization of both motherhood and domesticity are profound, for alternative roles and identities are not easily achieved.

In Chapter 3, "Conjugal Connectivity," the politics of marriage among the Egyptian urban poor are explored in light of the problem of childlessness. Contrasting marital ideals, expectations, and realities are highlighted in an attempt to explain the divergent outcomes of actual infertile marriages. That most poor infertile women face marital uncertainties, including the ever present possibilities of repudiation or polygyny, should become abundantly clear in that chapter. But what will also become apparent are the common demonstrations of love, affection, compassion, and commitment between many infertile couples, whose marriages seem to resemble the "companionate" form thought typical only of the middle and upper classes. Such conjugal connectivity and resilience in the face of sometimes overwhelming external pressures force us to rethink our worn-out notions of Middle Eastern sex segregation and the purported great gulf between men and women, husbands and wives. Furthermore, it challenges notions of Middle Eastern family life: that is, that the supposed corporate nature of family groups in the Middle East requires the subordination of individual desires to the "will of the group" (Rugh 1984), such that marital partners feel less connection to each other than to their families of origin. Although not every infertile marriage is harmonious or remains intact, the disproportionate ratio of marital success to failure speaks to changing marital arrangements, accommodations, and alliances among the men and women of the urban Egyptian underclass.

In Chapter 4, "Relatives' Responses," the nature of familial intervention in the lives and marriages of infertile women will be examined. Among the Egyptian urban poor, husbands' and wives' families play countervailing roles in their attempts at marital negotiation. Whereas husbands' kin often attempt to tear asunder the "useless" infertile union and are the first to stigmatize the infertile wife, wives' families are "stigma managers," protecting their infertile daughters, urging marital persistence and remediation, and even facilitating fostering arrangements with couples' nieces and nephews (although not adoption, which is culturally prohibited). The degree to which families succeed in their efforts to effect either positive or negative change in the infertile marriage will be examined in some detail. Although husbands' mothers and other family members may still succeed in instigating polygynous remarriage or divorce, overall their influence is waning in light of changing notions of the family and an accompanying diminution of senior women's relative social power over their sons and daughters-in-law. With the recent pronounced breakdown of patrilocal extended families in the urban setting, it is not unusual for couples to have relatively little sustained contact with the kin of either partner, freeing them from the connective claims and obligations that relatives may impose. For infertile women, however, liberation from the subordination of female in-laws may mean increased reliance on their husbands, with implications for women's marriages that may be profound.

In Chapter 5, "Endangered Neighbors," we shall see that infertile women's female in-laws are not the only women who may band against them. The experience of overt stigmatization and ostracism is most evident in poor urban neighborhoods, where female community members may engage in malicious gossip about the infertile woman and strategies of covert and overt avoidance. It is in their relationships with neighbor women, who rarely perceive them as normal, that infertile women feel perhaps most acutely the pity and hostility they arouse. At home in their crowded neighborhoods and apartment buildings, infertile women must shield themselves from accusations of *hasad*—the giving of the evil eye—of which they are suspected by virtue of their childlessness and by which they are thought to endanger their neighbors. Although not all fertile neighbors subscribe to such traditional beliefs about infertile women's inherent, destructive envy, infertile women must be on guard for this eventuality in every neighborly relationship and must find ways to manage the social tension engendered in mixed contacts with "normal" women and their children.

In the concluding chapter, "Child Desire," the stigmatization of infertile women is examined in light of pronatalism, or the intense ideological emphasis among Egyptians of all classes on the desirability of having children. Although Egyptian pronatalism has received much attention from scholars and population policymakers, it has been viewed primarily as a demographic issue manifested in soaring population growth rates, the failure of family planning campaigns to curb significantly such growth, and the continued large size of the average Egyptian family. However, Egyptian pronatalism is also a social and cultural issue inextricably linked to the psychosocial and various relational problems facing infertile women. Infertility would not be such a grave social onus for women were it not for pronatalist ideologies extolling the virtues—indeed, the necessity—of producing offspring. Thus, in Egypt, pronatalism—and the patriarchal ideologies that underlie it—is at the root of both population growth *and* infertility stigmatization, throwing into relief the intimate connection between the domains of fertility and infertility. In order to reveal this connection, the desires for children among the Egyptian urban poor must be examined from a sociocultural perspective that takes into account three related levels of analysis: the individual psychosocial, the social structural, and the political-economic. In this concluding chapter, the importance of children—and, by extension, parenthood—on all three levels will be explored. The intent is to shed more light on the uncertain future of poor urban infertile women in an increasingly pronatalist, Islamic Egypt.

2. Missing Motherhood

Paradise lies under the feet of mothers.
—An Egyptian proverb from the hadith

Fayza's Story

As Fayza sees it, fate and the wishes of her father conspired against her to lead her life down a childless path devoid of happiness and the material pleasures that might ease her suffering.[1] For Fayza, her troubles began in early childhood, when her father promised her in future marriage to his only sister's only son. At that time, Fayza was her father's only child. Seven children that followed either died in utero, in childbirth, or in early infancy to the ravages of disease. (Two additional children, a girl and a boy, survived these neonatal perils and are married adults today.) Thus, Fayza was a precious child, coddled by her parents and grandparents and allowed to play while other young girls her age were expected to help their mothers and raise their younger siblings.

However, Fayza's misery began when she was sent to the neighborhood elementary school, which had been built with Nasser's largess after the 1952 revolution. There, it became widely known that little Fayza was already promised to her cousin Sami. As Fayza recalls, "Even the teachers picked on me. They would tell me, 'You're engaged to the son of your paternal aunt. You're getting married. You're still too young for this. What is this engagement they're talking about? Why aren't you wearing your wedding ring?' They drove me away from school. And all my friends in the street said, 'You're engaged. You're the bride.'" So, when the teasing became too much for Fayza to bear, her mother and father took pity on her and withdrew her from school in the fourth grade, before Fayza had learned to read or write. From that point on, Fayza stayed at home with her mother, whose days had frankly been lonely without her beloved daughter, and Fayza was not permitted by her parents to venture out into the streets where the other children played.

Although Fayza's late childhood and early adolescence were spent in virtual seclusion, she and a young man who lived across the street began to glance at each other from their balconies, where Fayza occasionally sat to gaze at the world of the street below. As Fayza explains, "You find his looks full of admiration for you. Your heart feels that he's attached to you. And he used to, whenever he saw me, to stand on purpose in the place where he stands. But it was loving each other at a distance. We didn't talk or walk together or sit together, because I was very young, an adolescent. I was very happy [as an adolescent], because I was very beautiful—more than now. And my body was always full."

Unfortunately for Fayza, fate took its course, and she became officially engaged at the age of sixteen to her cousin Sami. Sami's mother brought the bridewealth *shabka*, a gift of bracelets and a wedding ring, and the two families threw an official engagement party to which family and neighbors alike were invited. But following the engagement, Fayza, who was plump, fair-skinned, and lovely and had never been ill a day in her life, began losing weight rapidly, describing herself as a skeleton. "I didn't lose weight and become skin on bones except when I got engaged," she explains. "Through the year when I was engaged, you wouldn't know me. Whoever saw me would say, 'No, this is not her. What happened?'" Fayza's concerned parents took her to a doctor, who examined her and told them, "She has no physical illness. She doesn't like the groom." And then he asked Fayza in front of her mother and father, "Don't you like the groom?" She responded, "No, I like him," modesty precluding an honest reply. When she returned home, her mother asked her in private, "Indeed, do you really not want him?" When Fayza did not respond, her mother repeated the question, "Don't you want him, Fayza?" Following Fayza's continued silence, her mother finally said, "Then *you* tell your father. I can't tell him such a thing. He never breaks your words, so you go and tell him."

As Fayza's mother knew all too well, her daughter did not have the courage to defy her father's wishes or to admit that she was in love with a total stranger instead of her father's nephew. Thus, Fayza remained in her depression and engagement for a period of a year, which ended with her marriage to Sami. "When I felt that I lost the other young man and that he lost me, I started to hate Sami more," Fayza explains. "I didn't want him. In my mind, I didn't want him, but I couldn't confess it to anyone, because all of them wanted me to marry this one, meaning that I *would* marry this one

... I had no idea about the story of sex and I had no idea about these things at all. Except that a man would marry a woman to serve him and that's it. To see to the affairs of his house and that's all. I had no idea [about sex]. Even when I got married, I had no idea. No one told me about anything."

Not surprisingly, given Fayza's feelings of aversion toward the groom and her complete lack of knowledge about sex, the wedding night was a disaster. When Sami came to bed bearing the white defloration handkerchief given to him by Fayza's grandmother, Fayza was in a panic, thinking "Oh, my God! No, I don't want him!" But she knew that if she tried to run away, the families would say, "She's in love with someone else. So that's why she doesn't want this one." Thus, Fayza was trapped. She and Sami stayed awake all night, with Sami repeatedly attempting to penetrate his new wife in order to bloody the piece of cloth and prove his wife's "honor" as an untouched virgin. Because of Fayza's fear and recalcitrance, the *dukhla*, or penetration, eventually occurred by force at six in the morning. Until that moment, Fayza had still "defeated him." But the early-morning loss of her virginity to a man whom she did not love and who took her by force "is what defeated me," according to Fayza.

Amazingly, given the inauspicious advent of her marriage, Fayza's feelings began to change over time. For one, Fayza's mother-in-law, who loved Fayza's father very much, took Fayza "into her bosom," making her feel part of the family in whose home she was now living. Neither Fayza's mother-in-law nor father-in-law said a word to upset the young bride and, at least initially, let her sleep late into the morning hours after the others had already awakened. Furthermore, Fayza began loving her cousin Sami "bit by bit." Whereas in the beginning she had "hated him as a husband," but "loved him as a brother," after months in his presence she began "loving him as a husband very much, to the extent that today he's everything in my life."

Indeed, although Sami sensed his wife's initial antipathy, he never spoke a harsh word to her nor made her feel diminished by the fact that no children were forthcoming in their marriage. As the months passed, Sami and his family could not help but to notice that Fayza's belly did not grow and that she continued to wash her menstrual rags. Although Sami himself was patient, believing God would provide them with a child at the appropriate time, Sami's mother became concerned, fearing a cold draft or some impurity might have deleteriously affected Fayza's reproductive organs.[2] Once two years had passed, Sami's mother began saying things to both Fayza and her mother about Fayza's continuing childlessness. Fayza's mother was nonchalant, attributing the lack of children to Fayza's youth, for she had not yet turned twenty. But Fayza's mother-in-law was impatient to see the child of her only son. So, without consulting Fayza's parents, she decided to take her daughter-in-law to a *dāya*, or traditional midwife, who was renowned in the area for her ability to cure the maladies of the infertile.

Without examining Fayza, the *dāya* told her that she had an infection that was preventing pregnancy. She made three *ṣūwaf*, or vaginal suppositories of herbs and honey wrapped in gauze, which she inserted deep inside Fayza's vagina. In the morning when Fayza was supposed to remove the *ṣūwaf*, she could find only two of the suppositories and told her mother-in-law that she was also experiencing considerable pelvic pain. Her mother-in-law brought the *dāya* to their home to examine Fayza. When the *dāya* could not find the third suppository upon a manual examination of Fayza's vagina, she told Fayza and her mother-in-law that it must have fallen out without Fayza's knowledge. Fayza, who was in so much pain that she fainted during the examination and had to be revived with onions and cold water on her face, knew that the third suppository was still missing inside of her. Once the *dāya* had left, Fayza's worried mother-in-law took Fayza straight to a doctor. Too ashamed to tell the doctor what had happened, Fayza said, "I feel something bursting inside my tummy. I feel the part that has burst. It's hurting me, oh doctor." Without examining Fayza, the doctor told her that she probably had appendicitis, and he recommended that she have an X ray and an operation to "open her belly."

Eventually, after the pain had subsided and she had recovered her strength, Fayza went to another doctor, who recommended that Fayza's husband undergo a semen analysis and that Fayza undergo a laparoscopy, a surgical diagnostic procedure to examine the interior of her pelvis by way of a scoping device. The semen analysis revealed that Sami was quite healthy and fertile and thus could not be the source of the couple's childlessness. However, the laparoscopy revealed the effects of a severe pelvic infection that had scarred Fayza's fallopian tubes beyond recognition and had blocked at least one tube completely.

As Fayza explains, "My tubes are blocked as a result of this bad *dāya*. Believe me, my mother-in-law didn't feel anything. She didn't feel she'd made a mistake, except that she kept telling me, 'Don't tell your father that we went to a *dāya*.' And, indeed, I didn't tell my father or my mother. But I blame my mother-in-law because she took me to the *dāya*. I blame her only when she took me to the *dāya*, because she went in a wrong way. I mean, I think if she took me to the doctor, this wouldn't have happened to me."

As a result, the last thirteen years of Fayza's marriage have been spent seeking a cure for her infertility. Initially, Fayza sought the treatment of three Alexandrian gynecologists in private practice, who prescribed a multitude of ineffectual treatments, including tubal surgery, which Fayza underwent willingly despite her family's opposition. Eventually, she made her way to the University of Alexandria's Shatby Hospital, where she had learned on the radio that they planned to make "babies of the tubes," or in vitro fertilization (IVF) "test-tube" babies. Although she had always believed that only one of her fallopian tubes was completely blocked, she was shocked to learn from the physicians at Shatby that both tubes were blocked and that her only chance of conceiving was via IVF—a procedure that would cost much more money than Fayza could presently afford.

Indeed, just as Fayza had no luck getting pregnant, Sami had no luck making a living for himself and his wife. Although he had once driven a taxicab, he had been forced to quit two years earlier when doctors discovered a potentially life-threatening heart valve condition secondary to childhood rheumatic fever. Because he tired easily, Sami was forced to give up his taxi to another driver, who split the profits with him. Although Sami's income as a cab driver had never been sufficient to raise his family above the poverty line, the new arrangement was even less satisfactory financially, causing Sami and Fayza to sink further and further into destitution. As Fayza laments: "I'm living in a house that I don't want to tell you that it's collapsing. It's very old. Whenever my husband puts it up for sale, nobody gives him the price that he wants. I mean, I'm living in depression, between me and myself. I have no electricity. I have no television. And I don't have a refrigerator. And I don't have a washing machine. I wash with my hands. Sometimes I sit with myself, between me and myself, I cry by myself. Sometimes I say, 'God deprived me of everything. Even the joy of life, he deprived me of it.' But I can't talk to Sami because he, too, is unable to do anything. We wanted to apply for electricity, but they said, 'No, the house is about to fall down. There should be no electricity in it because it's about ready to fall.' We are sitting in depression . . . and we're living."

Yet, Fayza admits that, despite her infertility and her poverty, her life could be much worse. Perhaps most important, her marriage to Sami is stable and loving. Not only does Sami treat Fayza well, but he has told her repeatedly that "children are not important" and that he will never replace her with another wife, even when she has encouraged him to remarry so as to have children. Recently, he told Fayza that the first thing he plans to buy her when he accrues some extra money is a gold wedding band to replace the one she pawned in order to support her infertility treatments.

As Fayza admits, "We've become very good together, and now he's every-thing in my life. He's very precious to me to the extent that if he gets a little sick, I say, 'God, please make it be me, not him.' If he's a bit sick and he sleeps, I try to feel his heartbeats to see if they're too many or what and to examine his pulse. But I don't show him my anxiety so that he doesn't worry about himself. Since the day he had his sickness, I'm scared to upset him. And he's very good to me."

In addition, unlike so many other infertile women, Fayza's in-laws and neighbors have never bothered her about her childlessness nor made her feel that they fear her for potentially giving their children the evil eye. On the contrary, her neighbors "throw their kids at me," according to Fayza, who has entered into an informal fostering arrangement with a particu-larly friendly neighbor, whose birth control failed and who delivered a son after her other children were already grown and married. The little boy, now two years old, spends most of his time with Fayza and Sami, calling them "Mama" and "Baba" and sleeping most nights in their bed.

Yet, despite this good fortune, Fayza feels that the women who know her are kind to her out of pity. "Whenever I put my face in front of some-one else's face," she explains, "they say, 'May God give you compensation.' I have the wife of my maternal cousin, whenever she sees me coming, she says, 'Your son, after a while, he will appear.' These words make my psy-chology below zero. I think if she hadn't told me this, it would have been better.'"

Fayza admits that her self-esteem has suffered tremendously because of her infertility. "I used to feel that I'm lacking something more than other people," she says. "My feelings, I feel that I'm missing something and I'm lacking something, between myself and me, unlike other women. But I don't confess it to anyone that I'm lacking this thing. I mean, I show people that I'm very strong—I'm not feeling that I'm lacking anything. But sometimes, something comes up between me and myself, and I sit and think and cry and I say, 'Why God, why?' Why did God give me this lack-ing? In everything. I don't know. . . . I consider myself good—very good. But, sometimes, because of the problem of children, I feel that I'm smaller than all other people."

Motherhood and Identity

For Fayza and for thousands of other infertile Egyptian women like her, becoming a mother is more than a desire; it is a mandate. Without motherhood, a woman is perceived and perceives herself to be lacking something so fundamental that her very personhood is at stake—making her, as Fayza states so poignantly, "smaller than all other people." For, among the urban Egyptian poor, motherhood "completes" a woman on multiply meaningful levels—as a whole human being with a normal social identity and self-concept, as a true female with the proper feminine parts, processes, and inclinations, and as a real woman who has passed beyond the transitional state of newlywedness to assume the normal rights, duties, and responsibilities of married womanhood. In other words, the achievement of motherhood implies both individual and social completion, the importance of which cannot be underestimated.

Infertility, as a barrier to motherhood, threatens such completion, throwing into question a woman's gender identity, her sexual identity, and her very sense of selfhood. Thus, the particular situation of infertile women illumines the social construction of gender and the politics of identity in Egypt, throwing into relief the ways in which the socially constructed categories of "person," "female," "woman," and "mother" are inextricably linked and emotionally charged.

The importance of motherhood to the construction of gendered identity for women in Egypt is perhaps best understood from the perspective of the infertile—from those who are barred entrance into the "cult of motherhood" (Bouhdiba 1985). To wit, by virtue of their uncontrollable childlessness, infertile Egyptian women fail to uphold a special category of social norms called "identity norms," or "norms of being." Goffman (1963), who was the first to typify such norms, notes that "failure or success at maintaining such norms has a very direct effect on the psychological integrity of the individual. At the same time, mere desire to abide by the norm—mere good will—is not enough, for in many cases the individual has no immediate control over [her] level of sustaining the norm. It is a question of the individual's condition, not [her] will; it is a question of conformance, not compliance."

In other words, identity norms differ from behavioral norms, in that the latter involve human volition, or a willful decision to act in accordance with or defiance of normative standards. Identity norms, on the other hand, are nonvolitional; they involve "being," not "doing." As such, they draw attention to personal attributes, or "identity pegs," that are not subject to easy alteration, especially when they involve aspects of one's physical being, such as racial features, height and weight, or various "abominations of the body" (e.g., homeliness, deformity, physical disability) (Goffman 1963).

Because those individuals who fail to conform to such identity norms invariably value these norms as members of the society in which such norms are shared, they cannot help but to perceive their own failing and to experience subsequent feelings of shame, incompleteness, self-hate, and self-derogation (Goffman 1963). Goffman has argued that individuals sharing the same failing or stigma will experience similar "moral careers," or learning experiences regarding the consequences of their plight and changes in their self-conception. Furthermore, the moral careers of those stigmatized late in life have a particular poignancy, for these individuals have thoroughly internalized what it means to be "normal," and thus are likely to have special problems reidentifying themselves as abnormal and a special likelihood of developing disapproval of themselves. As Goffman (1963:132–33) put it, "The painfulness . . . of sudden stigmatization can come not from the individual's confusion about [her] identity, but from [her] knowing too well what [s]he has become."

Such is the case of poor infertile Egyptian women, who do not violate identity norms until they come of reproductive age and enter into marriage. For them, the physical inability to conceive a child—let alone to bear one—represents much more than an unfortunate failing of a woman's reproductive body. More momentously, it represents the inability of a woman to achieve a normal social identity, or those categories and attributes of a person that are felt to be ordinary and natural (Goffman 1963). This failure to achieve normalcy occurs on three related levels, for infertility serves to spoil a woman's personal identity as a human being, her sexual identity as a female, and her gender identity as a woman.

First and most fundamentally, infertility throws into question the very nature of a woman's humanity, making her less than a normal adult human being. Almost by definition, women who are biologically ready (i.e., neither pre- nor postmenopausal) but are unable to bring forth a child from their bodies are seen as not quite human, for the ability to reproduce biologically is viewed by poor Egyptians as one of the most basic and inherent attributes that unites people as human beings. Consequently, women who are infertile are seen by others and see themselves as "lacking" a vital component of personhood—or, as they put it more metaphorically, "A flowerpot without flowers is not a flowerpot."

The metaphor of the flowerless flowerpot points to what infertile women often feel about themselves and what they are not infrequently told by others who wish to hurt them—namely, that they are "unproductive" persons and that their lives are of "no use." In other words, for poor urban Egyptian women, producing children is tantamount to living a worthwhile life. Thus, women who fail reproductively are often taunted for leading lives that are viewed as barren, unaccomplished, and wasted.

One fertile Egyptian woman explained this widespread view as follows: "Women want children to give them a value in life, to make the woman of value. If she has none, she is not of value. . . . She is like a piece of land not producing plants or a tree not producing fruits. It's for nothing."

Another fertile woman added: "Of course, not having children is a *big problem*. Some people think a wife is no good if she doesn't have any children. It's like having a cow and feeding it, and she doesn't give you anything, milk or calves. People think that if a woman has no children, a man is feeding her for nothing."

In addition to the problem of precarious personhood, infertility casts doubt on a woman's sexual identity in a society where "maleness" and "femaleness" are well bounded categories and gender ambiguity is not easily tolerated. Indeed, infertility threatens to overturn the perceived differences between men and women—differences that are assumed to be natural and whose subversion is thus deeply threatening.

To wit, by virtue of their childlessness, infertile Egyptian women are viewed as not quite female and are even seen by some as pseudo-males, more masculine than feminine. Just as lack of female circumcision is thought to produce gender ambiguity vis-à-vis the eventual prolongation of the clitoris into a male phallus (Inhorn and Buss 1993), a female body whose internal organs are unreproductive is an ambiguous body, suspected of having some hidden male attribute(s). Thus, a woman who is childless is seen as inherently unfeminine and is even called a *dhakar*, or male, to her face.

As one woman with seven children explained: "Some people talk and say, 'Two men are living together. She's the same as he is. She's like barren land.'"

Another fertile woman added: "People hurt her. They tell her, 'You don't have children. You are like the rooster that does not break the hen and doesn't have children. You are a homosexual rooster.' Lots of people say these things."

Although few infertile women view themselves as masculinized by their infertility—knowing what they know about their own bodies, physiological processes, and feelings toward the opposite sex—they often admit that they feel less feminine than other women, for the achievement of a truly feminine persona can only be reached through the birth of a child. Pregnancy and childbirth are perceived as the most natural demonstration of a woman's femininity, for they can never be shared by men and they offer tangible evidence that a woman's internal organs are present and properly functioning. As one woman put it, "We are created into this sex just to be mothers." Without such proof of motherhood, it is feared that a woman may not be a true female, in terms of her biology and sexual orientation.

In addition to doubts about infertile women's true sexual identities, infertile women are also deemed incomplete as women. Although marriage itself is a vitally important marker of womanhood—turning a virginal *bint*, or girl, into a sexually awakened *sitt*, or woman[3]—becoming the wife and lover of a man is not enough to prove one's womanhood. Rather, a woman's adult gender identity can only be completed through motherhood, since what makes a woman a woman is ultimately her ability to *khallafa*, to produce offspring for herself and her husband,[4] and to demonstrate her ability to mother these progeny appropriately.

Women are seen as "naturally" performing the roles of childbearing and mothering, due to their God-given "maternal instinct," a kind of primordial drive fueling women's motherhood desires and their capacities to care for and love their children with affection. Women are thought to be born with this instinct "in their blood," and, as part of their constitution, it remains with them their entire lives. This is why little girls love playing with dolls and why old women relish their grandchildren. This is also why women, upon marriage, hope to have children immediately. Motherhood allows women to replicate the care, affection, and compassion of their own mothers and to complete what is seen by most poor women as their primary "mission" in life. For them, children *are* their life; women live for their children, with all else, including their husbands, their relatives, and their work if they are employed, paling in comparison in terms of relative importance.

Although men, too, are thought to have a natural paternal instinct, women see their own feelings toward their children as being much stronger than those of most men. This is despite the fact that women do not bear their own children in a hereditary sense, according to the widely held theory of male monogenesis described in the preceding chapter. Yet, the fact that women do not see themselves as playing a major role, if any, in the biological production of their offspring does not mitigate the sense of connection they feel to the children they bring forth from their bodies. Women still feel physically connected to their children through the joy and suffering of pregnancy, childbirth, and lactation—events that only a woman can share with her child. Once men have ejaculated their fetuses into women's wombs, they have "nothing to do" with pregnancy, childbirth, and breast-feeding, as women are proud to report.

It is during the gestational period that a woman first "feels," first gets to know, the child growing in her belly. Once the child is born, it becomes, for all practical purposes, a woman's responsibility. Among the Egyptian urban poor, fathers are deemed responsible for a child's financial support and usually for its discipline, responsibilities that are deemed complementary to those of a woman. But, beyond that, the role they play in their children's lives is deemed optional and varies considerably from man to man. Some Egyptian fathers are extremely involved in their children's upbringing, spending considerable time with them, helping them with their homework, teaching them about religion and morality, and displaying love and affection openly. However, according to women, most fathers are much more distant, leaving the upbringing and care of their children almost entirely to their wives.

In fact, many poor women believe that men want children not for the sake of the children themselves or for the joys of being a parent, but rather for the special kind of ego satisfaction that men derive from proving their procreativity and virility in a society where manliness is valorized.

As one woman explained: "A man wants children to be proud, to say he has children, to feel he is a man. He sees that his friends have children, so he wants [them], too. It's like an envy in each man that he wants to have children and a family. It makes him feel complete; exactly like the woman, he feels incomplete without it."

Because men are seen by women as lacking a strong paternal instinct and wanting children for their own egos (as well as a number of instrumental reasons to be described in Chapter 6), it comes as no surprise to women that there are so many bad fathers among the urban poor—men who frankly "don't deserve" to be parents. Such men fall into three categories, with some particularly bad men displaying features of all three. First, some men "can't carry the responsibility" of taking care of a family. These are men who fail to provide even the most basic subsistence needs of their wives and children, either because they are unwilling to work hard enough or because they think only of their own foolish pleasures, squandering their money on selfish habits such as cigarettes, alcohol, hashish, prostitutes, or gambling. As one woman put it, "These are the 'destroyed people'— drunkards or drug addicts who forget all about God and the whole world." Second, some men are thought to be lacking a paternal instinct altogether or to have minimal natural feelings of affection toward children. According to poor women, these are the "hardhearted ones," who "throw their children into the streets" and who beat their children, "making them grow up in fear." Third, some men are bad fathers because they know no other way to parent, replicating as they do their own childhood mistreatment at the hands of their fathers.

Bad mothers, on the other hand, are seen as rare, even nonexistent. Mistreatment and neglect by a mother, although they occasionally occur, are said to result when a woman has too many children to care for or is experiencing domestic problems, rather than from lack of love. As poor Egyptian women are fond of saying, "No woman doesn't love her children." Even women who are "unnatural"—who feel less for their children than they should because of the incorrect way in which their own mothers raised them—are thought to have much stronger feelings of affection and concern for their children than the average man. Whereas a man may be able to work all day and entertain himself all evening with his friends, rarely bothering to see his children, a woman would be unable to stand this, needing to be with her children as much as possible and to know that they are safe. As a popular Egyptian expression puts it, "The mother makes a nest and the father drives away what's in it."

The strong maternal feelings that virtually all women are thought to have for their children are described by poor Egyptian women in a number of ways. As one fertile woman explained: "It's the best feeling there is and when a woman has a child, she waits for the day when he pronounces the word, 'Mama.' It's something natural. No matter how stupid she is or nasty she is to others, when it comes to her kids, she's different. No woman doesn't love children. If the child is a black beetle, as long as it's out of her own belly, it's precious. And if she has one hundred kids, they're all the same to her."

Like their fertile counterparts, infertile women themselves believe in the inherent rightness of motherhood and all that it entails, for they, too, see themselves as endowed with a God-given maternal instinct that has yet to receive expression in their own lives. Indeed, infertile women's own discourse on the beauty and naturalness of motherhood constitutes an ardent poetry of its own.

As one infertile woman explained: "God creates the woman to be a mother and to handle the motherhood, to have all of it in her. She has to be affectionate. She carries all the affection, the love, and she's the one who, whenever her child is sick, she stays awake to take care of it. The mother's role is *very* big. She carries him [in her womb] for nine months. She suffers when delivering him. She breastfeeds him. She raises and teaches him. She helps him in his education, and she helps him in everything."

Another woman put it this way: "When a woman has a child, she feels she's a woman of substance, and she's always very happy when carrying her child. Anyone wants to feel motherhood, because it's substance. It's a woman's most important role, in my view. If I had a child, I would bathe it with cologne, not just soap. I would make my children shine."

Because women are seen as having a maternal instinct that makes them naturally loving and nurturant toward their children, it is believed that every woman must experience the love of motherhood in order to be "complete." When a woman cannot have children, whether the infertility stems from her or her husband, she is viewed as "incomplete," as "less than" other women, as "not normal." In other words, in order to be a "normal woman," one must be a "normal mother," which is tantamount to bearing a child of one's own. One's gendered identity thus revolves around being the mother of the child of one's body. Surrogate mothering, which amounts in Egypt to either babysitting or fostering, is sometimes tried, but it can never take the place of normal motherhood. Nor is it perceived as completing a woman in the same way. In order for a woman to be normal according to widely accepted normative standards, she must be a mother to the *children of her husband*. All other substitutes—including continuing childlessness, fostering others' children, and the development of a working career—are deemed unacceptable. Thus, among the urban Egyptian poor, infertility, the inability to bear the children of one's husband, is a tragedy of immense proportions *for women*, who are usually blamed for failures in the reproductive realm.

In Egypt, infertility is a "woman's problem," even though Egyptians of all social backgrounds acknowledge that men, too, may be infertile because of "weak worms" and other forms of sperm pathology (Inhorn 1994). Yet, men are seen as suffering from only one potentially resolvable problem—their "worms"—whereas women are seen as suffering from a host of sometimes intractable problems of the female reproductive equipment (Inhorn 1994). Therefore, poor Egyptians are often quick to assume that a couple's childlessness derives from the wife rather than from the husband. Even in cases of known male infertility, a woman's in-laws and neighbors may continue to blame her for the childlessness and expect her to take steps to overcome it, under the assumption that there *must* be something wrong with her, also.

As one infertile woman explained: "They usually reserve the blame for the woman. They always blame the woman and say she's like a tree without dates. Usually when it's known to be from the husband, they don't tell him anything, because it would make him feel embarrassed and his manhood would be shaken. So they always blame the woman, even when it's from the man. They talk badly about these women. 'She isn't able to have kids.' Women are on the lookout for these things."

The degree of woman-blaming and the internalization of that blame on the part of childless Egyptian women—even those without an identifiable female infertility problem—are often quite remarkable. Almost uniformly, poor infertile women tell of their inadequacy and incompleteness, of the fact that they are "missing" something that normal women have. This missing something, in fact, refers to two things, one tangible, the other not. On the one hand, it is children that are missing in these women's lives, creating an emptiness, a void, that is difficult to fill. Among the urban Egyptian poor, the infertile woman may be called *Umm Il-Ghāyyib*, "Mother of the Missing One," *Umm Il-Ghāli*, "Mother of the Precious One," or *Umm Il-ʿIwaḍ*, "Mother of Compensation." This *kunya*, or teknonym, reflects the fact that her as-yet-unborn, or "missing," child will be truly precious, a great compensation for all that she has suffered, in a society where children and hence a woman's fecundity are highly valued. Although such teknonyms are felt to be expressions of respect and sympathy for the infertile woman—who would normally be called by her eldest son's name (or eldest daughter if she lacked sons) in a society where women's first names are rarely used—they often prove hurtful instead, highlighting as they do the absence of that which is most precious to other women.

Such teknonyms also highlight the lack of connectivity in infertile women's lives. That women are typically identified not by their own names but by those of their children is indicative of the degree to which selfhood is defined relationally in Egypt (as well as in other parts of the Middle East) (Boddy 1989; Dwyer 1978b; Joseph 1993, 1994; Rugh 1982), and the way in which children are thought to complete a woman's identity, serving as her primary ego extensions (Hatem 1986c). For women without children, their relational selves are viewed as incomplete, and thus the relational teknonyms that index a normal woman's motherhood and connectivity to her offspring must be reinvented for the infertile, tying them to the future imagined completion of their personhood.

But it is not only children that are deemed missing from infertile women's lives. It is motherhood itself—with all that it entails for a woman's daily existence and her gendered identity—that is missing and that cannot be found until a woman experiences the birth of a living child. For poor urban Egyptian women, motherhood is more than a role to be fulfilled along with many other roles, some more or less important. Motherhood is a primary identity, the very source of one's being as a woman.

Infertile women who are "missing motherhood" experience their diminished identity most painfully in comparisons made to and by fertile women with children. In an infertile woman's everyday social world, she inevitably mingles with many mothers, some of whom are her allies and some of whom are her detractors. Yet, it is often in interactions with those physically or emotionally closest to her—usually her own or her husband's married sisters and sisters-in-law or friends and neighbors who married at nearly the same time and went on to have children—that an infertile woman feels most acutely her own inadequacy and incompleteness, especially if her husband or his relatives point to her comparative infecundity.

As one infertile woman explained: "I feel collapsed when I see all the people who have children surrounding me. My husband's sister, she's newly married, not even nine months. From the first month she got pregnant; ten days ago she delivered. My husband's other sister is very close to me. She's pregnant. She showed me her belly and said, 'I hope you get jealous to get pregnant.' If I'm going to be jealous, I would have been pregnant a long time ago."

Another infertile woman put it this way: "I'm lonely. I have no one to talk to. I see all my neighbors with kids and I feel something missing and I worry that my husband will leave me. I'm alone between four walls, no baby to talk to. A woman [without children] will be missing something, and she'll feel broken. Children are the essence of life. If no children, your life is broken."

Motherhood and Domesticity

Poor urban infertile women's lives are "broken" in part because of the isolation and utter despair these women experience as domestic shut-ins, trapped all day in small apartments without children to keep them company. The loss of life meaning and profound loneliness shared by many poor urban infertile women are reflections of changing domestic and economic realities in Egypt that have left fertile women alone with their children and infertile women alone with themselves. The construction of women's identity in Egypt must be historically situated in the household, for recent urbanization, nuclearization of the family, and the dramatic loss of roles for women in the household economy have drastically affected women's sense of self and purpose in the urban Egyptian setting. This is especially true of poor women, whose lives of enforced domesticity make mothering their central occupation, a kind of "career" by default (Hatem 1986c; Youssef 1978).

As noted in the last chapter, the past three decades have been a time of profound demographic transformation in Egypt. Millions of Egyptian villagers have moved to the cities, causing strains on urban infrastructure and absolute shortages of housing space. Such nationwide rural-to-urban transition has been accompanied by two changes on the level of the urban Egyptian household that have been of tremendous significance to women's lives: first, the loss of household economies characteristic of rural areas and, second, the increasing nuclearization of the urban Egyptian family with a concomitant loosening of extended family bonds (MacLeod 1991; Rugh 1984).

With regard to the loss of household economies, among the urban poor, women's productive skills, which were and still are essential to survival in the rural economy (Lane and Meleis 1991), have been largely lost. Indeed, women's loss of *both* productive skills and domestic responsibilities in the urban setting has been quite dramatic. Today, most urban women, unlike their contemporary rural counterparts, are no longer involved in domestic food production. Because their husbands no longer plant crops, they no longer assist them in the fields, nor process the garden crops into food for their families. Because their families no longer have land, they no longer keep large numbers of rabbits, chickens, and other fowl for eggs and for meat. Because their husbands no longer own livestock, they neither tend to these animals, nor milk them, nor process this milk into cheese. In short, women's traditional food production skills, which are still central to rural Egyptian life and complement the agricultural production activities of men, have all but been lost in urban areas, where food processing has passed into the capitalist factory system.

Furthermore, unlike their rural counterparts, who often live in nucleated, extended-family compounds with adjacent stables, poor urban women tend to live in small, nuclear-family apartments, often consisting of only one room. Thus, they no longer spend long hours in household domestic labor, including sweeping and cleaning each room, removing manure from the household stable, washing the earth from their menfolks' clothing, and fetching pails of water in order to carry out these tasks and to quench the family's thirst.

As a result, poor urban Egyptian women's household life now revolves around what Ehrenreich and English (1978:10) have called "the most personal biological activities—eating, sex, sleeping, the care of small children, and (until the rise of institutional medicine) birth and dying and the care of the sick and aged." Indeed, the loss and devaluation of poor urban Egyptian women's productive labor in the household economy has led to an intensive, almost exclusive focus on their "production of people" (Tong 1989), with biological reproduction being central to women's identities and mothering being central to their daily existences. In other words, at the present historical moment, most poor urban Egyptian women are wives and mothers only, who are referred to and refer to themselves as *sittāt il-bait*, or housewives.

This creation of a large corps of poor urban housewives is a historically recent phenomenon in Egypt (as it is in most of the developed and developing world),[5] and is tied to two major forces: first, the rapid growth of the migrant urban underclass in the past three decades and, second, the rise of industrial capitalism in Egypt, with the accompanying growth of labor-intensive factory jobs that have gone mostly to men. Although Egyptian women have not been officially banned from the industrial workplace and, in fact, have been entering it with increasing frequency (Ibrahim 1985a, 1985b), multiple patriarchal ideologies, including a long-standing cultural ideal of female seclusion, the Islamic valorization of women's domesticity, the widely held dogma of "man the provider," and the imported bourgeois capitalist ideology of the "leisured" woman removed from the workplace,[6] have all served as barriers to women's widespread participation in nondomestic wage labor. Despite Egypt's relatively progressive labor laws regarding women, including a comprehensive maternity leave policy (Azzam, Abu Nasr, and Lorfing 1985; Smock and Youssef 1977; Sullivan 1981),[7] demographers and development personnel continue to lament Egypt's overall low female labor force participation rates, especially in industrial production (Azzam, Abu Nasr, and Lorfing 1985; Jemai 1993; Moghadam 1993; Warren and Bourque 1991). Although official labor statistics continue to underestimate the true extent of women's labor—especially in petty commodity production in the informal sector (Hatem 1986c; Jemai 1993; Fluehr-Lobban 1990; MacLeod 1991; Rugh 1985)—it is quite clear that economic activity rates among Egyptian women remain low. More specifically, less than one-quarter of all Egyptian women were defined as "economically active" during the 1980s (when the last official census and labor survey results were reported), and less than 15 percent received salaries for their work (Fluehr-Lobban 1990; Moghadam 1993).[8]

When all is said and done then, it would appear that poor urban Egyptian women have been effectively "domesticated" (Moore 1988), to the extent that they extol the virtues of domesticity and feel considerable pity for women wage laborers, as well as for their hardworking rural counterparts. This "cult of female domesticity" has been noted by other scholars working in urban Egypt (Bowen and Early 1993; Tucker 1993), but has been said to characterize women of the middle class rather than the urban poor (Hatem 1987b). However, the valorization of domesticity and the consequent feminization of the domestic realm are as operative among the urban poor as they are among the middle class, and they serve as a more effective barrier to women's labor force participation among the poor, who are proportionately underrepresented in the formal work force in comparison to their middle-class counterparts.

On the one hand, freedom from work, be it agrarian, industrial, or domestic labor, has come as a boon to many poor urban women, who are able to devote most of their time to their children, to keeping their small living spaces tidy, and to enjoying leisure time, especially the "company" of the radio or television (but not telephones, which are uncommon in poor households). On the other hand, such freedom has meant restrictions on women's mobility and economic independence. No longer able to rely on subsistence crops to feed their families, poor urban women have become almost totally reliant on their husbands for the cash necessary to buy food and other staples.[9] Yet, husbands may be notoriously unreliable in the provision of economic resources to the household and may put in domestic appearances as little as possible (Hoodfar 1988).

For some poor women, dire economic circumstances at home may force them into the wage labor market, usually as domestics in the homes of the urban affluent or as unskilled workers in repetitive, exhausting factory jobs. But, because resistance to women's work is still extremely strong among the urban poor, and especially among poor urban men, women are likely to enter the wage labor force only out of dire necessity. Particularly among married women with children in the household, work is viewed as a last resort, something to be given up as soon as the household returns to its former economic solvency.[10]

From women's standpoint, the reasons why they do not work—and may never even consider it if their husbands are adequate providers—are

Photograph 1. An urban housewife baking bread. (Photograph by Marcia Inhorn)

many. For one, the patriarchal ideology of "man the breadwinner, woman the homemaker" remains strong and receives support from the Islamic scriptures, which deem fathers fully responsible for the support of their wives and minor children (Schleifer 1986). Among the urban poor, this notion of a financially responsible husband is upheld as a laudable ideal, and deviations from it are deeply threatening, serving to emasculate a man who is exposed as a poor provider.[11] Because women's work outside the home is seen as highly degrading to men, women believe in their husbands' inherent right to keep them at home, for work, if undertaken, must always receive a husband's permission. In most cases, husbands refuse, even if the family is impoverished and the wife volunteers to work in order to raise the family's standard of living.

As one infertile woman explained: "I thought about working because we have financial problems and I wanted to help out, but he refuses the idea totally. He tells me, 'After marriage, a woman should never go to work. Do you expect me to wear a [woman's] scarf and sit at home and you go out to work?' He thinks like his father and the older generations. He's very backward. To them, if a woman goes out to work, it's a shame."

Not only does a woman's work affect a man's pride, but it is thought to bring shame upon a woman, who will be exposed to other men in the workplace and who will potentially be "corrupted."[12] Thus, a man who allows his wife to work is thought to have too little "jealousy" over her and too little concern for her honor, which may be marred by mixed-sex contacts. This notion of the impropriety of women's work, with its accompanying stigma,[13] is particularly pronounced among migrants from culturally conservative Ṣaʿīd, or Upper Egypt,[14] where women's nondomestic wage labor is virtually taboo.

Speaking of her Ṣaʿīdī origins, a poor urban infertile woman explained: "For us in Ṣaʿīd, it's a shame for a woman to work. Maybe she would want to, but they would never let her—her husband, her parents, his relatives. In Ṣaʿīd, women don't work; they never think of this possibility."

Another woman commented: "Ṣaʿīdī men are worried their wives will talk with men, and they think whenever a woman works, she has more power than he does. For example, the woman can tell him, 'I work outside, too. I make money, too. You should help me at home.' This will create problems."

Although the stigma surrounding women's work may be diminishing somewhat as men, including men of Ṣaʿīdī background, see more and more women in their workplaces,[15] women view their husbands' refusal as only one of many practical barriers to obtaining employment. Among poor women, most of whom are uneducated and illiterate, the lack of education—often construed as "lack of a certificate"—is seen as a major obstacle to finding a job, even in a factory. This, coupled with (1) poor salaries that barely cover the cost of overcrowded, unreliable transportation to and from work, (2) poor work shifts, either early in the morning or late in the evening, (3) poor working conditions and repetitive jobs that lead to fatigue and illness, (4) the potential need to purchase work clothes and meals outside the home, (5) problems of daycare for women with children, and (6) the inability to tend to one's daily chores, including food preparation,[16] are often viewed by women as creating overwhelming obstacles, which make work, ultimately, seem unworthwhile.

Furthermore, poor women, who are usually equipped only for manual labor, view work outside the home as what it is—namely, work, rather than a "career." Not only is the concept of career poorly developed in

Egypt, where most people work for money and money alone, women who want to develop working careers are seen as deviant, because, for women, the proper career is motherhood. Women who prefer to spend their days at work—especially in the boring clerical jobs that are the norm among the newly educated lower-middle class (MacLeod 1991)—are shirking their primary responsibilities for their children and their household, according to most lower-class women.

Given these ideological and practical obstacles, it is not surprising that most infertile women are effectively barred from the work force after marriage, even though they have no children to "form their whole lives." Because they are "missing motherhood," many infertile women experience extreme boredom at home and believe that work would relieve their emptiness. But, despite their desires, few poor urban infertile women do, in fact, work outside their homes, for in the vast majority of cases their husbands have refused this idea. Even sewing for others from home, the major form of socially acceptable work,[17] is an impossibility for most poor infertile women, who have neither the skills nor the money to buy a sewing machine.

For most poor infertile women whose husbands disallow their working, their daily lives are spent at home, often in one room, often impoverished, often alone. Living life in a one-room apartment, sometimes far from other family members who cannot be reached by telephone, has in reality been a mixed blessing. On the one hand, nuclearization of the family and the loosening of family bonds, which will be described further in Chapter 4, have allowed many poor infertile women to enjoy relative freedom from familial obligations, especially the tyrannical reign of in-laws. On the other hand, most poor infertile women spend much of their time in solitary activities, such as cooking, sweeping, and watching television.

Being infertile is perhaps the loneliest status of all for a woman. Deprived of the company of children, the infertile woman is often also deprived of the company of other women, for reasons to be explored in Chapter 5. Thus, loneliness is an abiding theme in infertile women's lives, as are feelings of purposelessness and questions about life's meaning. Because the care of children has become the poor urban woman's only legitimate role, childlessness usually generates an existential crisis—one that is played out in women's emotional lives and seeks resolution through religion.

Motherhood and Alienation

Infertility can be seen to affect—quite profoundly—poor urban Egyptian women's gendered subjectivity. Cut off from other life options and legitimate roles, infertile women bemoan their "empty," "meaningless," "unfulfilled," "unaccomplished," "useless" lives as homemakers trapped in their small apartments, as wives trapped in childless and sometimes loveless marriages, and as infertile women trapped in a child-centered society. Because they have no children to mother, infertile women are unable to fill their time, which makes them bored and causes them to brood over their situations. For many poor infertile women who are unable to read and write, the television, radio, excessive sleep, or excessive eating are their only relief from loneliness, depression, and despair.[18]

Although the lives of poor urban infertile women in Egypt differ in the various ways to be described in this book, what is shared by these women is their tremendous sense of alienation. Individuals are alienated "if we either experience our lives as meaningless or ourselves as worthless, or else are capable of sustaining a sense of meaning and self-worth only with the help of illusions about ourselves or our condition" (Allen Wood cited in Tong 1989:44). Furthermore, the effects of alienation may differ according to one's sex. As Ann Foreman has argued:

> Men's objectification within industry, through the expropriation of the product of their labour, takes the form of alienation. But the effect of alienation on the lives and consciousness of women takes on even more oppressive form. Men seek relief from their alienation through their relations with women; for women there is no relief. For these intimate relations are the very ones that are essential structures of her oppression. (Foreman cited in Tong 1989:45)

As Foreman argues, women experience themselves only as the fulfillment of other people's needs. Thus, in the absence of their friends' and families' needs of them, and particularly those of their children, women are left with no sense of self—experiencing their personhood as fragmented and splintered.

Indeed, for infertile Egyptian women, the self is experienced as "broken," "collapsed," "destroyed," "lost"—or, as one woman put it, "I feel like I don't exist." For, as we have seen, personhood is completed only through the birth of a child. Although *all* poor Egyptian women may view themselves from time to time as *ghalāba* (subdued, conquered, vanquished, or defeated) or *maksūrit il-gināḥ* (broken-winged), infertile women are seen by others and often see themselves as particularly pitiable and downtrodden. Not only do infertile women face an array of emotionally distressing experiences in their personal lives and as patients, but by virtue of their childlessness, they are seen as unable to achieve emotional fulfillment and may, in fact, experience identity crises of major proportions. As one infertile woman put it succinctly, "Why am I living if I don't have any children?"

This crisis of women's "ego" or "felt" identity—namely, women's subjective sense of their own situation, continuity, and character (Goffman 1963)—can be seen in infertile women's emotional discourse, which, although reserved for private moments with intimates,[19] bespeaks the magnitude of women's suffering. Among infertile women, talk of emotion revolves around the word *nafs*, a polysemous term referring to the human being, to the self or personal identity, as well as to the soul, psyche, spirit, or mind (Cowan 1976). Popular psychological discourse emanates from this core term, such that women speak of their *nafsīya*, that is, their individual "psychology" or frame of mind; their *hālti il-nafsīya*, their psychological state, or mood; and *nifsi*, an intense personal desire or wish, as in "I *wish* for a child." In a sense then, when one's psychological state is "upset," "tired," or "sick," as it often is among infertile women, then one's self, or *nafs*, is thought to reflect this unhealthy condition. Infertile Egyptian women sometimes speak of themselves as having a "psychological complex"—a problem, or sickness of the psyche that prevents them from experiencing themselves and their worlds in a normal way.

As one infertile woman explained: "You could say I have a psychological complex. I feel I'm nothing without a baby, useless. I feel that I'm empty and especially when I return home [from appointments at Shatby Hospital], I feel very miserable; you can't imagine how I feel. Frankly, I can't imagine how I can live without a child."

Another woman put it this way: "I'm already sick, uncomfortable. All the time I'm sad. Most of the time, my psychology is bad, and I sit and cry for hours when [my husband] is away. I feel sorry for myself, because God said in the Qur'an, 'Wealth and offspring are the adornments of earthly life,' and having a child keeps the woman company and his laughter makes a difference instead of having fights with a man all the time. A child would give some flavor to life. So what would it be like if I know that I cannot have children [ever]?"

As reflected in these women's statements, exacerbating infertile women's psychic turmoil is their anxiety and stress—experiences so common that many women say that they worry about their situations almost continuously. Feelings of worry are exaggerated for most women around the time of the menstrual period, when hopes for pregnancy are heightened and then dashed. Although some infertile women believe that anxiety of this sort can *cause* infertility and that, therefore, they should worry about their situations as little as possible, most infertile women admit to feeling "upset," "uncomfortable," and "tense" almost continuously. Some women use the language of "suffocation" to describe tension and anxiety so great that the very act of breathing becomes difficult.

As one infertile woman expressed her situation: "I am desperate, and desperation makes you ready to kill yourself because a child makes a difference in a home. It makes the father happy, even if he comes home exhausted from work. But if there is no child, there may be a divorce. Even though I wouldn't think of committing suicide for such a thing, when you're desperate, you feel suffocated and you do things you wouldn't do otherwise. Because I have nowhere else to go and I have no work, I can't just go and live by myself. He can do anything he wants, and I have nowhere else to go. So I worry all the time. It makes me cry, and I faint sometimes from the suffocation. The biggest problem is not having children, and I worry about this."

As suggested by this woman's statement, overwhelming fear often underlies infertile women's heightened anxiety. Many infertile women describe feelings of fear so pervasive that they see themselves as "living in fear." This fear generally derives from two sources: first, uncertainty about the future of their marriages and, second, uncertainty about the future of their reproductive lives.

As we shall see in the following chapter, women's fears about their marriages are often legitimate, given the duress many women experience in their relationships with their husbands. As many women note, being infertile increases feelings of insecurity in the marriage, which, in turn, makes them timid around their husbands and more likely to acquiesce to their husbands' wishes. Whereas fertile women are seen as being "self-confident" around their husbands when these men issue unreasonable requests, very rarely do infertile women experience such aplomb, and most fear that being infertile has made them less "precious" in their husbands' eyes. As one woman stated, referring to her own marital insecurity, "My life is in the palm of an *'ifrīt* [a mischievous spirit]."

Perhaps even more significantly, infertile women fear for the future of their reproductive tracts, including the horrifying possibility of permanent sterility. Such fears are especially pronounced among three groups of women: those who have been undergoing infertility therapy for extended periods of time with "no results"; those who are in their late thirties and early forties and are approaching menopause; and those who have been told by doctors that their only hope of conception lies in in vitro fertilization or some other arcane reproductive technology (Inhorn 1994).

Yet, some infertile women deny being afraid, because whether or not they become pregnant and whether or not their marriages last are matters to be decided by God. As they explain, to experience fear would be to deny God's wisdom and will; thus, fear serves as a clear sign of lack of religious faith. Similarly, to experience self-pity is regarded by some infertile women as sacrilegious. Although many infertile women admit to posing the existential question "Why me?" the answer ultimately lies with God. Because most infertile Egyptian women, both Muslim and Christian, consider themselves to be religiously pious, this is a question that, for them, has only one possible answer—that is, God's will. Consequently, even when infertile women feel sorry for themselves, their self-pity rarely turns to doubt in God, as we shall see.

However, God cannot prevent women from feeling their wounded pride. Clearly, infertility is a condition that is thought to affect rather profoundly a woman's *karāma*, or her sense of self-esteem, pride, and dignity. A woman's *karāma* stands diminished by her inability to conceive, especially when she compares herself or is compared to other fertile women. On the other hand, infertility cannot diminish a woman's *sharaf*, or honor. Only moral improprieties of a behavioral nature, such as a premarital loss of virginity or an extramarital relationship, can dishonor a woman. Because infertility is seen as being beyond a woman's control, as "out of her hands," it is never perceived as morally discrediting.

As one infertile woman explained: "Most of the time, it affects the wife's pride, because whenever they talk, most of the time there are discussions about children, and it hurts her pride. The pride of the wife's family is also hurt, because maybe people will see that their daughter has something missing. But honor is not like pride. [Not having children] has nothing to do with honor, because [infertility] is not in your hands."

In addition to its effects on women's self-esteem, infertility is a source of considerable grief for most women, who mourn the absence of the children they have never known. In private moments, infertile women often weep and experience dysphoria so great that they believe that happiness has escaped them forever. Happiness and infertility are seen as mutually exclusive categories; until a woman bears a child, she cannot possibly experience this positive emotion.

Although profound sadness is an abiding theme in infertile women's lives, it is unclear how many women experience true clinical depression, since there are few studies of this problem in Egypt and few resources for dealing with it.[20] In fact, psychological services for infertile women are entirely lacking in Egypt, because psychotherapy is reserved only for the most serious mental health problems, such as schizophrenia. Because such cases are usually referred to physicians and result in hospitalization in state psychiatric facilities, Egyptians fear mental illness of any kind and the potential for institutionalization. Outpatient psychotherapeutic services—of the kind that are now widespread throughout the United States—are unavailable in Egypt, and even if present, would probably attract few patients, given the tremendous stigma of mental illness. Thus, anxiety, grief, depression—the kinds of problems handled in outpatient psychotherapeutic settings in the West—are handled "at home" in Egypt and, among the urban poor, are taken to traditional healers only when they become somatized as bodily complaints.

Clearly, psychotherapy might be of great benefit to many infertile Egyptian women, especially those who are forced to deal with their emotional, relational, and biomedical problems entirely on their own. Likewise, a nationwide infertility support group would allow infertile women to share their experiences with sympathetic others in a supportive environment. Occasionally, infertile women are able to confide in other infertile women, who may be relatives, neighbors, or other patients met in clinic waiting rooms. Some infertile women also share their emotional lives with their husbands or female relatives, who, as we shall see, may be their best friends and confidantes. However, in most cases, infertile women remain isolated in their suffering, and some admit that they have experienced fleeting thoughts of suicide. But, because suicide is deemed sinful in Islam, few infertile women consider this to be a reasonable solution to their plight.

Motherhood and Islam

Although Islam disallows suicide as a final solution to human suffering, Islam does provide great solace to infertile Egyptian women who seek understanding of their misfortune. Indeed, the emotional lives of infertile Egyptian women cannot be understood without reference to their religious lives as women who believe in God, his power, and his omniscience. Despite the fact that most poor urban Egyptian women are religiously illiterate, they are nevertheless religiously pious, and they turn to their religion to sustain them through times of trouble. Infertility, like other major life problems, is widely acknowledged by Egyptian women to be the type of misfortune for which the religiously based interpretations described here (and in Inhorn [1994]) are to be sought. Thus, most poor urban women, the vast majority of whom are Sunni Muslim, not only take great comfort in their religion and their faith in God, but they also attempt to explain their infertility according to the nature of their beliefs in God and God's role in their lives. For them, infertility is a condition "from God," which he bestows upon certain human beings for a reason. This reason is something that infertile women admittedly ponder; but, as they are quick to point out, they ask the question "Why me?" without intending to question the wisdom or righteousness of God's creation of them as infertile. This is a reality that they accept and that they attempt to overcome with God's help, since he, too, created medicine for this purpose.

To understand the nature of infertile women's subjectivity, it is therefore necessary to understand the fundamental character of their beliefs about Allah, the one and only God according to Islam.

First, most poor urban Egyptian women see God, who is referred to as male, as the creator of the universe and of all life in it. Egyptian women are fond of saying that "God is everything" and "everything is from God." All creation, including the creation of human beings, is ultimately in God's hands; or, as Egyptian women say, "human beings are incapable of creating even a fingernail." Most important to this discussion, God is seen as orchestrating human procreation. Not only does God decide who will be fertile and who will be infertile, but he also imbues each fetus with a soul and decides which ones will be male and which will be female. The proof of his creative force, according to women who know the approximate translation,[21] can be found in the following Qur'anic verses:

> Unto Allah belongeth the Sovereignty of the heavens and the earth. He createth what He will. He bestoweth female [offspring] upon whom He will, and bestoweth male [offspring] upon whom He will;
> Or He mingleth them, males and females, and He maketh barren whom He will. Lo! He is Knower, Powerful. (42:49–50)

Thus, human procreation is divinely guided, and, as such, it is ultimately beyond human control.

As one infertile woman explained: "He creates pregnancy. He creates children. And he makes liquid water into a fetus."

As another put it: "He's the one who created children from the beginning to the end. It's with his power. He's the one who gives the fluid to the husband, and God is the one who is creating the baby inside us, and he makes the baby move, for example, its fingers and everything."

Because God ultimately controls procreation, it is his decision to give children or not to give. Thus, women who use birth control may still become pregnant because God wants this. Likewise, a husband and wife may never have a child, because God wants this, too. These decisions are his and his alone, because God is the ultimate creator. Women express this variously, with formulaic phrases such as, "It's in God's hands," "God decides," "God has his reasons," "It's God's judgment," "It's when God wants," "God permits," "It's God's wish," "It's God's will," and "God gives his permission." Or, as they are particularly fond of saying when referring to their own inconsequential role in such matters, "There is nothing in our hands."

Thus, God, who is omnipresent, is the one who decides everything, and these decisions are made by him before an individual's life begins. Once born, an individual's destiny has already been determined. As many poor urban Egyptian women explain it, on the tree of life, each person has a leaf upon which his or her life is written; included on this leaf is the time of birth, if and when marriage will occur, if and when children will be born, and how and when a person will die, at which time the leaf falls from the tree.

Because each individual's life is "written" by God (with the help of his angels) in this manner, life occurrences can be seen as being under God's control, according to his wishes and his will. Events are not random; rather, they occur at predestined times according to a plan, the purpose and meaning of which can only be known by God. For example, if God does not allow a woman to become pregnant, God knows that her time for motherhood has yet to come. Furthermore, he has his reasons for waiting—for example, to prevent the birth of an abnormal child or one who will grow up to lead a bad life. God has his reasons for everything he does, including "approving the timing" of life's events. This is the nature of God's wisdom and judgment. Thus, women who fail to become pregnant often remark, "My time hasn't come yet."

Yet, just because life is "written," human beings are not passive creatures, devoid of volition and will. God expects human beings to exercise their minds and to make choices, including decisions about how to lead their lives.

As one infertile woman explained: "God is the one who decides your life, but he gave you a brain, and when he gave you a brain, he showed you good and bad. It's the person himself who decides to go the right or wrong way."

Although human beings have been divinely endowed with intelligence and morality, God is seen as making the important decisions about humans' lives, overruling and reversing human decisions at any time, for reasons known only to him (since he does not "reveal his secrets").

As one infertile woman explained: "You can think and imagine and wish for lots of things, and God may have in mind something totally different for you. We have a saying, 'The worshipper is in a state of thinking, and God does the action.'"

And, according to another woman: "Each person has twenty-four wishes, but God doesn't grant them all. There is always something missing, including possibly children."

Some women argue that the more a human being wishes for something, the less likely God is to grant that wish. Therefore, those who are "dying for children" do not get them, and those who do not want children get too many.

One woman put it this way: "Those who have children suffer from responsibility, and those who don't search. Neither is happy. It's his [God's] ability and greatness that no one should question."

Although God decides the important matters of humans' lives, he is seen as disapproving of human passivity and indecision. Therefore, it is argued that God expects those who are sick to seek treatment. Infertile women take this notion very seriously (see Inhorn 1994).

According to one infertile woman: "He's the one who decides and gives. The human beings have nothing in their hands. It's God who makes the doctors. He creates the medicine, and he's the one who showed us to go to doctors."

But if and when "medicine" takes its effect is God's decision. God may choose to heal or not to heal, to give life or take life away. Thus, in matters of life and death, sickness and health, God is seen as having the "final word." Final outcomes, such as irreversible infertility or even death, are always under his control and "out of the hands" of humans. God may grant or deny human wishes for wellness, cause or alleviate human suffering. These are his choices, and his alone. Although humans may attempt to overcome their problems—and, in fact, are expected to do so—they cannot, ultimately, overcome God's will regarding their health and well-being.

When deciding who will bear children and who will remain barren, who will live and who will die, God is not whimsical. All of the decisions made by God, even when they cause human suffering, are made for a reason and are meaningful. For example, in his actions, God may be reminding human beings of his power, strength, and omnipotence. Or he may be setting an example, so that human beings may learn from one another. Or he may make human beings suffer for something so that, when they finally receive it, they will be grateful and caring. Or he may deprive individuals of happiness in their earthly lives so that they will be rewarded in Paradise or suffer less on the Day of Judgment. As one infertile woman put it, "A needle prick in life lightens some suffering in the afterlife."

Or God may be testing human beings. According to most poor urban Egyptian women, infertility is best viewed as a test of both patience and religious faith. When God fails to grant a husband and wife a child, he is testing their faith in him and their ability to endure hardship—just as he tested Ibrahim (Abraham) and Zakariya (Zacharias) in the days of old, giving them children when they were elderly and their wives were barren or postmenopausal. Indeed, God is thought to have tested the Prophet Muhammad himself, whose first wife, Khadija, was the only of his wives to bear living children. Although 'A'isha, one of the Prophet's wives, was infertile, she was deemed "the Mother of the Worshippers of God" by the Prophet and was held in great favor by him (Fernea and Bezirgan 1985).

According to poor urban Egyptian women, when God tests husbands and wives in this way, he seeks to determine: Will they continue to believe in me, even if I allow years to pass without granting them a child? Will the wife give up her quest for therapy? Will the husband divorce his infertile wife in haste? Do they have faith in my ability to help them overcome their problem?

As one infertile woman put it: "He tests the strength of their faith and the slavery of humans to him to see if they will be patient or not. He can give a person a child after twenty years. He means something by infertility, but we don't know what it is."

Those who are impatient or without faith will never be granted a child by God. But whether God punishes humans for their misdeeds by depriving them of his gift of children is a point of great contention. According to most women, infertility is a test but *not* a punishment. They argue that God only punishes in the afterlife and that during one's earthly life, God is forgiving and merciful.

As one woman stated: "God never does anything bad like that. He's all goodness. He's big. He never harms. He's generous. He forgives. God has his own wisdom."

Those women who disagree with this view tend to be ones who feel that they (or their husbands) are, in fact, being punished for their mistakes and improprieties. These include, *inter alia*, failing to pray; refusing an arranged marriage; committing adultery, premarital sex, or prostitution; engaging in malicious gossiping or wishing harm to one's enemies; using birth control before having children; being tyrannical or abusive to one's spouse; divorcing a spouse and abandoning one's children; interfering in a sibling's wedding plans; and committing a heinous crime, such as beating, raping, or killing someone.

Obviously, there are levels of difference between these misdeeds, with greater misdeeds being punished more severely, according to those who view God's punishment in this way. For example, a woman who underwent three abortions shortly after her marriage to a coercive husband who eventually divorced her is certain that her continuing infertility in her second marriage is God's way of punishing her. "I cry all the time now that I did them," she laments. "I'm afraid from God that I'm going to hell. But I think I was too young then, and I did as I was told by my husband."

Furthermore, God is seen as punishing those who doubt his wisdom. Thus, infertile women who lament their fate and ask repeatedly "Why me?" are considered unlikely to receive God's favor of children. As one woman explained, "God gets angry and will never give you."

As apparent in the Qur'an, God regards children as a great favor to believers, extolling their virtues and proclaiming them the "allurement of earthly life." Yet, he reminds believers that wealth and children are also human beings' greatest temptations, and he cautions that good deeds are more deserving of reward in his eyes.

Thus, according to poor urban Egyptian women, religious faith and devotion to a merciful and compassionate God are the only *true* hope for overcoming a problem that he created, for reasons that only he can know. Because the gift of fertility is ultimately incumbent upon God's divine wisdom and will, convincing God of one's worthiness as a (re)productive member of society and as a parent is viewed by many Egyptian women as essential. How one seeks to demonstrate one's worthiness depends to some degree on one's religious orientation, level of religiosity, and religious education. For most poor urban Egyptian women—who tend to be minimally schooled, religious but not devout, and who often do not pray regularly because of their lack of knowledge of the formulaic prayer verses as well as the culturally grounded belief that prayer is an activity restricted to men and older women—leading an upright life is seen as the best demonstration of one's worthiness in the eyes of God and one's ongoing devotion to him. Many women attempt to pray informally, if not frequently and correctly, and generally attempt to be good Muslims by following widely accepted religious codes of behavior.

For some women, the experience of infertility also makes them more religious, given their conviction that they and their husbands are being "tested" by God in order for him to determine the sincerity and strength of their faith and patience. In fact, heightened religiosity is common among infertile women, for faith in the kind of religious arguments cited above provides a convenient coping mechanism for women who find themselves in a situation of profound uncertainty. The belief that "God will compensate" relieves many infertile women of their self-doubts and emotional distress, which would certainly be exacerbated were it not for their religious convictions.

Nonetheless, religion can be shown to be a counterbalancing force in the lives of poor urban infertile women. On the one hand, Islam is the source of infertile women's greatest consolation, providing powerful and convenient rationales for why some women are infertile while most others are not. On the other hand, Islam permits both divorce and polygyny, which as we shall see in the following chapter allow Muslim men to replace their infertile wives with both ease and rapidity. And, more important to this discussion, Islam glorifies motherhood and all that it entails, serving as a constant reminder to infertile Muslim women of their comparative maternal deficiency.

Indeed, the Islamic scriptures, including the Qur'an and the hadith, as well as the Islamic *sharīʿa*, venerate mothers, viewing motherhood as the perfection of the Muslim woman's religion and the special vehicle by which she attains respect in this life and ultimate reward in the afterlife (Schleifer 1986). As Aliah Schleifer explains:

> The mother in Islam is placed in a lofty position, that of the greatest respect, but this does not occur in a vacuum. It involves her active participation in the affairs of her family. In Islam, there are two aspects of the characteristics of the mother: that which aligns itself to responsibility, and that which is attributed to natural, God-given qualities, including both the physical exertion of childbirth and the expression of positive emotion. These two aspects are not mutually exclusive, but rather supportive of each other, thus buttressing a state of equilibrium which is the desired atmosphere in the Muslim household. (Schleifer 1986:47)

For example, Islam supports the widely held Egyptian belief that motherhood is a "natural instinct" and considers a mother's affection for and generosity toward her children to be "normal emotions" and a blessing from God (Schleifer 1986). The Islamic scriptures, furthermore, stress the importance of the mother's task in raising her children and the great hardships that she must endure for the sake of her family—for which she will be amply rewarded in Paradise upon her death. One of the most famous passages from the hadith places Paradise "under the mother's foot," while another deems the mother thrice more entitled to a son's companionship and support than the father (Schleifer 1986). The fact that these scriptural passages are known—if not exactly—by most poor Egyptian women attests to the potency of their message and the way in which Islamic ideology serves to strengthen the aforementioned non-Islamic cultural messages valorizing motherhood.

Furthermore, the glorification of motherhood in Islam—or what Bouhdiba (1985) calls the Islamic "cult of motherhood," which has a long Arab-Islamic history—is being felt increasingly today with the revival of Islamism in Egypt. Namely, Islamist discourse promotes conservative views of women as wives and mothers only—effectively essentializing them as "breeders" and "family keepers" (i.e., the raisers of good Muslims), according to one observer (Helie-Lucas 1994). In its Egyptian variant, this discourse praises the beauty of women's domesticity and the ills of women's work and even condemns women's emancipation for its harmful effects on women's reproductive organs (Stowasser 1993). One of the most popular and influential of the Egyptian Islamists, the televised cleric Shaikh Muhammad Mitwali al-Shaarawi, has published a popular guide for the Muslim woman, outlining the ideal paradigm by which a woman's life may be measured as truly Islamic (Stowasser 1987). In al-Shaarawi's guide,[22] as well as in other examples from Egypt, the notion of woman's sole identity as "Wife-Mother" remains central (Haddad 1980; Moghadam 1994), and is receiving increasing popular support, including from women themselves, as the country becomes more and more visibly Islamic (MacLeod 1991).

Although few poor urban Egyptian women are Islamists, viewing the Islamic movement in their country with some skepticism and even downright amusement,[23] the increasingly vocal messages of Islamists have served to reinforce women's own ideological convictions about the mandatory nature of motherhood. As a result, it is not uncommon today for infertile women to worry openly about their fate as "nonmothers" in an increasingly Islamic and matrifocal society. Unfortunately for them, their concerns are probably legitimate. As patriarchy intensifies in Egypt under the legitimizing cloak of Islam, the fertility mandate characteristic of classic patriarchy, too, will probably intensify, making women's claims to esteem and support incumbent upon their deliverance of men's children. Thus, under this new Islamic scenario, motherhood may prove to be the key—and perhaps the only—source of women's power. And, for those women who are "missing motherhood," it remains to be seen whether their lives will take on an even more tragic cast.

The Cultural Construction of Motherhood

Given the rapidly changing cultural climate in Egypt today, the need to understand the new ideological and practical forces affecting women's lives is greater than ever. As patriarchy intensifies under a revival of religious conservatism, it is likely that the renewed emphasis on motherhood and mothering will be felt by all Egyptian women. But perhaps it will be felt, in particular, by poor urban women, whose other avenues for fulfillment are already quite limited by the economic obstacles and deeply engrained cultural proscriptions described in this chapter.

In reality, too little is known about the meaning of motherhood and the practices of mothering in Egyptian women's lives, either before or after the recent Islamic resurgence (Hatem 1986c; 1987b). Although Hatem (1986c) attributes this "silence" to a lack of cross-cultural analysis in feminist theory, part of the problem would appear to lie within the discipline of anthropology itself and its continuing tendency to see the mother as a "natural" category—hence one that requires little scholarly consideration (Moore 1988).

However, as reflected in this chapter, notions of motherhood and mothering are culturally constructed. Not only do they take their meaning from within specific cultural milieus, but the meaning of motherhood itself may vary within any given cultural milieu depending upon such factors as class position, rural versus urban residency, degree of religiosity, and fertile versus infertile status. Furthermore, the meaning of motherhood may shift over time in response to such culturally metamorphosing events as political revolutions, mass migrations, and religious revivals, all of which have profoundly affected Egypt during the past half century.

When all is said and done then, the need for finely nuanced cultural contextualizations of motherhood across place and through time seems quite clear. As Kay Warren and Susan Bourque state so aptly:

> We need to contextualize "motherhood"; that is, to analyze the ways in
> which various images of motherhood are constructed, imposed, subverted,

manipulated, enshrined, and doubted in the everyday life and ideologies of other societies and our own. This reformulation calls for culturally sensitive research on the multiple meanings of motherhood (and, obviously, of other gendered identities): when and how constructions of gender are used to exclude women from the workplace, when they are used by women to mobilize politically, when they are evoked to identify failures in the sexuality of young women, and how constructions and practices vary by class, race, and age within particular social systems. (Warren and Bourque 1991:287)

Furthermore, the meaning of motherhood may vary under different forms of patriarchy. Feminist scholars in the West have argued that the institutionalization of "biological motherhood"—namely, the need for women to mother the children of their own bodies—is one of Western patriarchy's overwhelming successes and has led many desperate infertile women down the slippery slope of technologically "assisted" conception (e.g., Oakley 1974; Rich 1976; Rowland 1992). The imperative for biological motherhood is operant in Egypt as well and has led many infertile women on relentless quests for therapy including the utilization of various forms of reproductive technology (Inhorn 1994). However, the cultural construction of many other aspects of Egyptian women's gendered identity—such as what it means to be a "virgin," what it means to be "feminine," what it means to be a "worker," what it means to be a "woman," and most important to this discussion, what it means to be "infertile"—may differ considerably from those gender constructions found in the West. Therefore, one cannot assume the existence of a universal patriarchy that oppresses all women everywhere in the same way.

Unfortunately for poor urban Egyptian women, their oppression as "mandatory mothers" derives from a number of sources, only one of which is patriarchy. We have seen in this chapter that Egyptian motherhood must be viewed through the multiple lenses of patriarchy, class, urbanism, and religion, sources of oppression that intersect in ways that have yet to be fully understood. However, what is clear is that for poor urban infertile women in Egypt, their failure to become mothers can only serve to magnify the other forms of oppression that they may experience in their daily lives. For such women, the ones who are seen as "missing motherhood," infertility serves as the major source of their suffering—marring their identities, testing their faith in God, and enveloping their lives in sadness.

3. Conjugal Connectivity

The shadow of a man is better than the shadow of a wall.
—An Egyptian proverb

Aida's Story

"I used to hear about cases like mine, but I never could feel what they felt. But now that I'm in it, it's lots of problems, problems, problems." So says Aida, an Egyptian woman whose infertility has brought on a marital tragedy of epic proportions.

From a poor, rural farming family, Aida was allowed to remain in school through the sixth grade, completing six more years of vocational education through a secretarial and bookkeeping correspondence course. Following years of illness, including hospitalizations for the removal of her spleen (the complications of childhood schistosomiasis),[1] kidney stones, gallbladder stones, two bouts of severe jaundice, and a high fever, Aida was finally engaged at the age of twenty-two to her *ibn 'amm*, the son of her paternal uncle, who, according to *fallāḥīn* tradition, was deemed the preferred marriage partner. Because Aida's cousin Samir was still young and virtually penniless, he migrated to Alexandria to take a relatively well-paid job as a textile factory worker prior to their marriage. Finally, after four years of working, Samir was able to accrue enough money to secure a small Alexandrian apartment, a few pieces of furniture, and a modest *shabka*, or gift of jewelry, to present to Aida upon their marriage.

Although Aida was neither happy nor sad about marrying Samir, whom she had known since childhood, the chance to join Samir in the city and to find her own secretarial job in a government office excited the young bride. Indeed, the first six months of their marriage were extremely joyful. Samir was kind and, unlike so many men of his poor rural background, he did not object to Aida's working in a Ministry of Health office. In fact, he welcomed the extra income, which they utilized to buy additional furnishings. However, Aida soon came to realize that Samir's parents were becoming increasingly concerned about the fact that she was not yet pregnant. Indeed, Samir's father, Aida's uncle, had been unable to have children by his first two wives, whom he had promptly divorced, eventually marrying a woman who had borne him six sons, including Samir. Samir himself was nonchalant at first, taking Aida to doctors who could find no apparent cause for the infertility. However, Samir's father eventually intervened after one and a half years of their marriage, insisting that Samir take his wife to the university hospital in order to "get her examined."

At the University of Alexandria's Shatby Hospital, the physicians recommended a diagnostic laparoscopy, a surgical procedure that would allow them to view the interior of Aida's pelvis and to assess the condition of her fallopian tubes. Seeing herself as having little choice in the matter, Aida formally consented to the procedure, and Samir and his father accompanied her to the hospital for the surgery. When the results of the surgery came back, both Samir and his father were present to receive the bad news: Aida had "sticky things" (i.e., peritubal adhesions) around both of her fallopian tubes as well as a scarred ovary, which, according to the doctors, would make it difficult, if not impossible, for her to get pregnant without further surgery, which might not be successful.

From Aida's perspective, this crucial moment in the hospital was the beginning of the downfall of her marriage. Samir's father took the news very badly and began almost immediately to tell Samir to divorce Aida and remarry a fertile woman. Toward Aida, he became verbally abusive and took every opportunity to degrade her in Samir's eyes. With the bad news and his father's pressure, Samir himself began to change. As Aida explained:

> It all started when I did the diagnostic laparoscopy. He [Samir] told himself, "This woman, she won't get pregnant," and he started to behave badly toward me. We haven't reached the point where he hits me, but he always shouts. He tells me, "What do you do? You're just a woman who cleans and washes for me." Whenever I'm home and he comes in, I feel my brain circling round and round. I don't argue with him, because I don't want to get divorced. Because it's bad if a woman gets divorced, bad for her reputation. So, from right after the laparoscopy, the problems were from children only. He's exactly like his father, like a pharaoh.[2] It's hereditary.

Although Aida spent all of her own salary—£56 ($22.40) a month— and sold all of her gold jewelry except her wedding band in order to finance various infertility treatments with the "biggest professors" in Alexandria, she was unable to become pregnant, as the Shatby physicians had suggested. During a three-and-a-half-year treatment period, she noticed that Samir's behavior toward her had changed rather dramatically. He no longer wished to have sex with her, and he began working night shifts, which he had never done before. Extremely suspicious, Aida went to his workplace and asked Samir's supervisor if the employees really worked overnight. When he told her no, she was *extremely* upset and went to her sister, who attempted to calm her down. Aida's sister and her husband told Aida, "Don't do anything. You go back home and we will keep track of him, see where he goes." Aida did go back home as her sister recommended, but she confronted Samir, accusing him of having an affair, which he denied. Yet, it was evident to Aida that Samir was also removing his clothes from their apartment; when she questioned him about this, he told her that they were at the factory, where he was having them laundered.

Eventually, Aida began to suspect that Samir had, in fact, taken a second wife without her knowledge and that both his and her relatives knew of this fact but were keeping it a secret from her. Indeed, over time, Aida became quite certain of this, as she explained:

> I know [that he is remarried]. And my family knows that he has a "relationship" with his colleague [i.e., a fellow factory worker], but my sisters and my mother don't want to tell me. But I know. They don't want to tell me because they know I will ask for a divorce, and they want to see what is the first step he will take. Sometimes, when I tell them, "I want to divorce Samir," they tell me, "It's up to you. If you want to get divorced, leave him." But, on the other hand, they tell me, "Don't forget, what will you do after you leave him? Your reputation. Like this, still nobody is talking about you. Let *him* pronounce the words [of divorce]. Don't ask for a divorce so nobody blames you."
>
> It's very difficult to live with someone who hates you. And I hate him, too. At the beginning, I didn't hate him, but after what he did to me and he's denying it, so that's why I'm hating him. And I'm sure that he wishes that I die. He didn't tell me [this], but I know. Two weeks ago, he came home and I had prepared food [for lunch]. He asked for lunch and made a small fight and told me, "Like this we can't continue. We should get divorced." So I said, "Okay, let's get divorced." But he wants me to write a paper that whatever I have, I will give it back to him and won't demand all my rights. So I refused. But I know that if not now, later he will *definitely* leave me, because when the other woman delivers a baby, he will want to be with his child.
>
> You know why he didn't tell me he's remarried? Because when the husband gets remarried, usually the *shaikh* [who certifies marriage and divorce contracts] then sends a paper in which it says that the husband has taken a second

wife, so she [the first wife] has to sign that she knows.[3] But in my case, my identity card address is Samir's family's address, so this paper came and I had no idea about it and someone at his house forged my signature. But if I go to court and tell them I didn't receive that paper and someone signed for me and they check the two signatures, they will know it's not my signature, and I can send Samir to prison. There is a program on the radio every morning that shows some of the problems of life. One of the problems was like this— a husband remarried and the first wife doesn't know. So I told my husband, "Did you see that man what he did to his wife? He should go to prison!" He agreed with me, but you should have seen his face! I hate him. I don't care where he goes. I *wish* he goes to prison, but I'm not going to do that because his father is still my uncle and my sister is married to his brother and they have kids and it would make problems for her.

Hurt and angry at Samir for his colossal deception, Aida simply decided to "make him suffer as he has made me suffer." Namely, Aida decided to remain in her now loveless marriage, pretending that everything was normal. Her reasons for remaining in the marriage were threefold. First, she needed time and energy to accrue the evidence of his remarriage and deception, so that when she finally asked for a divorce from him, she would win everything in the court settlement. Second, Aida still hoped to become pregnant with Samir's child, so that when she divorced him, she would at least have a child to "live for" and to ease her suffering and loneliness. Perhaps most important, Aida hoped to seek revenge: She wanted to bear Samir's child, divorce him, and make him live in guilt-ridden torment over his cruel betrayal of her, his cousin, and his lack of faith in her ability to get pregnant. The question, however, was how to get pregnant by Samir, given that they were now "living like brother and sister."

Reading the newspaper one day, Aida learned that Shatby Hospital— where she had once undergone the disastrous diagnostic laparoscopy—had initiated a new artificial insemination "by husband" (AIH) program. Thus, she decided to return to Shatby, this time for treatment of her infertility. Reviewing her case, the physicians at Shatby agreed that Aida might be a good candidate for AIH. Because her fallopian tubes were not completely blocked, it might be possible for her to be artificially inseminated with her husband's sperm. Aida agreed to the procedure, without telling the doctors of her current marital predicament. For her, the only problem would be obtaining Samir's semen for insemination, which she was told to bring to the hospital in a test tube provided to her for that purpose. Although Samir, with whom she had not had sex in weeks, initially refused to provide his semen, Aida played on his guilt, telling him: "What kind of a husband doesn't want his wife to get pregnant?" Still clinging to his marital cover-up, Samir finally consented, and, over several months, he provided "samples" for Aida to take with her to Shatby for what he believed would be semen analysis only. Unfortunately, Aida lived more than an hour and a half from the hospital, so that by the time she arrived there, Samir's sperm were usually dead. When she begged Samir to come with her to the hospital, he simply replied, "Don't go. We'll just stay at home together. Why do you want to go there again when the treatment brings no results?"

After several failed AIH attempts, the Shatby physicians recommended that Aida become a candidate for in vitro fertilization. They prescribed for her a very expensive medication costing £750 ($300), which Aida knew she would have to finance on her own, as she explained:

> I will try to get this medicine, one way or another. Last month's salary, I didn't touch it. And I'm going to sell my wedding ring and buy a shoe so that I can walk on his wedding ring [she laughed]. Actually, I'm not going to buy a shoe; I'm just going to sell it so I can buy the medicine. And my sister will give me some money, too, *if* it's going to be used for in vitro fertilization. I will do it, but I'm not going to tell Samir that, because *if* he wanted a child from me, he would get the money from *anywhere*. And by not telling him, I'm not going to give him the chance to hurt me. But if I get pregnant and I ask for a divorce, he won't be able to do anything. I will show him, "I am pregnant," and he will feel sorry. If I get pregnant, I'm going to go and tell him right away that I'm pregnant so that he will feel sorry for *everything* he did to me. All his life he will suffer.

Unfortunately for Aida, her ploy did not work. Before she had saved even a fraction of the money required for the expensive IVF medication, Samir's second wife had her baby: a son. When his son was born, Samir finally stopped his charade. After work one day, he returned to the apartment where Aida was waiting for him, threw some of his new son's baby clothes in her face, and stated contemptuously, "Look! I have the child now that you couldn't give me." He then told Aida that he had, in fact, remarried almost a year earlier and that, if she knew what was good for her, she would ask for a divorce and give him back the furnishings and home appliances.

Seeing their daughter's suffering, Aida's parents finally advised her to seek a divorce, quit her job, and come back to the village to live with them. The divorce occurred only a few months later. Although Aida was unable to realize her dream of having a child, she received a favorable divorce settlement from a sympathetic judge and the satisfaction of knowing that Samir's conscience will never be clean because of the way he treated her. Meanwhile, she moved into the home of her sister in Alexandria, and, although she vowed she would *never* remarry so as not to repeat "this ordeal," she received a marriage proposal from a polite widower with four small children. At last report, Aida was thinking about the proposition.

Marital Insecurity

Divorce and polygynous remarriage—both permitted in Islam, described very clearly in the Qur'an, and institutionalized through the Egyptian state's Muslim personal status laws—are the institutions that strike fear in the hearts of infertile Egyptian women. Because marriage and family-building are perceived as inseparable objectives in adult life, marriages that are childless are inherently insecure because of the looming threat of divorce or polygyny. It is this threat of marital collapse—or, as most women put it, "the collapse of the home we built together"—that is the greatest source of stress for infertile women, who hear cases like Aida's and can only wonder if a similar tragedy lies in store for them. Thus, in an attempt to rescue their marriages, infertile Egyptian women are likely to embark on therapeutic quests foddered by fear, insecurity, and the deleterious intervention of unsympathetic in-laws and community members. These external social pressures on the infertile marriage are the subjects to be explored in the following two chapters. In this chapter, the infertile marriage itself will be examined, because it is the marital relationship—that microstructural dyad of husband and wife—that is most profoundly affected by the problem of infertility, as suggested by the poignant story of Aida.

In Egypt, the distinctly Western notion of the "couple" is not well developed; in fact, a word for the human "couple" does not exist in either classical or Egyptian colloquial Arabic. The absence of this concept from the Egyptian cultural vocabulary, particularly among the rural and urban poor, is manifest in the way men and women think about and relate to one another both before and after they are married. But, the absence of a culturally constructed concept of the couple is particularly problematic in infertile marriages, because, in social structural terms, a husband and wife without children do not constitute a socially recognized, definable unit within Egyptian society. Rather, to reiterate an earlier point, marriages are viewed as vehicles for family-building; thus, a marriage that is not productive in this sense—and, ultimately, not productive for society at large—is considered, at best, pathetically deviant and, at worst, dangerously useless and something to be destroyed, usually by the husband's extended family (which, as we will see, has its own reproductive agenda). Hence, the social pressures on both the husband and wife in an infertile marriage are in many cases quite intense, and these pressures naturally affect the dynamics of the marital relationship, as seen in the story of Aida.

These marital dynamics—or what might best be called the gender politics of the infertile Egyptian marriage—provide the major substance of this chapter. However, to make sense of the actual social interactions and conjugal negotiations taking place within infertile Egyptian marriages, it is necessary to understand the differences between marital ideals, expectations, and realities among the urban poor: namely, what marriage is supposed to be, how Egyptians expect marriage to be, and how Egyptian marriages actually differ from what they are supposed and expected to be. Most important, we shall see how poor urban Egyptians' perceptions about the potential success of fertile versus infertile marriages—and their widespread belief that children "tie" a man to his wife—often diverge markedly from social realities. Even without social recognition or support, many childless husbands and wives view themselves on a practical level as committed couples, despite the absence of such an officially authorized concept. Thus, among the urban poor of Egypt, marital praxis seems to be shifting away from traditional marital ideals, despite the lack of recognition among poor urban Egyptians themselves of this drift toward increasing conjugal connectivity.

Marital Ideals

Among the urban poor in Egypt, marriage is a highly valued and normatively upheld institution. Islam extols the virtues of marriage, regarding it as *Sunna*, or the way of the Prophet Muhammad; as the proper vehicle for procreation; as "protection" for both a woman and a man, especially against illicit sexuality on the part of the latter; and as the "completion of half of the religion" (with worship and service to God completing the remaining half) (Mernissi 1985; Omran 1992; Schleifer 1986). Thus, most Egyptian Muslims—like Middle Easterners in general, who are among the "most married" people in the world (Omran and Roudi 1993)—take the call to marriage quite seriously and marry at least once in a lifetime. Remaining single is a deviant status and is socially penalized for both men and women (Smock and Youssef 1977); thus, permanent bachelors and spinsters are rarely found in Egypt. Furthermore, cohabitation between unmarried adults of the opposite sex, a historically recent pattern in the West, is unheard of among Egyptians of any social class or educational background.

ARRANGED MARRIAGES

Marriage is insured for most men and women, because marriages among the urban poor in Egypt are usually arranged by families. Under ideal circumstances, a young man (aged twenty to thirty-five) identifies the woman whom he would like to marry. She may be a cousin (first or beyond, from either patrilateral or matrilateral relatives), or she may be a "stranger" from an unrelated family, usually from the same neighborhood. Ideally, she is young (aged fourteen to twenty-five), slightly plump, and attractive.[4] Whether or not she is formally educated or literate is irrelevant, because her domestic skills and maternal capabilities will be much more important in insuring the success of the marriage than any of her other attributes— including her pulchritude, which will often decline rather rapidly after marriage and childbirth. Nevertheless, before she is engaged, her physical attractiveness in the eyes of beholding males will be *the* key factor in whether or not she receives suitable marriage proposals,[5] because the marriageable man identifies the woman he would like to marry based on sight. An "honorable" young woman, who is necessarily a virgin before marriage, does not interact socially with men, including her suitor, until she is engaged. Hence, marriages based on "love," as achieved through social interaction and the development of emotional intimacy between a man and a woman, are rare and, in fact, are frowned upon, because they are considered "shameful" and less successful in the long run.

THE ENGAGEMENT

Once the young man has spotted a young woman he finds attractive, the engagement, or *khuṭūba*, is arranged when he and his parents (or some other representative adult party from his family) come to ask the young woman's parents (or some other representative adult party from her family) for her hand. She may or may not be asked by her parents whether she "accepts" the suitor, and even if she is asked, she may feel too timid to reject the young man, especially if he is a relative. Thus, in most cases, marriage proposals are accepted by the authority figures in a young woman's life—usually her father—rather than by the young woman herself. Ideally, she will grow to "feel something" for the man to whom she is engaged and who will visit her and her family on a formal basis during the engagement period. Interactions with her husband-to-be during this period are limited by her parents, who normally sit with them during the young suitor's visits. As a result, many young women never speak to their husbands alone before the wedding day.

In order for an official engagement to take place, the parents of the future bride and groom must agree on the marriage payments. These include, from the groom's side, an official bridewealth payment in cash, called the *mahr* (which has increased from the £0–1,000 [$0–400] range to the £1,000–3,000 [$400–1,200] range over the past ten years, but which is often minimal in marriages between cousins); a gift of gold jewelry, called the *shabka*, which usually includes a pair of earrings, one or more bracelets or necklaces, and the bride's and groom's gold wedding bands; other optional presents, including clothing; and various home furnishings, particularly the large electrical appliances (stove, refrigerator, washing machine). From the bride's side, her parents may provide the bedroom set or other furniture, or agree to use all or part of the *mahr* for this purpose. Ideally, the young man has accrued enough money not only to make these bridal payments, but also to pay for the wedding festivities, including an engagement party at which the *shabka* is presented, as well as the major wedding party. In addition, since urban newlyweds have come to resist the notion of living with their parents after marriage—a change in residential pattern that has occurred over the past ten to twenty years—the young man is expected to put the key money down on a room or apartment that will be prepared by the wedding day.

If the families cannot agree on these marriage arrangements, if the groom is unable to provide everything that the bride's family expects, or if some unforeseen problem between the two families arises, the engagement may be called off at any time during the engagement period. The engagement officially begins when a Muslim cleric reads the opening passage of the Qur'an with the two families present and may be followed at that time by the writing of the marriage contract, called the *katb il-kitāb*. In some cases, families wait to write the marriage contract until the day of the wedding itself, because, once the contract is written, the young man and woman are officially married and must seek a divorce, even if they have never lived together as husband and wife. Furthermore, the marriage is usually not consummated until the night of the wedding party, even if the marriage contract has been written months or even years earlier.

THE WEDDING AND WEDDING NIGHT

If all goes well and the engagement continues (usually over the course of several months and ideally no longer than one or two years), the wedding party, or *farah*, followed by the wedding night defloration, or *dukhla* (meaning, literally, "the entrance") take place. The wedding consists of a party with food and loud music and, in some cases, other forms of entertainment (e.g., bellydancing, acrobatics). The bride, who wears an ornate, Western-style, white wedding gown, and her husband, who wears a suit, are displayed on chairs throughout the event, which usually takes place during a weekend evening, often in the family home in poor urban neighborhoods.

After the wedding party ends and the newlyweds return to their bedroom suite in their new apartment, the virginal bride must be deflowered. In most cases, the groom deflowers the bride, using either his penis or his hand, which is covered by a piece of white gauze or a handkerchief. Large amounts of blood are expected to appear on this white cloth, which must be produced either immediately or the next day for inspection by both families. This piece of bloodied cloth, which is the ultimate confirmation of the young woman's honor, or *sharaf* (also known as *'ird*), will be kept by the woman for life. However, if the virginal bride is too frightened and her husband is unable to penetrate her hymen, a midwife, or *dāya*, is often called in to deflower the bride by hand and to produce the requisite blood.[6]

THE EARLY DAYS OF MARRIAGE

Following the wedding night, the newlyweds have frequent sexual intercourse (at least once a day) in order to satisfy the groom's sexual appetite and to make the young bride pregnant. (The bride's sexual appetite is irrelevant.) Ideally, conception occurs during the first month, as evident when the bride's first postmarital menstrual period fails to arrive. If conception does not occur immediately, it is eagerly awaited by the new wife, her husband, and their families, who will experience feelings of relief when conception finally occurs, ideally within the first year of marriage.

During the early months of marriage, the husband and wife, who, up until the wedding day are barely on speaking terms, must become accustomed to one another—which women usually describe as "the creation of understanding." It is in these early months that patterns of behavior are

Photograph 2. A bride. (Photograph by Marcia Inhorn)

established, with the wife learning how to accommodate the husband's needs.

THE WIFE'S DUTIES

In fact, a woman's major goal in her marriage is to make her husband as "comfortable" as possible, both with her and with their home environment. From the female perspective, the major ways in which women "create comfort" are as follows, although not necessarily in this order:

1. By cooking well on a limited budget and by having the major meal of the day prepared by the time the husband returns from work.

2. By keeping the apartment or room tidy.

3. By bearing two or more children—and, ideally, at least one son—in the early years of marriage.

4. By taking care of all of the children's needs (other than the financial ones) and by keeping the children from annoying the husband when he is not in the mood to interact with them.

5. By making do with the husband's salary and by placing no additional financial demands on him.

6. By being a polite and generous hostess to the husband's relatives, especially his parents, and by acquiescing to his mother's wishes.

7. By accepting the husband's absences from the home, especially at night, when he may prefer to pass his time with his male friends.

8. By avoiding quarrels with the husband, his family, and neighbors.

9. By maintaining a mild to moderate state of obesity, which the husband will continue to find attractive.

10. By always accepting the husband's requests for sex, which he, alone, initiates.

THE HUSBAND'S DUTIES

Wives who are successful creators of these measures of comfort, even when they must sacrifice many of their own needs and desires to do so, are more likely to enlist their husband's continued loyalty and support. From the female perspective, a loyal and loving husband will reciprocate by "taking care" of his wife in these ways:

1. By providing enough money to cover the basic needs of the family (e.g., food, clothing for the children, school supplies), as well as occasional luxury items (e.g., material for a new dress for the wife, a television, a sewing machine).

2. By being willing to migrate outside of Egypt to insure the continued economic security of his wife and children and to allow his wife to remain a *sitt il-bait* instead of a second-income earner.

3. By allowing his wife to visit her family (especially her mother) regularly and allowing them to visit her in their home.

4. By keeping the visits to (and of) his relatives to a minimum and taking his wife's side in arguments with his family, especially those involving his mother and her demands on his wife.

5. By assuming paternal responsibilities, which include spending time with the children, helping them with their homework (if he is literate), providing their discipline and religious education, and showing affection to both his sons and daughters.

6. By being a "good husband," which means showing occasional appreciation of his wife's culinary and other domestic skills, feeling "jealous" and protective of her, especially around other men, and cooperating with her in overcoming financial, familial, and other problems that arise in the marriage.

7. By limiting his time spent outside of the household to a reasonable level and informing his wife of his whereabouts.

8. By avoiding "bad influences," including morally corrupt friends, alcohol, hashish, and "bad women."

9. By demanding his wife's sexual services at a reasonable rate (i.e., no more than once a week) and being sensitive by not asking her for sex when she is tired.

10. By remaining in the marriage—and with her as his only wife—until death do they part.

In this ideal scheme of things, spousal friendship, intimacy, and emotional support remain optional. Even if a wife is able to satisfy her husband with her service to him and his family, and he responds by providing financial and marital security, communication between them—in the form of an egalitarian dialogue about ideas, events, and life issues—may remain rather limited. Husbands and wives are not expected to spend time together talking or socializing. Rather, time together is spent eating, napping (especially on the part of husbands and especially after the midday meal), watching television, and visiting relatives. In fact, visiting may be the only time in which a husband and wife form a cohesive social unit, since men and women are not expected to socialize with one another otherwise.

This lack of an ideal notion of the "couple"—of marriage as an egalitarian partnership between a man and a woman—is central to the understanding of how lower-class Egyptian marriages can go wrong and what kinds of problems lower-class Egyptian women actually expect to face in their marriages. These more realistic expectations of marriage—as compared to the ideals outlined above—are the subject to which we now turn.

Marital Expectations

Romantic notions of the ideal marriage are illusory for most poor urban Egyptian women, who, given the sometimes grim realities of their

Photograph 3. A husband and wife. (Photograph by Marcia Inhorn)

own marriages and those of the women around them, are realistic about this institution and the men who are expected to uphold it with them. From the vantage point of married women with some experience in this realm, marriage—the institution that serves as the source of their childhood fantasies, but the major source of patriarchal control in their adult lives—is expected to differ from the ideal situation described above.

Nonetheless, most women wish that the aforementioned marital ideals were achievable, because marriage itself is an institution that they support, even though they are often given little choice in the matter of marriage partners. For them, marriage is a necessary and laudable institution, which is not, in and of itself, oppressive in nature. Rather, when married women sometimes describe themselves as "broken-winged"—which is as close to an emic definition of "oppressed" as can be found in this setting—they are referring to the result of their husbands' treatment toward them. It is men as husbands—and not marriage itself—that Egyptian women view as problematic. Yet, marriage is the arena in which men's culturally condoned assertion of patriarchal power over women is most readily apparent, including to Egyptian women themselves. The gender politics of marriage are a subject that Egyptian women have much reason to ponder, since their own lives after marriage are often lived out *in reaction to* their husbands' behavior toward them. Thus, women's reflections on marriage, which constitute the theme of this section, are actually reflections on how poor urban Egyptian women view men in general and more specifically men as husbands.

MALE CHARACTER

Essentially, Egyptian women view the success of a marriage as dependent upon the man who happens to fill the role of husband. Whether any given situation will become a problem in a marriage is largely dependent, in the eyes of women at least, on what kind of man a woman has for a husband. In a very general sense, Egyptian women tend to categorize men as being of two types: predominantly "good" or predominantly "bad," with some men having made a transition from one category to the other at some point in their lives.

In this scheme of things, the qualities of a good man are as follows: He is *aṣīl*, or of noble origins, which implies that he is of good upbringing, is well-mannered, and has a strong, unswerving character. He is also *mu'min*, or faithful, both to God and to his wife and family. Thus, he stands by his wife, even if she is infertile, and assumes responsibility for the welfare of his children, to whom he is affectionate, kind, and loving. In addition, a good man is not easily influenced by others, be it his peers or his natal family; thus, his decisions are his own, and he is not subject to either moral corruption or the pressure of opinion. In overall disposition, he is calm, even-tempered, and *dammu khafīf*, or "light-blooded," which is the Egyptian way of saying that a person is pleasant, amiable, and a pleasure to be around.

Conversely, a bad man exhibits the following characteristics: He is egocentric, thinking only of himself and his own pleasure and failing to assume responsibility as a husband and a father. He is weak in character, such that he may be easily swayed toward evil (e.g., alcohol, drugs, gambling, illegality) or may be unable to stand up to others. In addition, his "eyes are never full," which means that he is never satisfied with what he has, especially his wife, and is therefore inherently untrustworthy as a marital partner; "empty-eyed" men of this sort are known to "wander" toward other women. And, although he may profess his religiosity, he is not truly faithful, because he is not pure in heart. Finally, in terms of disposition, he is *shadīd*, or severe and even violent with others, and because his bad moods and temper induce others' fear, he is not pleasant to be around and is considered to be *dammu ta'īl*, or "heavy-blooded."

Naturally, individual men do not display all of these good or bad qualities simultaneously. Nevertheless, women tend to view men as leaning in one direction or another. Furthermore, some men are thought to experience life-transforming events that turn good men into bad ones and bad ones into good. Good men are known to "fall" when they try alcohol or drugs under the influence of friends (often during periods of labor migration), or when they become bewitched by a seductive, "bad woman," who tries to steal the man from his wife. Conversely, bad men are known to leave their troubled pasts behind them when, for various reasons, they "find their religion" and become devout, or *Sunnī* Muslims.[7]

Because women often have so little control over the choice of their marriage partners, the quality of a woman's marriage is most often a reflection of the quality of the man she happens to marry. Or, put another way, marriage is only as good as the man; good men can make women's marriages relatively happy, while bad ones can make them miserable.

The degree of control that men have over marriage—or that women *perceive* them to have—is apparent in women's discussions of their expectations of marriage, which differ rather considerably from the ideals described above. As should be evident in the following discussion, most women expect problems to arise over the course of a marriage, but the way these problems are handled and resolved depends largely upon the man's character. Moreover, in some cases, men themselves are viewed by women as the catalysts of marital problems, especially with respect to the issues of polygyny and divorce.

LOVE

Because marriages are arranged by families and the development of premarital intimacy is considered shameful among the urban poor, love, or *ḥubb*, between a man and a woman is expected to develop after marriage and over time. As women explain, love comes from living together as husband and wife, rather than from feelings of premarital passion, which may or may not last. Thus, mutual premarital infatuations that lead to marriage do not constitute "true love," and such "love marriages," as they are called, are often considered less stable than strictly arranged marriages. This is because the realities of married life are never the same as young lovers' dreams of romantic, postmarital bliss, and, according to women, high expectations before marriage lead to greater disappointments after marriage. Thus, love developing before marriage is believed to vanish after marriage, even turning into hatred. The clear bias *against* love marriages—based on beliefs about their inherent unsustainability in the face of difficult life circumstances—is apparent in women's strongly held opinions about why such marriages are often ill-fated. Although women acknowledge that such marriages are increasingly common with the entrance of young women into higher education and public workplaces, most women ardently defend the rationale for arranged marriages, which remain the widely observed norm among the poorer classes.

As one woman explained: "These days, you see people walking together and *then* they get married. But fifteen years ago, it wasn't like that. Now they love *before* marriage. If they *really* love each other, their relationship after marriage continues this way. But usually it's artificial before marriage and after the woman shows her faults and is not so decorated as before, he may not be able to stand her. With arranged marriages, if the man is good and kind in his treatment, even if it's totally arranged, she can't help loving him. What more would a woman want?"

As another woman put it: "Some people love each other before marriage, but they're not necessarily happy after because they change later on. *Any* love ends, because after marriage they come up naturally as they really are; they show their true selves. If they don't love each other before marriage, maybe it happens after. The main thing is fidelity and sincerity. If these exist, love must exist even if there was no love before, and if they don't exist, there will be no love even if it existed before."

According to another woman: "Those who love each other [before marriage] never last. Those in love before marriage have lots of problems.

I know of people who didn't love each other before [marriage], and after marriage, they just worship each other, and I wonder 'How come?'"

Although women's discourse speaks to the superiority of arranged marriages, poor urban women are also quick to acknowledge that feelings of attraction of a woman to her future husband are not necessarily strong, since it is the man who chooses the woman based on her appearance and reputation and not vice versa. Thus, women can only hope that their feelings of love for the man designated as future husband will grow over time. In large part, this is dependent upon the man's behavior toward his wife after marriage. Men who are good, as defined above, show their wives by their deeds that they love them, and this love is usually reciprocated, even if the husband is not particularly physically attractive. Thus, women who obviously love their husbands often remark, "He's not handsome, but he's good"—with the implicit addendum, "and, therefore, I love him."

On the other hand, women acknowledge that love may never develop after marriage, although marital partners may "get used to one another" and even "collaborate" as a couple without real love between them. This lack of love may emanate from either partner or from both. For a woman, feelings of love may fail to emerge when she has been truly forced into a marriage—and especially if she had hoped to marry another man—or, as is most often the case, when her husband is bad and mistreats her in any way. When a man is abusive early on in a marriage, a woman may ask her parents to help her petition for a court-ordered divorce. Unfortunately, however, many women have already become pregnant and/or given birth to a child by the time they decide that the marriage is truly loveless, and, for this reason, they may opt to stay in the marriage for the sake of the children.

The same is true of women whose husbands take a turn for the worse —that is, move from good to bad—later in the marriage. Such women usually remain in the marriage for three reasons: (1) for the sake of the children; (2) because a woman's request for a divorce involves legal difficulties, shame, and loss of property, long-term economic security, and, potentially, custody of children; and (3) because, as women are apt to say, "the shadow of a man is better than the shadow of a wall"—that is, even a bad man is better than no man, given the stigma and difficulties surrounding the status of divorcée. Nevertheless, women acknowledge that, in these cases, which are not uncommon among the urban poor, love often vanishes. The decline in love after marriage is reflected in such popular Egyptian phrases as: "If problems enter from the door, then love jumps from the window."

"It begins with honey and ends with onions." "Love cools down after the honeymoon." "Marriage kills love."

Thus, to summarize, women expect love to grow *after* marriage, and, for most women, love is a product of their husbands' behavior toward them and the growth of mutual understanding. Good men who show their love through kindness will usually be loved well in return, even if they are poor and/or unattractive. Bad men who make their wives suffer will generate their wives' indifference and/or animosity. Thus, some marriages are loving and some are not, but, according to poor Egyptian women, loving marriages are more common in Egypt.

As one woman concluded: "Even if they don't get married for love, love happens after marriage. As long as they treat each other well and are faithful to each other, love will be there."

COUSIN MARRIAGE

Although anthropologists have long been fascinated with the purportedly unique Middle Eastern preference for *bint 'amm*—literally, "father's brother's daughter" (FBD) or patrilineal parallel cousin—marriage, this is an endogamous preference that probably remains a societal ideal rather than a statistical reality in most Middle Eastern populations (Eickelman 1989).

Such is the case among the urban Egyptian poor. From the point of view of poor urban women, the son of the father's brother (or the *ibn 'amm*) does, in fact, take precedence over other suitors, should there be a choice of marriage partners and an *ibn 'amm* is among them. However, for most women, the choice never presents itself, due to a lack of interest on the part of these particular male cousins in exerting their rights over the *bint 'amm* cousin (which is probably related to lack of concern over inheritance among the unpropertied urban poor).

Rather, any male cousin may propose, often under the advisement (or, in some cases, pressure) of his parents. And because a young woman may feel compelled (sometimes through direct coercion by her parents) to accept a cousin's marriage offer, endogamous marriages do occur and, in fact, are commonplace (see Rugh [1984] and Inhorn [1994]).

Yet, in the opinion of women, cousin marriages are a mixed blessing. On the positive side, familial loyalty certainly plays a role in securing such marriages, since male cousins often tend to feel protective toward their female cousins in general, and female cousins often feel an obligation to "take care of their husbands' name" (i.e., the family reputation).

Photograph 4. A husband and wife. (Photograph by Marcia Inhorn)

Furthermore, the "background" (i.e., family and upbringing) of a cousin is generally known to all, ensuring that the future husband/wife is a known quantity. In addition, it is widely believed that fertility may be enhanced in cousin marriages, due to the salubrious mixing of the "same blood" (Inhorn 1994).

As one woman from a highly endogamous family described these positive attributes: "In our family, it's a shame that a girl says she loves someone [from outside the family] and wants to marry him. In my case, an agricultural engineer proposed to me, but my family said that I shouldn't marry outside the family. So I was married to my cousin. Whatever my family says goes. *All* my family prefers to marry cousins, except if someone can't find one, then he searches outside the family. In our own family, there is no preference for one cousin over another; we all grew up together. No one ever makes his wife angry or divorces her or remarries [polygynously]. It runs in the family. My brother married from outside the family two times and he divorced two times and didn't have children from them, because there was no one of his age to marry in the family. But he married a cousin the third time and had children. So, if a cousin is available, it's better."

On the negative side, women view endogamous marriages as being plagued by three potential problems. First, cousins are often united in marriage under familial pressure; thus, they may bring resentments with them into the marriage, especially if one or both partners had hoped to marry a "stranger." Second, aunts and uncles—or the parents/in-laws of the husband and wife—may intervene in their children's marriage in a way that they would not were their son/daughter to be married to a nonrelative. As noted by many women, an aunt may make a particularly nagging mother-in-law, given the aunt's perception of her inherent rights to assert control over a niece who also happens to be her daughter-in-law. Finally, many women view their male cousins as "brothers"; thus, taking a cousin as a husband may feel semi-incestuous to a woman, who may demonstrate her feelings of repulsion through sexual resistance.[8]

As one woman caught against her will in a first-cousin marriage explained: "Because he's my *ibn 'amm*, he tried to stand in the way of any other suitor. He told them, 'She's not getting married to anyone else.' It was his right, because he is my *ibn 'amm*. But, in truth, I didn't want him. I'd never considered him for marriage. I was embarrassed that my 'brother' would become my husband. By the time he was about to finish the army, he kept saying that he loves me. I kept saying, 'He's having the problems that young men have.' But he said, 'If you get me a million other brides, I'll only take this one.' He said, 'I don't consider you to be a sister. I love you and I want to marry you.' He saw other young women outside and he didn't find anyone like me. So after our marriage, I accepted that he's my share [in life]. He takes care of me, and I take care of him."

As reflected in this woman's statement, although the practice of endogamy is certainly accepted among poor urban Egyptians—and may, in fact, be preferred among culturally conservative groups within Egyptian society (i.e., rural *fallāḥīn*, Upper Egyptians, Nubians, Bedouins)—it is viewed with some ambivalence by women, who see it as having its own unique set of problems. For this reason, on the continuum from *bint 'amm* marriages, which are the "closest," to other forms of cousin marriage, to marriage with a total "stranger" (Bourdieu 1977), many poor urban women today are adamant in their preference for "stranger marriage," which has become by far the most common type.

Sex

Although sex and sexuality among the urban Egyptian poor are topics worthy of extended discussion (Inhorn n.d.a.), suffice it to say here that sex may be a problem area in a marriage, precisely because women have absolutely no idea what to expect about sex before they are married. Sex education is not offered in Egyptian schools, and, even if it were, the majority of Egyptian women never reach the junior-high-school level, where such education would most likely be provided. Furthermore, information about sex is not passed on from mother to daughter, given the fact that unmarried women are expected to be totally naive about sex and virginal on their wedding nights. Thus, wedding-night defloration experiences are often reported by women as being harrowing, wounding, and even violent due to a bride's understandable resistance.

After marriage, furthermore, the decision-making process regarding sex is entirely under the control of the husband. He is the one who is culturally prescribed to initiate sex and to determine the quantity and quality of the sex act. A woman's request for sex is considered shameful, and a woman's refusal to have sex with her husband sinful. However, in the view of most women, the husband's control over sexual frequency is problematic, since men "naturally" desire sex more than women. Thus, women report that sex is an arena for marital disputes, given that women are (1) less interested in sex than men, which may derive from their "coldness" following female circumcision; (2) often exhausted from domestic chores and child-rearing and therefore lacking energy for sex; (3) concerned about privacy, especially considering that children usually sleep in the same room and often in the same bed as their parents and relatives may be in rooms nearby; and (4) required to engage in ritually purifying bathing, often in the absence of a private source of running water in the household. Given these perceived obstacles, issues of sexual frequency may become a major source of problems between a husband and wife—the former of whom feels he is being denied adequate sexual satisfaction, while the latter yearns for sex that is infrequent and "finishes quickly."

Part of women's lack of desire may also extend from expectations about the quality of the sex act. Namely, a woman is considered by her female relatives and peers to be lucky if her husband happens to be a skilled and sensitive lover, which, given men's own lack of sex education and knowledge, is often not the case. Lovemaking may revolve largely around vaginal penetration, with many husbands experiencing problems of immediate ejaculation or impotence (probably as a result of nutritional deficiencies, diabetes, and hypertension, all growing problems in the urban Egyptian setting). Furthermore, because foreplay is often limited, many women experience problems of dyspareunia, or pain upon intercourse, probably due to a lack of vaginal lubrication. And, not surprising given the high rates of female circumcision among the urban poor (Inhorn and Buss 1993), very few husbands are able to induce true orgasms in their wives; indeed, neither partner may have any idea what this would entail. In addition, men's increasing exposure to pornographic videos and prostitutes during periods of labor migration has led them to request sexual practices—particularly fellatio and anal sodomy—that most wives find repugnant and even sinful. Thus, from the perspective of women, the pleasure to be derived from sex may be quite limited, and passion for one's spouse may be virtually nonexistent.

Speaking of her own dissatisfying sex life, one woman summed up the situation as follows: "Sometimes I feel that I want sex but I'm too shy to ask. He's selfish; even if I'm sleeping like a log, he wakes me up, but if I want, I sleep upset and he never asks me why. It's shameful for a woman to ask [for sex], but how my sisters do it, if they are upset and want it badly, their husbands would notice because they're sensitive. But my husband, he's not too good. He's very good at talking, but not at this. I don't feel anything during sex, because I'm down there under him, and I don't like it, and he finishes quickly and gets up. He doesn't move me at all; he doesn't touch me or coax me. When I hear about that from other women, I find that mine is no good. And it's not that I'm cold. I heard of women who are cold in this respect. But when I see a [romantic] movie, I feel like it but I can never ask. He's not romantic at all—not like men in the movies."

MONEY

Money—or lack thereof—is also a source of expected difficulties in marriages among the urban poor. Although a young woman's parents are often concerned that she marry a man with a steady income, poor urban women generally marry poor urban men, whose earning power is therefore limited. Thus, poor urban women usually begin marriage with the expectation that their economic situation and life-style may not improve substantially from premarital levels. But what many women do not anticipate is how their economic situation may actually worsen after marriage.

In many poor urban households, money is always in short supply and making ends meet is a constant struggle—one that may prove to be a major strain on the marriage. Because men are usually the sole wage earners, as described in the last chapter, they control the financial resources of the household in an absolute way, although they often relinquish all or part of their wages to their wives. Women are usually expected to manage the household finances, budgeting the money that their husbands provide. But men differ in this respect. Not only do lower-class men vary in terms of their real earning power, but they also differ in their willingness to turn over their wages to their wives (Hoodfar 1988). Given that most Egyptian men have expensive smoking habits (which may eventually lead to debilitating illness or death) (Inhorn and Buss 1994), they are thought to require their own supply of "pocket money," which they spend on cigarettes, food and tea taken outside the home, and transportation. "Responsible" men make an effort to limit their pocket-money requirements—even going so far as to cut down on (or, in exceptional cases, stop) smoking for the sake of the family finances. However, many men are considered by women to be "selfish," pocketing a significant portion of their wages and distributing the rest as they please to their wives.

Furthermore, even men who provide their wives with the bulk of their wages may simply be unable to earn enough money to meet the needs of their families. This is especially true when there are many children to support and the children are entering their young adult years when their economic needs (for school supplies, marriage, clothing, and so on) are greater. For this reason, many poor but responsible men are forced to migrate outside of Egypt in an effort to send remittances that are greater than what they could be earning in similar jobs back home.

As described in the last chapter, most men would rather migrate abroad than see their wives enter the wage-labor force. Because men are expected to be breadwinners, sending their wives into the work force is more than most men's egos can tolerate. Therefore, women who are willing to work to help support their families often meet with vehement opposition on the part of their husbands, who would be "ashamed" to let this happen. This opposition, in turn, is interpreted by women as a sign of their husbands' love for them, because, in their view, only a husband who "doesn't care" (i.e., is not "jealous") would allow his wife to enter the labor force and therefore mingle with other men.

Given these realities and the fact that the economic situation in Egypt has grown steadily worse in recent years, money is a major source of worry for most women. Women tend to characterize the Egyptian economy in terms of *khair*, which means both "goodness" and "wealth." They note that there is now less *khair* than in the time of their parents, which is why, in part, they view their poverty as increasing. Furthermore, they point to spiraling inflation—particularly evident in the constantly rising cost of a loaf of bread—and to the fact that wages do not increase at the same rate as prices. Because women do most of the shopping on limited budgets, they are extremely sensitive to increasing prices and are just as concerned about the Egyptian economy as their wage-earning husbands. Indeed, the price of staple items is a major topic of women's conversation.

Men who are frustrated by their inability to support their families are liable to take out their feelings of economic impotence on their wives. Not infrequently, this takes the form of domestic violence, ranging from occasional slaps or slugs to severe battery, which may or may not be instigated by a wife's complaints over lack of resources or requests for additional money. Men who are simply prone to violence may beat their wives at the slightest provocation, which many poor urban women are only too willing to rationalize and accommodate by virtue of their understanding of their husbands' economic frustrations. Furthermore, men's abandonment of their families—lasting from days to months—is not unheard of among the urban poor. "Bad" men who are seen as "unable to carry responsibilities" may leave their wives and children without the necessary provisions for survival, usually until they are discovered by friends and relatives who pressure them to return. Furthermore, abandonment may be largely emotional, as in cases where husbands who leave send money to cover basic household expenses, but rarely return home or communicate with their spouses (especially in cases of extended labor migration).

Thus, when all is said and done, it is women who bear the double burden of poverty *and* their husbands' anger about that poverty. For women who have spent their entire lives in a more or less impoverished state of existence—and have seen problems over money played out in their parents' marriages—money is expected to be a source of postmarital trouble. But, as with most other issues, how troubling the problem of money becomes is largely dependent on the man to whom a woman is married. "Good men" work as hard as they can to put food on the table and generally cooperate with their wives as their major "economic associates" (Tucker 1985). "Bad men" tilt the economic balance of power away from their wives by keeping their wages for themselves and failing to take economic responsibility for their families. Although most men, ultimately, are relatively poor providers, women tend nonetheless to be charitable toward their husbands and to view most men as "trying to be good" by virtue of their hard work for low wages in an economic climate where little more is to be expected.

CHILDREN

Without a doubt, having children is one of the major goals of marriage among poor urban Egyptians. As discussed earlier, men and women do not generally marry because they love each other; rather, marriages are arranged in such a way that the development of mutual love can only occur after marriage. As a result, men and women usually enter marriage as virtual strangers to each other; under these circumstances, having children together is perceived as one of the major ways of overcoming these feelings of estrangement and fostering love between a man and a woman.

In fact, in the view of many poor urban Egyptian women, having children is *the* major way a woman "ties" her husband to her, a view that is reflected in the popular Egyptian expressions "Conquer him with children," "Cut the husband's tail with lots of children," "Love doesn't last but a house with children does" and "When the love goes, the children tie them together."

As one woman who takes this view of marriage explained: "A child can prevent a lot of problems between a man and a woman. They tie them together. If he has a baby, he doesn't need to look or even have time to look at another woman, because he has a wife and a kid. Some actually marry for love, but if they just married without love, then they married for children."

"She ties the man with children," another woman commented. "That's what makes him stay with her. It takes up all his money so he can never remarry. It's because she's scared he will remarry any time, the one who has no confidence in herself. *All* women want to tie the man; that's the *real* reason for having children. It's just for the man, the reason why women have so many children."

The perceived "tying power" of children is, in part, a reflection of the lack of other bonds and feelings of affinity between partners who do not truly know each other when they wed. However, additionally, both men and women in Egypt are seen as loving and desiring children. In fact, Egyptian men and women perceive themselves as loving children more than adults in other countries, which is why Egypt has "too many people." And many women contend that this love of children is the major reason why men and women want to marry.

As one woman explained: "People marry for children, because instead of having only two persons alone for better and for worse, and instead of finding nothing to do but fight together, a child can change their lives. Both get busy with the child, and whatever happens, the child's smile makes all the difference to them. This is the system of life. One wishes to have his own house and children when he marries."

This desire to have children, which propels men and women into marriage, is reflected in the saying that "a man buys a woman for children." The verb "to buy" is not used here in a literal sense. Rather, it is linked to the concept of desire—namely, that men desire women as mothers for their children. This use of the verb "to buy" to connote desire occurs in other contexts as well, but is especially powerful in the context of marriage and family-building.

Although both men and women are believed to be ardent in their desires for children, their reasons for wanting children are considered to be somewhat different. As noted in the last chapter, motherhood is viewed as a natural condition for women, with their maternal feelings being instinctive. Thus, children complete a woman by allowing her maternal nature to be expressed. In addition, caring for children is the major role of most poor urban women in Egypt. Children occupy a woman's time, provide her with joy and friendship, and make her proud as they grow into adults. Essentially, raising children is the endeavor that gives a woman's life meaning. Children are viewed as an extension of a woman's self and personality, and, when they turn out well, they are her major accomplishment in life. Furthermore, given the nature of the marital relationship among the urban poor, it is usually the children—and not the husband—who provide a woman with consistent intimacy and affection. In women's words, children provide "the taste in life."

Men, on the other hand, are viewed as having primarily ego-gratification needs for children, given that they are not as directly involved in the caretaking aspects of parenting. On a most basic level, children are proof of a man's virile ability to bring life into this world, the basis of his patriarchal authority. Men are also seen as wanting to be fathers, because having children makes them equal to other married men. Furthermore, although their "paternal instinct" is considered less intense than a woman's maternal one, most men enjoy the "noise of children in the home" and desire affectionate interactions and emotional involvement with their children. In addition, men's economic interests are tied to their children, especially their sons, who may begin assisting their fathers from a relatively early age in various forms of income generation and, hence, family support. When a man dies, furthermore, he hopes to leave his inheritance to his own children rather than to other relatives, and it is his children who are his "memory after death," since all of them, including his daughters, will carry his name.

Indeed, just as women are teknonymously named after their children, men both receive the names of their children and impart their names to them. In the Arab world, naming practices are considerably different from those found in the West. Family surnames are often not used. Rather, an infant is given a first name and his/her second name is the first name of his/her father, whose own second name is the first name of his father, and so on. Thus, if a man named "Ahmed" has a son whom he names "Karim," the boy will usually go by the name of "Karim Ahmed," although, later in life, he may choose to use his patriline's name as a professional surname. Likewise, if Ahmed has a daughter "Karima," she will be known as "Karima Ahmed" throughout her life, because she does not adopt her husband's family name after marriage. However, her children will be named after their father rather than her father, which is one of the reasons why it is claimed that men prefer sons—that is, so that their names will not be "lost," as is the case when their daughters have children. Furthermore, if the child Karim is his father's first son, his father will no longer be known as "Ahmed," but rather as "Abu Karim," or "Father of Karim," since teknonymy is employed for both men and women.

Given these mutual but divergent desires for children, two potential problems can arise in this area. The first one is the problem of hyperfertility, or having too many children. The second one is the problem of infertility, or having none at all.

Hyperfertility

Because Egyptian men and women love and want children, those who are able to reproduce tend to do so immediately after marriage, setting in motion a reproductive process that, in many cases, becomes out of control. As a result, a husband and wife may find themselves with more children than they can effectively support, and, according to women, when this happens, problems in the marriage are sure to follow.

Although issues of fertility are not the direct subject of this book (see Inhorn 1996), it is important to note here that two distinctive patterns of hyperfertility can be found among Egyptian women: one involving women's loss of reproductive control (e.g., through unavailability of effective birth control, through a husband's refusal to let his wife use birth control, or through birth control lapses or failures); and one that was actually intended but that, after the fact, resulted in more children than the husband's income could support.

Which pattern is more prevalent in Egypt is unclear, although it appears that, among poor urban women, birth control failures and incorrect use of birth control methods account for numerous unwanted pregnancies today. Although many poor urban women desperately attempt to control their fertility in an effort to prevent the birth of children they cannot afford, many accidental pregnancies continue to occur, for which husbands—most of whom do not participate directly in birth control decision-making— often blame their wives. As a result, women in these situations may be faced with two choices: to abort with either traditional means or to obtain an illegal and expensive medical abortion in a clinic run by a physician; or to bear a child that is unwanted and that will remind the husband of his inability to meet the financial needs of his family.

Furthermore, it is important to point out that with the growing Islamic movement in Egypt, more and more poor urban men are becoming convinced that birth control is sinful from a religious perspective—a view that accords well with traditional cultural dictates against limiting family size. Yet, even men who refuse to let their wives practice family planning may take out their economic frustrations and inability to provide for their growing families on their wives—and, in some cases, on the hapless children themselves.

Although some men may forbid or discourage the use of contraception, most poor urban women are in complete agreement with official state policy suggesting that two children is the ideal number for any nuclear family. According to women at least, two children are the most any husband and wife can expect to feed, clothe, and educate properly, given today's taxing economic conditions. Yet, for various reasons, limiting family size to two is difficult for most women, and many of them end up having more children than they intended. Furthermore, even when pregnancies are planned and exceed the now official number of two, women are apt to state: "If I knew then what I know now, I wouldn't have had so many kids."

Having more than a manageable number of children is believed to put strains on a marriage. In these situations, women expect men to have anxiety about supporting their children, which they may express in any number of the following ways: (1) by working even harder and consequently becoming more exhausted and morose; (2) by fleeing their families, either without the intention of providing support or for an extended period of labor migration, which they hope will lead to improved support; (3) by taking it out, either verbally or physically, on their wives; (4) by resenting their children and/or mistreating them in various ways; (5) by forcing their wives to enter the wage labor force to help support the family; and (6) by denying the needs of their families and drifting toward "irresponsibility."

Furthermore, women say that having too many children is exhausting for them, both physically and emotionally. The expenditure of energy necessary to care for multiple children causes women to "lose their looks," to be physically drained at the end of each day, and therefore to become less attractive as wives. When all of a woman's energies are directed toward the care of her children, her husband may become frustrated, including in the sexual realm; in the worst case scenario, this may cause him to desire a divorce or, if he has the economic resources, to take a second wife. As women are quick to point out, not even children are completely effective in "tying" a man to his wife, because, when a man becomes fed up with his home life, nothing can stop him from taking action to remedy his own situation.

Although most poor urban women extol the tying power of children, they nonetheless recognize that children cannot tie a man in an absolute way, which is why some men with children still divorce their wives. Having too many children, furthermore, may be the factor that pushes an unhappy husband over the marital precipice.

As one woman explained: "Some women like lots of kids to tie the man. If she has fights with her husband, she thinks she's tied him. But it doesn't really, because if he wants to divorce her, he will do it—children or no children. Children do not, *never* tie the man, no matter what they say. It's the wife. If the man is not comfortable with his wife, he would leave her even if he had thirty kids. He would say, 'They will grow up anyway.'"

Given their expectations about the potential outcomes of hyperfertile marriages, poor urban Egyptian women tend to view hyperfertility as folly—for themselves, for their husbands, and, ultimately, for the children who suffer from the lack of resources and the problems between their parents. However, as apparent in the discussion that follows, having too many children is considered by women to be far more preferable to having none at all.

Infertility

In the view of poor urban Egyptian women, infertility can only be problematic in a marriage; therefore, it is an outcome that they believe must be greatly feared by all women who have married but have not yet conceived. Because the desires for children and the marital protection they afford are perceived as so great, most poor urban Egyptian newlyweds (as well as newlyweds of other social classes) hope to conceive a child immediately, which, in their view, means well within the first year of marriage. This is why Egyptian newlyweds, especially among the lower classes, rarely practice immediate postmarital contraception, and why anything less than almost immediate conception may be viewed as a sure sign of infertility. Although doctors in Egypt often try to comfort panicked brides by assuring them that at least a year and up to two years of "trying" is within the normal range, many new brides begin their conceptive quests almost immediately if six months of marriage have passed without any signs of pregnancy (Inhorn 1994).

This conceptive pressure on women can be great, as one infertile woman explained: "Here in Egypt, as soon as a woman is married, they like her to have children right away. So, if she doesn't, the talk starts. They start watching her to see if she's pregnant or not. They scrutinize her."

As another infertile woman put it: "Here, all [people] want children right away. It's our way; we're in a rush. Some people are afraid they will have problems [with infertility] and if they use birth control, they will increase the problems. The environment, the people around them make them want [children] right away. Even if you're working, educated, here in Egypt that's the way."

Given these pressures on women to prove their fertility immediately, any significant delay in childbearing is considered by women, fertile and infertile alike, to be a big problem, the *biggest* problem, according to those who are experiencing it, and one that is perceived to be bigger in Egypt than in other countries because of the aforementioned cultural expectations. The amplified magnitude of the infertility problem for Egyptian women is a common perception, described by one woman as follows: "In any country, infertility is a problem, because people want children so that they will be happy. But a woman's problems are worse here, because in other countries, women work or leave him and marry someone else she likes, not like us Egyptians. And Egyptians like children more."

Although most women agree that the actual rate of infertility in Egypt is low in comparison to the overwhelming fertility and population growth, some women believe the percentage of infertility cases is increasing, as reflected in the outnumbering of fertile women by infertile ones in hospitals and clinics.[9] Furthermore, they argue that, when infertility strikes, it is nothing but a problem for the afflicted couple, who will feel like they are "missing" something important, will become "fed up" and "bored" with each other, will fight all the time, and will be influenced by their families, possibly to seek divorce. A "wall" will grow between them, one that may eventually cause "their house to collapse." As one woman summed up the situation, "It's the biggest problem, of course. How can it be other than a problem? It fills the married life with fighting and boredom."

Although infertility is perceived as a problem for women themselves for all the reasons described in the last chapter, infertility is most commonly viewed as problematizing marriage, usually with dire consequences for infertile wives. When the problem of infertility besets a husband and wife, one or more of the following marital problems are expected to ensue, although not necessarily in this order.

First, women who do not conceive immediately are expected to begin worrying and eventually to experience many of the psychological ramifications of infertility described in the last chapter. Men, too, are expected to experience a range of negative emotions, although their concern over and emotional response to the situation are expected to lag somewhat behind those of their wives, who live their delayed conception in a bodily way. According to Egyptian women, infertility is a problem known to affect the "psychology" of both a husband and wife. The predominant emotion is expected to be profound sadness over dashed hopes, especially when the husband and wife have grown to love each other. However, men are often expected to become increasingly impatient with, resentful of, and hostile toward their wives if resolution of the infertility problem is not achieved relatively quickly.

Second, women who have not conceived within the first year of marriage are expected to begin searching for an explanation and a cure for their infertility, and this quest for therapy usually involves their husbands, who are requested by one or more treating physicians to undergo evaluation (Inhorn 1994). However, men and women are expected to differ in their willingness to embark upon the therapeutic quest. Out of fear for their reproductive health and the future of their marriages, women are expected to be eager participants, whereas men are expected to be less willing to undergo biomedical testing and intervention, including semen analysis. Furthermore, if, during the therapeutic quest, one or the other partner is discovered to be the cause of the infertility, problems of blaming, blame assumption, and guilt are expected to arise, especially if the woman's reproductive system is implicated. Additionally, biomedical therapy of any type is known by the Egyptian poor to be expensive; thus, they expect husbands and wives to argue over the costs of therapy. Accordingly, some men are expected to prefer remarriage over expending their economic resources on the treatment of a wife who may never become pregnant. Likewise, it is expected that some men will prefer remarriage over semen analysis, which they will refuse to undergo out of pride.

Third, whether or not a couple resorts to biomedical treatment of their infertility problem, infertility is expected to be the source of fighting between a husband and wife, especially when it has been determined that the wife is the cause of the infertility. Men are expected to be the primary initiators of these fights, which may be either unintentional or purposeful. For example, unintentional fighting may break out after the husband has received pressure from his parents, other family members, and/or peers to "do something" about the infertility problem, which, in turn, causes him to take out his frustration on his wife. Or, a man may compare himself to a brother or a friend who has just had a baby, and, feeling inferior, he may attempt to boost his own self-esteem by humiliating and blaming his wife as the source of their infertility problems. However, women contend that many of the fights instigated by men in infertile marriages occur for a reason: namely, that men set the stage for eventual divorce by making their wives' lives intolerable and forcing them out of the marriage through fighting.

Fourth, the husband's relatives—and especially his mother and sisters—are expected to be a significant source of interference in the infertile marriage and a catalyst for the fights that men tend to initiate. According to women, the mother-in-law is usually the one who pressures her daughter-in-law to seek treatment, and if, through the therapeutic quest, blame for the infertility problem should be assigned to the woman, the mother-in-law and others in the husband's family are expected to pressure the infertile woman's husband to divorce her and/or to take a second wife. Women contend that the husband's family is often the source of many of the problems that arise in infertile marriages; the only time the husband's family is perceived as being "good" is when it is known to them *and they accept* that the infertility problem stems from their own son and not his wife. On the other hand, the wife's family is viewed as being much more benign. The wife's parents are expected to take pity on their daughter and to rescue her from her marriage should it become unbearable. Furthermore, women contend that the wife's family is generally much more understanding when the infertility problem stems from their son-in-law. Instead of encouraging their daughter to divorce her infertile husband, they encourage her to remain with him if he makes her happy. Thus, the husband's and the wife's families, and particularly their parents, are viewed differently by women in terms of levels of interference in the infertile marriage. Yet, both families are expected to intervene, as will be described in the following chapter.

Finally, the ultimate marital problem associated with infertility—and the one most commonly cited by poor urban Egyptian women as the probable outcome of the aforementioned problems—is collapse of the infertile marriage by way of divorce or the husband's marriage to a second wife. Although Egyptian women are quick to point out that divorce or polygyny "can happen to anyone," they also adamantly believe that men are much more likely to divorce their wives or to take second wives when children have not been forthcoming in the first marriage. The widespread belief among both fertile and infertile Egyptian women is that very few infertile marriages are successful, given that a husband and wife living alone for a lifetime "can never be happy" in such an unnatural state of affairs. Rather, they contend that most men eventually succumb to mounting family pressure to replace the first wife, even in cases in which the husband loves his wife very much and spends several years with her attempting to overcome their infertility problem.

According to women, when a man decides to change his marital status, his decision to divorce his wife or to take a second wife depends upon two factors: (1) whether he loves his first wife, in which case he will prefer to keep her and to marry a second woman; and (2) whether the first wife accepts such a polygynous arrangement or prefers to be released from the marriage by way of divorce. Given that most men are thought to love their wives, they are seen as preferring polygyny over divorce. However, divorce is viewed as being much more common than polygyny for three reasons: (1) the costs associated with maintaining two households are unaffordable for most lower-class men; (2) love may fail to emerge in an infertile marriage because of the lack of children and, in these cases, infertility is a legitimate and socially acceptable excuse for ending a loveless marriage; and (3) most women find the idea of sharing their husband with a cowife intolerable, especially if they love him. Thus, when a man decides to look for a new wife, he and his first wife are normally expected to divorce, and, if she is lucky and has parents to help her, she, too, may be able to remarry.

Although divorce may appear to be the preferable outcome, both divorce and polygyny are viewed with considerable trepidation by Egyptian women, and especially infertile women, whose fears of replacement loom large in their minds.[10] To understand why replacement of any kind is such a threat to an infertile woman, one must understand the expected implications of—and the stigma associated with—being replaced by another woman, and especially one who is fertile.

Namely, if the husband decides to take a second wife, the infertile woman's position in the marital structure will be as the elder—and childless—cowife in a polygynous marriage, one of the worst possible structural positions for a woman to occupy in Egyptian society. Although Qur'anic prescriptions about polygyny demand that both (or all if there are three or four) wives be treated fairly in terms of love, sex, and money, equitable treatment by the husband is widely acknowledged as being impossible.

For one, setting up two equal households is impractical for most Egyptian men, and especially men from the lower class. As a result, co-wives may be forced to live together, which, according to women, is a situation virtually guaranteed to generate conflict and jealousy.

Second, a man's affection for his two wives can never be the same, especially if the second wife bears him children. Given that the second wife is the mother of his offspring, a man's affinities will naturally lie with her. As a result, the first barren cowife may lose her husband's affections over time and with the birth of each of her fertile cowife's children. If she loves her husband, this will cause her great sadness and jealousy, and, as the "unproductive" wife, she will be viewed by others as a pathetic and dependent creature, who is living off her husband's charity.

Even if her husband loves her and tries to protect her from the negative valuation of others, she is a stigmatized woman. Her stigmatization is exacerbated, furthermore, by the fact that she and her reproductive failing are juxtaposed continuously to a reproductively successful cowife, who may flaunt her fecundity in an effort to affect change in the marital structure from a polygynous relationship to a monogamous one. Thus, a jealous cowife may actually exacerbate her competitor's stigmatization and, if she is effective, make the husband view his infertile first wife as devalued and unworthy of his attention.

Eventually, such stigmatization from within the polygynous structure itself may become intolerable for the infertile first wife, and she may request that her husband release her from the marriage by initiating divorce. Or, she may ask for the divorce herself, although, as the instigator of the proceedings, she may lose some of the tangible goods she has accrued over the course of the marriage.

Given these potential outcomes, most infertile women say they would prefer that their husbands divorce them from the outset, so that they do not become embroiled in the potentially devastating dynamics of an asymmetrically structured polygynous marriage. Yet, as with polygyny, divorce is an undesirable experience for women, and especially infertile ones.

One of the major problems surrounds the initiation of the divorce: Namely, whoever requests the divorce usually loses their rights to jointly held property and potentially to major gift items (such as jewelry) given by the other spouse. Moreover, when the request for a divorce comes from the husband, he is often legally obligated to pay his wife a lump-sum divorce settlement called a *mu'akkhar*, which is decided upon at the time the marriage contract is written. Because of this potential loss of money and/or tangible items, neither partner may want to initiate the divorce, and this may lead to maliciousness and, in some cases, even acts of cruelty designed to push the other partner over the edge of tolerance of the marital situation. In most cases, the husband, who resists paying the *mu'akkhar* and losing other bridewealth tangibles, is the one expected to act badly through insults, arguments, and even physical abuse; unfortunately, women may tolerate such mistreatment for extended periods of time, in order to retain their rights and because, on the ideological level, it is perceived as shameful, even sinful, for a woman to request a divorce. Indeed, a good woman *never* asks for a divorce, even if her husband mistreats her. A woman who initiates a divorce, no matter what the cause, sullies her own rather than her husband's reputation and will be blamed for her inability to keep her marriage intact. Furthermore, she may fail to rally familial support for her cause and therefore risks not being taken in by her family if she leaves her husband.

Even when the initiation of the divorce is not acrimonious and an equitable settlement is reached, a divorced woman suffers in multiple ways.[11] First, as suggested above, a divorced woman must have a place to live after she and her husband separate. Because the husband usually keeps the apartment, which he has obtained with his own resources (even though the law does not stipulate this), the wife is usually expected to return to the home of her parents—if they are still alive. In fact, because the most powerful figures in a woman's life are her husband and her father, a divorced woman is lucky if the reigning control over her life can be returned to her father, who is expected to support her during the liminal period of divorce and, with some effort, find her another husband. Unfortunately, a woman's father may have died during the period of her marriage, and she will therefore be dependent upon the willingness of other male relatives to accept responsibility for and support her. If she has no father and no other relatives willing to take her in, a divorced woman may literally find herself with nowhere to go, and, as a result, she may be forced to capitulate to a polygynous marriage because of what she sees as her lack of other options. Frankly, few women have the economic resources to support themselves independently, and, more important, unmarried women are culturally prohibited from living alone. An unmarried woman living alone, especially by choice, would be viewed, at best, as a pathetic social deviant with no one to "protect" her, and, at worst, as an immoral woman who uses her solitary living quarters to "entertain" men.

Even if a woman finds shelter and support following her divorce, her family will feel the burden of responsibility for her as a divorcée. No matter what the reason for the divorce, a divorced woman is never as "valuable" as a never-married woman, given that the latter still retains her honor (i.e., her virginity). Thus, divorced women are socially stigmatized—and considerably more so if they are known to have been infertile in their first marriages. Not only are childless divorcées "used property" like other divorcées, but they are used property that was "returned" because of "defectiveness" in the most important area of marriage, namely, reproduction. As a result, childless divorcées are doubly devalued as marriage partners and are expected to be desirable only to the following types of deviant men: (1) extremely poor men who cannot afford the normal marriage payments for a virgin; (2) extremely unscrupulous men who are willing to marry an infertile, nonvirginal divorcée until they find someone better to replace her; (3) widowed men with young children who need a stepmother; (4) old men, widowed or divorced, who want a woman to take care of them until they die; (5) married men with children who are willing to marry a second infertile wife out of pity; (6) men who are known to be infertile themselves; or (7) men with some other mental, physical, or behavioral defect.[12]

Moreover, if such a man can be found, an infertile divorcée's parents or other relatives in positions of authority over her are liable to marry her off as quickly as possible, for fear that she will never receive any other marriage proposals. Thus, a woman who has already been scarred—emotionally and sometimes physically—by the problem of infertility in her first marriage may be forced to enter almost immediately into a second, often suboptimal marriage arrangement with a man who views her as instrumental in overcoming his own difficult situation. Knowing that she is desired as a quick-fix to a man's own problems, an infertile divorcée may resist the notion of remarriage but may have little choice in this matter, given that she is viewed by her own family as a social burden and a problem child, even when they love her and want her to be happy.

The thought of remarriage may be untenable to the infertile divorcée for other reasons as well. For one, some women may ardently love their husbands; thus, the thought of remarrying a new man may seem implausible on an emotional level. More commonly, however, infertile women who have suffered at the hands of their first husbands may feel "fed up," that they have "had enough of marriage," and may vow, usually unsuccessfully, that they will never be made to marry again.

As one infertile woman remarked: "What if I remarry and my husband will be the same as the first one? My life will be a catastrophe."

Another woman commented: "I've developed a complex [about marriage]. If I left this one, I wouldn't remarry. I would think they're all alike."

Or, as one woman summed up her situation: "From what I've seen, I don't want to get married again. He made me hate marriage. It's true! Because we fight a lot over money [for treatment]. I can't take the risk. I wouldn't like to be 'exposed' to another man."

Thus, the thought of polygyny or divorce is horrifying to most Egyptian women, and especially to infertile ones. Yet, according to women, replacement is the probable outcome of an infertile marriage, simply because the children who tie a man to his wife are missing. Although few women are willing to initiate a divorce given the social penalties described above, the average husband in an infertile marriage is expected to remarry another woman.

As one infertile woman lamented: "How can you trust a man? He's like water in the flour sifter. One woman goes and ten others come."

Another woman remarked: "If [infertility] is from the wife, 100 percent he will go and marry and leave her. If it's from him, the wife always has to support him because there's nothing she can do."

Another infertile woman observed: "Most men don't accept the fact of not having children, which is why they get married one or two or three times to have children and build a family. The husband always has the power; it's in his hand if he wants to marry or remarry, because sometimes a woman asks for a divorce and still the husband doesn't divorce her. So the woman is always the loser, because he has the power."

Although most infertile marriages are expected to fail because of the attitudes and actions of Egyptian men, Egyptian women, who are anthropological observers in their own right, do acknowledge that a small percentage of infertile marriages (estimated at anywhere from 1 to 25 percent) "make it" and, in fact, are free from many of the problems described above. Such "rare" marriages are deemed successful for five major reasons.

First, women are normally expected to "accept" a childless marriage when the infertility problem is attributed solely to the husband. Although the double standard in this expectation is apparent to Egyptian women themselves, they rationalize women's acceptance of childlessness in these cases by noting that women are superior to men in their tolerance, compassion, patience, and faith—qualities that are culturally and religiously valued. These qualities are what allow women to accept frustration of their own motherhood desires for the sake of their marriages, as well as to hide the fact that the infertility problem stems from their husbands. Furthermore, as women note, men who are infertile often feel shame over their inability to impregnate their wives; such feelings of shame and guilt may make such men exceptionally accommodating and indulgent as husbands, which, in turn, will appeal to their wives. As women explain, a wife who knows that her husband is infertile will feel "comfortable," "relaxed," and "secure" and will be more likely to trade in her reproductive potential for the love and kind treatment that she receives from her husband. In addition, even when an infertile husband is not exceptionally kind, a wife may feel duty-bound to him because of what she considers to be the unfairness of divorcing a husband with a nonvolitional physical condition and because of the shame associated with a woman's request for a divorce. Thus, even though male infertility is socially recognized as a legitimate cause of divorce, women are expected *not* to exercise this option—which, according to women, speaks to their superior devotion, humanity, and *aṣl* (upbringing). That women perceive themselves to be far superior to men in these regards is readily apparent in their impassioned discourse on women's ability to accept male infertility.

As one woman remarked: "I would *never* make him feel that there's something wrong with him. I wouldn't even bring up the word 'children.'"

Another woman commented: "I'd never ask him for a divorce or be mean to him as he is to me now. There isn't a woman who would ask that from her husband. Children are important but not to the point of divorce."

Another woman put it this way: "I would love him more because I would feel sorry for him. If he loves me the same, I would never differ with him. I wouldn't care if there are no children. I wouldn't 'sell' him."

Second, although Muslim men are allowed to divorce their wives or to marry as many as four women simultaneously, men who are considered to be truly pious, or faithful, are not expected to exercise these rights because of their acceptance that infertility, even when it stems from the woman, is the will of God. Such men are not necessarily the most demonstrably religious (i.e., *Sunnī*), but they are believed to "know God," which makes them "good" as defined above. When both a husband and wife have accepted infertility as a test of their religious faith, they are considered more likely to remain together for a lifetime, especially when they love each other. One woman explained, "Some people are religious and accept what God gives [them], and God compensates them in some other way, for example, with health and people's love."

As another woman put it, "Sometimes the man goes and gets married, and some men think that's God's wish and they accept it. They have more faith. The ones who have faith in God don't consider [infertility] a problem."

Third, among poor urban women, it is believed that education and wealth, both attributes of higher-class men, prevent them from divorcing their wives. Education promotes understanding of the "scientific" reasons why either a man or a woman may be infertile, as well as the realization that many cases of infertility "can't be helped." Wealth, furthermore, is seen as making people forget their problems, including the lack of children. As one woman put it, "[The wealthy] say, 'As long as I'm healthy and I have money, I can enjoy my life.' But, if there is no money and no children, there is nothing to enjoy and life is depressing."

Fourth, infertile couples who live far from relatives or have no living parents-in-law are expected to have greater success in their marriages. Since in-laws are expected to be the bane of an infertile woman's existence, infertile women without in-laws nearby are expected to experience less familial interference and, ultimately, happier marriages, as will be described in the following chapter.

Finally, some infertile marriages are deemed successful because of the extraordinary love of a man for his wife. In these cases, which are considered to be rather rare, a husband feels so enamored of his wife that he refuses to part with her or to pit her against another woman in a polygynous marriage. Such extraordinary love is thought to occur when the husband has been in love with his wife since long before marriage (e.g., an infatuation dating back to childhood), and/or the woman has helped to create an ideal marriage by providing everything her husband could ever want. When a woman has "created comfort" in this way, a man may be unwilling to give up or to replace his wife's tenderness and affection, and such marriages may be even happier than those with children. As one woman put it, "If a man really loves a woman, nothing can separate them. He tells her, 'You're worth the whole world to me.'" Whereas infertile women are more likely to accept this as a possibility, such a loving scenario is deemed rare by fertile women, who often remark: "He may say 'I love you,' but no man can be trusted."

Marital Realities

From the previous discussion, it is apparent that poor urban Egyptian women's expectations of marriage are different—and, in fact, less—than what the institution of marriage should and could be for them under ideal circumstances. Given these marital ideals and expectations, a number of questions remain, including: What are marriages among the urban poor actually like? How do the problems that poor urban women expect to face manifest themselves in their marriages? Are women's predictions about the relative success of infertile versus fertile marriages accurate? And, ultimately, are children truly the tie that binds men to women?

Few poor urban marriages are ideal in the sense of being trouble free. Most marriages face at least minor problems, and, in some cases, marital problems are frankly severe. Yet, the most important point to be made here is this: Despite women's convictions that children are the key ingredient in securing the future of a marriage, having children is, in fact, no guarantee that a marriage will be unproblematic and ultimately successful. Rather, *both* fertile and infertile marriages face problems, although these problems tend to be of different kinds. In fact, having children in many cases may be more problematic and stressful to the marital relationship than having none at all (Inhorn 1996). As we shall see, many infertile marriages are among the most stable, with childless husbands and wives demonstrating a degree of commitment to one another that overrides their desire for children. Despite the absence of an officially authorized notion of the couple, many infertile husbands and wives do, in fact, view themselves as committed, loving partners for life, facing adversity together. The emotional enmeshment of these men and women, the friendships that they forge with one another, and their ability to withstand familial and other external pressures all speak to the strength of their marital bonds in a society where these bonds are expected by the poor themselves to be fragile.

In fact, the success of many infertile marriages among the urban Egyptian poor throws into question both lay and scholarly perceptions of marriage in Egypt (and the Middle East in general). As we have seen, infertile marriages are viewed by Egyptians as diverging so considerably from marital ideals that they are assumed to be almost inherently unsuccessful. However, what few poor urban Egyptians realize is that actual marital praxis does not support this contention, indicating that marital ideologies themselves may be in the process of liberalization. Furthermore, scholarly representations of Egyptian marriages, especially among the poorer classes, describe such unions as being attenuated and uncommitted, lacking partnership and companionability, and being plagued by the gender gulf that is said to separate men and women more generally. Although a shift toward the "companionate" marriage has been documented historically for the middle and upper classes in Egypt (Baron 1991), the scholarly assumption continues that marriages among the poor do not, and perhaps cannot, manifest such connectedness. Yet, such representations may be more stereotypical than real, given the changing marital arrangements, accommodations, and alliances evident among the urban poor.

Furthermore, the success of many infertile marriages and the fact that infertile couples are able to stand up to their families challenges, to some degree, the notion of familial corporateness in Egypt (and the Middle East in general) (Rugh 1984). Although the subject of families will be taken up in the following chapter, it is important to note here that the strong marital bonds forged by many infertile couples—a product of their own socialization into systems of familial connectivity (Joseph 1993; 1994)—allow them to resist the political tactics of family members, who may strive assiduously to destroy the infertile union.

This is not to say, however, that all infertile marriages are so resilient or resistant to family interference. Among infertile women in Egypt, personal reproductive and marital futures are topics of great concern, abundant speculation, fretful discussion, and agonizing distress. When infertile women express their most pressing fears about the future, they usually pose the question: Will my husband replace me with another wife if I do not bear a child? In some cases, the answer may be "yes" and may lead to the kind of marital catastrophe described for Aida at the opening of this chapter.

To explore this question, it is necessary to view infertile marriages from this indigenous perspective of replacement. Using the notion of replacement as the key definitional principle, it is possible to construct a typology of marital relationships that shows the actual range of marital experiences. As we shall see here, infertile marriages tend to be of four types, based on the probability of wife replacement. Some marriages are stable; others are not. However, stable marriages with minimal threat of divorce or polygyny are the most common type.

STABLE MARRIAGES WITH MINIMUM REPLACEMENT POTENTIAL

Contrary to expectation, the largest single proportion of poor urban infertile women (for example, 46 percent in this study) are involved in extremely stable, loving marriages, in which the actual potential of replacement through polygyny or divorce is defined by women themselves as being minimal. Women in these marriages not only feel secure with and loved by their husbands, but, in most cases, they have also been reassured repeatedly by their husbands that they will never be replaced by another woman and especially not because of infertility. In these marriages, husbands often insist that having children is not important, and that being married to a woman who is "precious" to them provides enough love and satisfaction for a lifetime. Typically, these are marriages in which husbands have "never said a word" about children; have never hurt their wives, either emotionally or physically, over the problem of infertility; and have never particularly encouraged them to seek treatment for their infertility, sometimes even discouraging their visits to doctors. These are also marriages in which the wife defines the relationship as extremely "close," "loving," "understanding," and "honest," and where husbands are described as "faithful," "patient," and "sympathetic." In these marriages, husbands make it clear that they "want" their wives, are "holding on" to them, and will "never let them go." And, despite their own profound love for their husbands, many women feel that their husbands love them even more.

Furthermore, in many of these cases, women have actually encouraged their husbands to remarry so as to produce offspring; but, in each case, they have been met with absolute refusal on the part of the husband, as well as professions of undying love and continuing devotion. Although few wives genuinely want their husbands to divorce them or take another wife, they feel sorry for their husbands, having deprived them of their "right" to offspring. Encouraging remarriage is thus a way for women to expiate their own guilt. But it generally occurs only in stable marriages, where women have some certainty that their husbands will resist such an overture.

As one woman explained: "Sometimes I discuss this with him, like I'm testing him. 'You want kids. Why don't you marry again?' But he tells me, 'I love you for you. It's no problem not having kids.'"

In addition, in these marriages, husbands tend to serve as "stigma managers" for their wives (Goffman 1963), protecting them from social harm (e.g., pressure from the husband's family) and physical pain (e.g., reproductive surgery with little chance of success). In many cases, husbands have made it clear to their own family members that any interference in their marriage is unwelcome and will lead to estrangement from the family if it occurs. Furthermore, a husband may refuse to reveal to his own family members any news about his wife's medical condition, so that she cannot be blamed by them for the infertility. Although it is widely known that wives may cover for their husbands in this way when the infertility problem is attributable to a male condition, it is rarely recognized that husbands, too, deflect the blame away from their spouses in successful marriages.

In general, in these marriages, husbands tend to form emotionally intimate relationships with their wives, confiding in them, working with them to overcome their infertility, and generally sharing life's problems. Clearly, such men are devoted husbands, and women are grateful to them for easing their fears of replacement. Thus, it would seem that in these marriages, husbands and wives look to each other for completion of their relational selves and are able to subordinate their desires for children, as well as forsake their ties to their families, in order to promote a kind of lasting conjugal connectivity.

But why are so many of these infertile marriages successful? On a general level, success is attributable to characteristics of the marital partners themselves. Namely, despite their inability to produce offspring, women in these marriages believe that they have succeeded as wives in other ways by making their husbands exceptionally comfortable in the marriage. Not only have they been able to fulfill most of the wifely duties of an ideal marriage, but they have loved their husbands well—providing them with affection, tenderness, and understanding that is viewed by their husbands as irreplaceable. Furthermore, because their husbands are "good men," according to the definition described earlier, they have repaid their wives in kindness and appreciation, despite the absence of children in their lives. Thus, in these marriages, women are, on the one hand, lucky to be married to responsive, kind men, and, on the other hand, they themselves have succeeded in accommodating their husbands as wives—even if they are unable to succeed as mothers. In fact, when speaking about their husbands, these women often beam with pride over their husbands' love, affection, and loyalty, and they deem their husbands especially wise for realizing that infertility is a problem of God's making (and not their own) and, hence, beyond their control.

Yet, it is apparent in studying the realities of married life among the urban Egyptian poor, that there are additional facilitating factors that lubricate marital relations and allow many infertile marriages to succeed in the ways described above. Six such factors—including being married to a cousin, being a Coptic Christian, being married "for love," being pregnant previously, being married to a religious man, and being married to an infertile man—stand out as being particularly important in stabilizing infertile marriages. (For example, at least one of these factors was present among 91 percent of the stable marriages in this study, and, in some cases, more than one factor was present.)

Cousin Marriages

In successful infertile marriages, familial loyalty appears to play the expected major role in securing the marital relationship. (For example, in this study, 35 percent of such marriages were between cousins.) When asked why they believe their marriages are more successful than others, infertile women married to their cousins are often quick to respond: "Because my husband is my cousin." Although not all childless cousin marriages are successful, as seen in the opening story of Aida, they are generally expected to proceed more salubriously than marriages between "strangers," because of a natural protective feeling that cousins have toward one another. More often than not, having a close cousin as a spouse does, indeed, appear to be a solidifying factor in the marital relationship, especially during periods of hardship and crisis. As one woman in a cousin marriage explained: "There's been no change in our relationship because we are cousins. Not having children has had no affect on our relationship because we are relatives. We have the same family. His family *is* my family."

Christian Marriages

Although little has been said to this point about infertile Coptic Christian women (see Inhorn [1994]), their marriages are deemed successful and secure by default, because, according to the Coptic Church's doctrine, marriages cannot be ended through divorce, annulment, or polygyny. Because of the legislated permanence of marriage, Coptic Christians in Egypt say they are especially careful to ensure that mismatched marriages do not occur. Instead, among Christians, it is considered important that a bride and groom are "comfortable" with one another *before* marriage, because, after marriage, they have "no way out." As a result, young Coptic couples are often allowed to get to know one another before marriage (although not in the biblical sense). Therefore, their marriages tend to be loving from the start and may be less affected by problems that arise, including infertility. Furthermore, because of the structural stability of Coptic Christian marriages, infertile Christian women admit that they do not suffer from the replacement anxieties of Muslim women, although they, too, may be sad about the absence of children in their lives. Although not all infertile Coptic Christian marriages among the poor are blissfully happy—since both partners may feel somewhat trapped in a marriage that is of "no use" reproductively speaking—most of these marriages are successful according to the criteria cited above. (For example, of the six Coptic Christian marriages in this study, four of them were extremely stable and loving unions that had not been significantly affected by the problem of infertility.) It would seem that the structural permanence of Coptic marriages eliminates the kind of ambiguity found in Muslim marriages, where both polygyny and divorce are continuing possibilities. Indeed, Coptic women often comment that they feel sorry for their Muslim counterparts, whom they believe (according to popular wisdom) will be replaced by their husbands if no children are forthcoming in the marriage.

Love Marriages

Contrary to popular expectations about the lack of success of love marriages, infertile marriages in which the husband and wife have married for love are among the most successful of *all* marriages among the urban poor. (For example, of the twelve infertile love marriages in this study, eight of them were not only stable but came close to the marital ideals described earlier in this chapter.) In these marriages, love present before marriage appears to intensify after marriage, despite popular convictions that premarital love either diminishes or vanishes in the face of life's exigencies. Instead, most love marriages appear to be based on authentic love, which remains present in the face of adversity and seems to bolster a couple's commitment when problems such as infertility arise. Even years after marriage, many of these couples—who faced the wrath of their families when they married—continue to protect one another from social censure. Furthermore, many privately profess their love for one another and exhibit a kind of public romantic affection, including hand-holding, kissing, and hugging, which are rare and even shocking among the urban poor and which are often missing in arranged marriages.

As one woman in a love marriage explained: "He's the one who takes my mind away. Even if I had a child, my first love would be my husband. When I go to the village [to visit kin], my neighbors tell me that my husband is lost without me. And even if I go to my parents, I would miss him after two days. When I'm at home, he's comfortable. Even when he sleeps, he wants me to be at home, since he feels more secure. I don't have dinner until he comes home. Even if someone gives me something sweet, even a sandwich, I take it home and we share it. We don't keep anything from each other." She added, "The husband of my sister gets jealous when

Photograph 5. A husband and wife. (Photograph by Mia Fuller)

he sees how I take care of my husband, because they didn't marry for love. Her husband hits her for this reason."

Previous Pregnancies

Infertile marriages also seem to be more successful when previous pregnancies have occurred—whether or not they have resulted in living offspring. According to women with so-called "secondary infertility" (inability to conceive following a previous pregnancy), previous pregnancies serve to strengthen hopes that future conceptions will take place, even when previous pregnancies have ended in early miscarriages, as is often the case. Women who have no children but who have miscarried at some point in the past are usually quick to establish the fact that they have been pregnant, even though, in terms of motherhood, they share the same structural position as women with so-called "primary infertility" (no history of conception). Likewise, women who are so-called "habitual aborters," having experienced repeated miscarriages or stillbirths, do not generally consider themselves to be in the same category as primarily infertile women, since, as they point out, they are at least *able* to get pregnant.

Among infertile women, however, a major distinction is made between those women (either primarily or secondarily infertile) who have no living children and those secondarily infertile women who have at least one living child. In other words, whereas all cases of secondary infertility tend to be lumped together by the physicians who treat these women, women themselves see the most crucial defining factor in infertility as revolving around the issue of motherhood: Namely, does the woman have a living child or not? Thus, secondarily infertile women *with* children are viewed by other infertile women—and by society at large—as being quite different from those women who have yet to become mothers. And, as such women with children admit, they tend to view their situations differently, although they, too, often seek treatment in order to conceive again.

From the perspective of infertile women without children, secondarily infertile women with children constitute an entirely different category. For example, when a woman comes to the University of Alexandria's Shatby Hospital with her child in hand, and it becomes known to other infertile patients that she is seeking treatment for infertility, those women without children often comment: "If I were her, I would *never* be searching for children!" Or, "If I were her, I would be satisfied!" Or, "Even one child like that would be enough for me!" Thus, from the standpoint of *childless* infertile women, secondarily infertile women with even one child have few grounds for legitimate complaint, and may even be viewed as selfish for wanting more children and ungrateful for not really appreciating those that they have.

Yet, secondarily infertile women with children often have compelling reasons for wanting additional offspring. In some cases, social pressures on them are just as great as on women who have no children at all. For example, women hailing from rural communities in which large families are the widely observed norm are quick to explain that having only one or two children is not "normal" for a woman from Ṣaʿīd or the *fallāḥīn*. Thus, such women may be under tremendous pressure from family and community members (and, in some cases, husbands) to bear additional offspring. For secondarily infertile women in these cases, having only one child—and especially a less valued daughter—is no different, structurally speaking, from having no children at all, at least from the perspective of one's community of reference.

Secondarily infertile women are also concerned about leaving their only children with siblings. For them, having more children means providing their child with future security, because, in Egypt, the family is the major source of social support. A child without siblings is considered by most women to be "lonely," and this loneliness will certainly intensify at the point when the child's parents die and he or she becomes an "orphan." Thus, many secondarily infertile women are desperate to produce at least one additional child, given their fears that they might die early, leaving their only child without a family, and given that other alternatives to family-building, such as adoption, are not culturally permissible.

In summary, then, although secondarily infertile women with children are often viewed—and may view themselves—quite differently from childless women, their reasons for wanting additional children must not be ignored, nor must the difficulties they encounter over their inability to conceive. Yet, it is true that these women are more likely to experience marital success, for husbands who have at least one child are more likely to feel satisfied with their children and with their wives, even though most would like to have additional offspring.

Nonetheless, hopefulness based on *any* history of conception seems to have a salutary effect on the marital relationship among the urban Egyptian poor. Women who through infertility treatment have been able to conceive at least once, even if they subsequently lose the pregnancy, often have the most hopeful husbands. And, although some husbands are known to lose hope over time, many desire to remain with the wife whom they have impregnated at least once and whom they believe, with God's help, they might impregnate again.

Religious Husbands

Religiosity on the part of husbands also seems to stabilize infertile marriages. As expected, men who "know God," and who accept God's role in human reproduction as it has been described in the preceding chapter, are more likely to remain in their marriages based on their conviction that infertility is "from God" and, hence, beyond human control. Like their infertile wives, many husbands believe they are being tested by God, who seeks to determine the husband's faith in God and his ability to endure with patience the absence of children in his life. According to such men, replacing a wife who cannot bear children is likely to anger God, for God has made the couple childless for a reason. Thus, it is better to accept one's fate and hope that God may someday provide the ultimate reward in the

Photograph 6. A husband and wife. (Photograph by Marcia Inhorn)

form of children. As one woman with a religious husband explained: "[My husband] encourages me to search [for treatment], but, if there is no baby, he'll accept this. He doesn't think of a thing like remarriage, because he's religious, faithful. He is allowed to have four wives, but he doesn't think of that. He thinks if God wants him to have children, he will have, even if it takes all his life with me."

Infertile Husbands

The final reason why many infertile marriages are successful is that the husband—rather than or in addition to his wife—is infertile, is apprised of this fact, and is willing to accept total or partial responsibility for the infertility. Although male infertility accounts for approximately 40 percent of all infertility cases and thus is a major subject of investigation in its own right (Inhorn 1994, n.d.b; Inhorn and Buss 1994), suffice it to say here that not all poor urban Egyptian men are willing to submit to infertility diagnosis or may view the results of such diagnosis as illegitimate if a male factor is detected. Thus, as noted in the previous chapters, Egyptian women continue to be blamed for infertility, even in the face of convincing evidence of a male infertility condition.

Nonetheless, with the advent of semen analysis in Egypt and with the widespread knowledge that men, too, may be infertile, many husbands today are willing to submit to infertility investigation and to accept their own responsibility for childlessness should a sperm or semen problem be detected. In these cases—and especially when the wife has been given a clean bill of health—marital relationships tend to be very stable. In fact, for a number of reasons anticipated by Egyptian women themselves, marriages affected by male infertility are among the most successful. (For example, male infertility was a factor in 41 percent of the successful marriages in this study.)

First and most important, husbands who acknowledge their own infertility problem and, in some cases, the absence of a comparable problem on the part of their wives are frankly unlikely to replace their wives over the problem of childlessness. Indeed, knowledge of their "secret failing" often serves to make such men more solicitous of their wives, largely because of the guilt that they feel over depriving their wives of children. In turn, wives of men with male infertility are usually relieved and happy to have at least part of the responsibility for the infertility displaced from them onto their husbands. Moreover, because of the gratitude and attentiveness of their infertile husbands, they are often extremely satisfied in their marriages, despite the absence of children. In fact, many women who find themselves in this situation are exceedingly protective of their husbands and of their husbands' "secret," given that male infertility is often confused with impotence and, like impotence, is both socially embarrassing and stigmatizing for men if exposed to the public. Thus, many Egyptian women with infertile husbands pretend that the infertility problem stems from them instead of their husbands and may even seek treatment under the assumption that something *might* be wrong with them, too. Their willingness to "accept the blame" socially is often very impressive to their husbands, serving to further cement the marital relationship.

Moreover, Egyptian women are socialized to be nurturant, compassionate caregivers and, if given the opportunity, will play this role with their infertile husbands, even if a husband's condition is responsible for permanent childlessness in the marriage. When a man's infertility condition is irreversible, some men take pity on their wives and encourage them to seek a divorce or offer to free their wives from the childless union. However, unlike men, who are known to leave their wives over childlessness, very few women choose this route and may be even more loving toward their husbands out of sympathy for their plight.

As one woman in this situation explained: "One day after the diagnosis, [my husband] told me, 'If you want to leave me, you can.' I was upset, and I went to talk to my mother—she's like my friend—and my mother wanted me to leave him! After thinking a lot, I refused this idea; I didn't want to leave him. My mother got upset and told all my brothers and sisters. They didn't—and can't—push me, but I felt *all* of them wanted me to leave my husband. And that's something up to me to decide. For example, my sister whose husband is very sick has three children. I told her, 'Can you leave your husband because you know he's sick? My husband, too, is sick. It's a sickness. You leave your husband and I'll leave mine!' A few times [my husband] told me, 'If you want me to leave you, I will. I'll leave you the apartment and everything. I just don't want to upset you.' He said he'd go to live with his father. Less than a month ago, again, he said this. He feels he's depriving me. . . . Others who can't have children have problems at home with their husbands, but I don't. I act at home as if he's my son, and I cuddle him a lot. . . . And if strangers ask me from whom it is, I say, 'Both of us are well and that's up to God.'"

SLIGHTLY UNSTABLE MARRIAGES
WITH MEDIUM REPLACEMENT POTENTIAL
Despite the many successful infertile marriages that have been described so far, not all marriages are as stable and may, in fact, undergo negative changes as a result of infertility. Although a few of these less stable marriages eventually become significantly disrupted—even ended—by infertility, the majority (for example, 37 percent in this study) may continue for some time or forever in a state of slight instability. In these marriages, threats of wife replacement are not imminent. However, for various reasons, women in these slightly unstable marriages contend that, if children are not forthcoming at some point in the not-so-distant future, their marital relationships will certainly change for the worse, and most fear (even if they are not certain of this) that their husbands will eventually replace them with another woman.

In short, marriages in this category are under stress, having moved from the ideal comfort zone of marital satisfaction to the socially expected realm of infertility-induced marital strain. Although the instability of these marriages is often subtle, it is manifest in a typical marital dynamic that can be characterized as follows:

A husband and wife have been married for a year or more, and, much to their dismay, they have been unable to produce a child. Both of them want children very much, and their families of origin also want them to produce offspring. Throughout their marriage and with each passing month, their failure to reproduce is noticed—first by the women (the wife, her mother, her mother-in-law), and then by the husband, his social peers, and other members of his family. In other words, the infertile husband and wife are increasingly aware of their "problem" and of mounting social scrutiny. Worried and pressured, the wife embarks on a therapeutic quest that takes her to both biomedical and traditional practitioners. If her husband loves her and supports these efforts, he encourages her to seek treatment, which he finances, and he agrees to undergo semen analysis. If, on the other hand, he views the infertility as his wife's problem, she must go it alone and must finance the therapeutic quest by selling her gold jewelry or borrowing money from her family. If, after some effort to be cured, pregnancy does not occur, the husband begins to feel impatient with the situation—impatience that is exacerbated by members of his family, and especially his mother and sisters, who begin to encourage him to find a new wife. Although, initially, he may resist the notion of replacement, especially if he loves his wife, he begins to contemplate the idea secretly, believing that his wife does not notice. However, already fearful of this possibility, she has begun to analyze his every action toward her, looking for any signs of change. Indeed, she notices an increasing distance between them and a coldness on the part of her husband, which may be manifest in the form of mild insults or emotionally wounding teasing. In some cases, her analysis of what her husband is thinking and what he might do if she cannot bear a child for him remains speculative. In other cases, her husband insinuates or tells her directly that "the time will come" when he will have no choice but to remarry. When this occurs, the wife's depression deepens, and she embarks on a more panicked quest for therapy. Although she prays for a happy ending, she realizes that her marriage is insecure, that her replacement anxieties are legitimate, and that her husband can no longer be trusted to remain in the marriage as it is. In short, unless she has a baby, her replacement may be realized.

Although this scenario may differ slightly from woman to woman, a number of shared features tend to characterize the lives of women who find themselves in this situation.

First, unlike many women in stable marriages whose husbands tell them that having children is "not important," infertile women in these slightly unstable marriages are made to feel that their husbands want and need children. Sometimes husbands tell their wives this directly. For example, one woman's husband told her even before marriage, "I want a baby." And, from the second day of marriage, he stated, "Pull your things together and get us a baby." More often than not, however, husbands index their child desire in other ways. For example, some men ask God for children during their daily prayers, making the request loudly enough so that their wives overhear. Some men comment repeatedly about "how nice children are" when children appear on television programs that they watch with their wives. Other men "become happy" when their wives take the initiative to seek treatment for their infertility. And many men show their wives how much they love children—hugging, kissing, amusing, and generally indulging the children of relatives and even total strangers. When undertaken in front of wives, such behaviors signal husbands' desires, even when such desires are never openly expressed. As one woman explained: "Even if he doesn't say it, it shows on his face. It's only the way that he looks at my sister's children or his uncle's children. I can understand that he wants [them]."

In addition, although many women believe their husbands still love them, they realize that their husbands may be contemplating other marital options. Again, such desires on the part of husbands may never be openly discussed. Instead, most women come to feel this because of increasing emotional distance from their spouses, especially following husbands' visits to kin, who often encourage the husband to remarry. Typically, verbal arguments instigated by the husband become more frequent over time and may be accompanied by frank insults concerning a wife's lack of fecundity. Such words remain indelibly recorded in women's memories. Not surprisingly, women are often able to recite their husbands' insults word for word. For example: "All the things I did for you are useless. I didn't see any results." "I spent so much money on you, and you're not getting pregnant." "All you do is eat and sleep." "I want someone who's healthy—nothing wrong with her." "You have no right to be tired. Have you exhausted yourself with your children?" "You live in humiliation."

In addition, during arguments, the issue of remarriage may crop up, although many husbands report to their wives afterward that they were "only joking." Whereas husbands in stable marriages reassure their wives that they will never replace them, husbands in these slightly unstable marriages offer no such assurances and, instead, exacerbate their wives' anxieties in some cases by raising the issue directly. Even when husbands offer apologies post hoc for "not meaning what they said," most wives believe that their husbands are frankly thinking about remarriage, which is why they raised the issue in the first place.

As one woman explained: "Now he's saying in jest, 'I give you three months. If you're not pregnant by then, I'll give you your piece of paper [divorce decree] and send you to your father's house.' I don't know if he's joking, or will it be serious in a couple of months? So far, I'm taking this as a joke, but I don't know if it will change. I'm only insecure about my marriage because he started saying things. He and his friends sit together and talk. He says, 'God allows us to have four wives.' It must be the talking around him by his friends. Buzzing around the ears is better than magic! One of his friends was infertile and had three children after a long time, so this is keeping [my husband] patient. But now all the time he's joking about 'I must have a child. I'm getting old. How many years do I have left?' Everything he says hurts, but I try not to think about it because it makes me very upset and sometimes it scares me that he might be serious."

In such slightly unstable marriages, women's love for their husbands is liable to decrease, not only because of emotional mistreatment, but also because of a basic lack of trust. Many women believe that, although their husbands still love them considerably, the ongoing childlessness has forced their husbands to consider the possibility of remarriage. This, in turn, makes women distrust their husbands and forces them to withdraw emotionally from the marital relationship.

Given that many women in these slightly unstable marriages no longer trust their husbands unconditionally, it is not surprising that many of them no longer confide in their husbands, especially about their infertility problems and about their fears of being replaced. For many of these women, being infertile (and therefore worrying about a husband's response) is described as their "only problem" in their marriages. However, it is a problem of major magnitude that is suffered alone once communication with the husband breaks down and increasing emotional estrangement takes place.

In summary, then, in these slightly unstable marriages, the conjugal connectivity typical of stable marriages is missing, as child desire and external pressures begin to overwhelm the husband. Wives in these marriages feel justifiably insecure, as their husbands behavior toward them begins to change and the issue of replacement (or at least its possibility) raises its ugly head. Even though some women in these marriages believe that their husbands love them very much, they also believe that their husbands cannot be trusted, ultimately, to remain in the marriage as long as there are no children. Although many such marriages remain in this state of ambiguity and uncertainty for years on end—given that many women do not achieve a "solution" to their infertility and many husbands are either unable or undecided about whether to remarry—some marriages do progress to a more advanced stage of instability, in which a wife's imminent replacement is presaged.

EXTREMELY UNSTABLE MARRIAGES
WITH MAXIMUM REPLACEMENT POTENTIAL

For a relatively small number of poor urban infertile women (for example, 11 percent in this study), their marriages do, indeed, progress beyond the stage of slight instability to extreme disruption because of infertility. Undeniably, these marriages are on the verge of collapse because of husbands' reactions to what they perceive to be their wives' infertility problems.[13] In all of these cases, the marital relationship is extremely tense, because of the husband's behavior in one or more of the following realms.

First, some husbands disclose their imminent plans to replace their infertile wives. Sometimes such disclosure takes place directly, whereas in other cases a woman learns of her husband's plans through relatives or neighbors. Either way, women in these marriages come to know that their husbands are actively seeking new wives (and sometimes new apartments if they plan to remarry polygynously). Often husbands are aided and abetted in this regard by their own relatives, as will be seen in the following chapter.

A variation on this theme is when a husband threatens to replace his wife if she does not become pregnant immediately (i.e., within weeks or months). In most of these cases, the husband tells his wife that he plans to change their marital status, but the wife bargains for a delay so that she can attempt some final treatment. Many women in these cases embark on desperate trips to multiple physicians, as well as to lay healers (Inhorn 1994). As such women in this desperate, reactive state of mind are liable to put it, "A person who is sinking will hold on even to a straw."

Second, when a marriage has reached this point of breakdown, some men completely abandon all emotional and physical intimacy, thereby making it clear to their wives that they soon intend to replace them. Whereas husbands in slightly unstable marriages may become increasingly distant and cold, husbands in these extremely unstable marriages may ignore their wives completely, either leaving them alone in the apartment most of the time or, when present in the household, treating their wives as invisible. Typically in these cases, husbands withdraw their requests for sex, since they are no longer interested in pursuing a marital relationship or conception with a woman whom they deem "useless," reproductively speaking.

Third, many husbands in such marriages verbally abuse their wives or instigate severe verbal arguments accompanied by shouting, cursing, and disparagement. Whereas in slightly unstable marriages such arguments take place occasionally and husbands often attempt to "make up" with their wives immediately afterward, in extremely unstable marriages such arguments occur more frequently and may end with little resolution, only to erupt again within a few days' time.

Unfortunately, for some women, arguments begin verbally but end physically, typically with the husband slapping or punching the wife, sometimes repeatedly. Physical abuse of the wife is not uncommon in these extremely unstable marriages. In some cases, battery of the infertile wife becomes part of the husband's behavioral routine, with infertility used as the "excuse" by a man to treat his wife as a punching bag. In one such case reported elsewhere (Inhorn 1996), an infertile woman's bitter husband literally tortured her over their lack of children—returning home to their one-room apartment on a daily basis to blacken her eyes, rupture her eardrums, break her bones, and terrorize her generally. Because this poor woman lived at a distance from her widowed mother and had no male relatives to "protect" her, she considered her options for escape from the marriage to be limited, although she had reported her husband's behavior to the police on more than one occasion. (Ironically, her husband considered himself to be a "religious" man, sporting an untrimmed *Sunnī* beard.)

To summarize, because of their husbands' behavior toward them and the knowledge that their replacement is imminent, women in these extremely unstable marriages are in a frantic, reactive state of mind, characterized by a mixture of desperation, despondency, and defiance. Despite blatant mistreatment by their husbands in some cases, most of these women are desperate to rescue their marriages by becoming pregnant; thus, in an effort to conceive and thereby reverse the course of the marriage, many women resort to multiple treatment modalities, both biomedical and traditional, which are often at cross-purposes with one another. As time elapses and these therapeutic efforts fail to produce a pregnancy, the women's feelings of despondency and hopelessness increase, and many begin resigning themselves to their "fate," commenting that "the rest is up to God." In these cases, women realize that it is only a matter of time before their husbands will accrue enough money to remarry. Thus, they are forced to decide whether they prefer to remain with the husband in a polygynous marriage or to instigate or accept a divorce. Having been forced into this compromised position, some women become extremely depressed and even suicidal in their thinking. Others become defiant, vowing never to marry again, because they have had "enough of marriage to last them a lifetime." And, in a number of cases in which women are being abused either verbally or physically by their husbands, direct acts of resistance are common, including women's returns to their natal families without their husbands' permission and reports to the police about their husbands' violence toward them. In short, all of these marriages are extremely unstable, and replacement of the wife by the husband, who has often become belligerent and abusive, is certain to occur if children are not forthcoming in the immediate future.

ENDED MARRIAGES WITH REPLACEMENT REALIZED

Given the emotional and physical punishment endured by many infertile women as their marriages decline, replacement in the form of divorce or polygyny may come as a relief to some. Yet, actual replacement of an infertile woman by reason of her infertility is relatively rare among the urban Egyptian poor. (For example, only 6 percent of the infertile women in this study had been replaced.) Not only do most men reject this option for the emotional, intellectual, and spiritual reasons outlined above, but the expenses of remarriage—and especially the costs of maintaining polygynous households—are prohibitive for most poor men, effectively barring their chances of remarriage on a practical level.

Nonetheless, in a few cases, infertile marriages do end. In each case, husbands' desires for children overwhelm their feelings of loyalty to their wives, and, eventually, divorces or polygynous remarriages occur. However, these marital endings vary significantly. Indeed, four distinct patterns of replacement among the urban Egyptian poor can be identified.

Polygyny

The least common option pursued by men who decide to replace their wives is to marry a second wife while continuing to retain the first infertile wife in a polygynous union. (For example, there were no cases of permanent polygyny in this study.) This option is not common because few men can afford it and few women will agree to it. For reasons described earlier, the thought of polygyny has become anathema to poor urban Egyptian women. Therefore, unless they have absolutely no other recourse, women will rarely agree to remain in a marriage as the elder infertile cowife and will exercise their legal option to divorce following notification of a husband's intention to take a second wife.

According to most poor urban women, becoming a cowife "is the worst possible thing that can happen to a woman" and is guaranteed to cause fighting and misery within the marital triangle. Although some men who love their infertile wives may prefer polygyny to outright divorce, few women consent to such an arrangement, because of the jealousy and conflict it is expected to arouse. As one infertile woman who was forced to contemplate polygyny explained, "I wouldn't have a second wife in the house with me, and she wouldn't either. Psychologically, I won't be able to stand seeing them together."

On the other hand, a woman who views herself as having no other residential, financial, or marital options may decide to remain in a polygynous union. So may an infertile woman who ardently loves her husband and wants him to be happy. However, as expected, such cases are rare and seem to be growing even rarer in urban areas of Egypt today.

Polygyny Followed by Divorce

In a few cases (for example, 2 percent in this study), husbands do not divorce their wives directly. Rather, they decide to hedge their bets by undergoing a trial period of polygyny; then, when their own fertility is proved by the impregnation of the second wife, they divorce their first wives, who may or may not want to remain in the marriage. As seen in the case of Aida at the beginning of this chapter, some men who polygynously remarry do this deceptively, notifying their wives of their remarriage only at the time of the request for divorce. However, because such tactics are illegal, most men who are contemplating polygynous remarriage ask their wives whether they wish to remain in or be released from the union. Sometimes men also inform their infertile wives that, if the second wife delivers a child, the first wife will be given up for divorce. This allows men who are unsure of their own fertility potential to prove themselves before casting off a woman whom they might not otherwise want to divorce. Although few women agree to such a compromising strategy, those who see themselves as having few alternatives may consent to such an arrangement on the hope that the second wife, too, will be unable to conceive. (Unfortunately, for the one woman in this study who agreed to such an arrangement, her cowife proved fertile, and her husband divorced her after the birth of his second child.)

Outright Divorce

When infertile marriages come to an end, most husbands divorce their wives directly. (For example, 4 percent of the infertile women in this study were divorced directly by their husbands.) In cases in which partners still love each other but the husband feels he needs a child, divorce may involve a period of negotiation, in which various treatment options are tried and the prospect of polygyny is at least discussed before a divorce takes place. However, more often than not, husbands issue divorce pronouncements to their wives with little if any specific advanced warning. In such cases, divorces tend to occur after particularly heated arguments or after periods of extreme marital instability. Although women may wish to remain in the marital abode, their inability to maintain a household financially (due in part to a lack of alimony payments), as well as the stigma of living alone, send most of them back to the homes of relatives following their replacement through divorce.

Divorce of, Followed by Remarriage to, the Infertile Wife

Yet, not all infertile marriages that proceed to divorce remain in that state for very long. Rather, in some cases, husbands who feel remorseful after precipitating a divorce over infertility are amenable to the idea of remarrying their wives. And, in some cases (for example, 2 percent in this study, or half of those who divorced directly), wives agree to be taken back.

Spouses who return to each other tend to remarry almost immediately, sometimes following reconciliatory efforts on the part of family members. According to Islamic law, a husband is allowed to remarry the wife whom he has divorced, as long as he has not pronounced the words of divorce to her three times in succession. Thus, a husband who has divorced his wife only once has time to reconsider his decision. In the case of some childless couples, a husband will decide that he prefers to remain with the woman whom he truly loves, even if he is unable to have children by her.

Women who find themselves in this situation usually report that marriage the second time around is much better, since husbands who have decided that they cannot live without their wives are more appreciative of them and are resolved about the lack of children in the marriage. Although it takes divorce for some men to realize their wives' worth, the very fact that

men *do* remarry their divorced infertile wives again speaks to the strength
of marital bonds in a society where these bonds are expected to be tenuous.

FERTILE MARRIAGES BY COMPARISON

As we have seen so far, infertile marriages among the urban Egyptian poor
vary greatly in terms of stability and replacement outcomes. Contrary to
Egyptians' expectations, many infertile marriages not only succeed, but
are quite happy. Husbands and wives who are emotionally connected may
decide that their love for one another overrides their desires for children,
and they may work together to search for therapy and to defend their marriage against external intervention. Even marriages that are less stable vary
considerably in their strength and resiliency. In some marriages, infertility
is only slightly disruptive, although wives may live in uncertainty about
the degree of their husbands' commitment to them. Other marriages are
tumultuous, with infertility providing the excuse for marital acrimony,
verbal and physical abuse of the wife by the husband and his family, and
eventual replacement.

Given the fact that nearly half of all infertile marriages are extremely
stable and another third are only slightly disrupted, the Egyptian adage
that "children tie the husband to his wife" must be challenged. Children
may *not* be the "glue," the major solidifying element, in marriages among
the urban Egyptian poor. Although evidence from infertile marriages supports such a conclusion, evidence from *fertile* marriages is equally, if not
more, compelling.

Although fertile marriages with children are not the subject of this
book and thus will be described only briefly,[14] approximately half of all
fertile marriages among the urban Egyptian poor (for example, 59 percent
in this study) clearly involve mutual love, respect, and loyalty, as well as a
commitment to work together to overcome the problems of being poor
and having children to support. These marriages are relatively stable and
trouble free, in that problems arising in the marriage are perceived by the
marital partners themselves to be minor. On the other hand, a relatively
large proportion of fertile marriages (for example, 41 percent in this study)
are strife-ridden and unstable, and threats of replacement are also a concern
for many of these wives. Thus, proportionately, serious problems contributing to marital instability—including uncontrolled hyperfertility, domestic violence (often related to substance abuse), husbands' abandonment of
the family, and destitution—are more common among fertile couples than
among infertile ones, and many fertile marriages may be affected by more

than one of these problems simultaneously. Furthermore, unlike infertile women who experience their problems alone, fertile women in such marriages may suffer from their problems more intensely, because of their desires to protect their children from the effects of relentless poverty, hunger, and the actions of disgruntled husbands.

Moreover, the most significant problem to be faced by fertile women —one that provides an appropriate conclusion to this discussion of marital ideals, expectations, and realities—is the problem of replacement. Having children does *not* necessarily "tie" a man to his wife, for, proportionately, more fertile women than infertile ones are replaced by their husbands. (For example, in this study, 9 percent of all fertile women had been replaced by their husbands either through polygyny or divorce, which was more common, and 8 percent feared this impending outcome.) Additionally, for these fertile women, the problem of replacement is made all the more difficult because of the presence of children. Unlike infertile women, fertile women may be forced to compromise their own best interests for what they perceive to be the best interests of their children. For them, this means either forfeiting their children to their husbands, keeping and supporting their children (and thereby diminishing their own chances of remarriage), or remaining with their husbands in polygynous unions. In each case, these "solutions" are not really solutions at all, given that they result in unmitigated suffering for these women.

The fact that husbands sometimes replace their wives who have born them children provides a grim reminder that, ultimately, men are able to assert greater control than women in the political machinations of marriage. Although women can request a court-ordered divorce under the limited set of circumstances described in Chapter 1, men have much greater legal and social latitude when it comes to replacing their wives. Furthermore, men may use their children—who, according to the patriarchal procreative ideology present among the urban poor, are truly their own as opposed to their wives'—in order to control their wives' reactions to threatened or actual replacement. Essentially, husbands who repeatedly threaten to divorce their wives and take their children away from them ensure their wives' subservience in marriages that are plagued by turmoil.

The Ties That Bind

In summary, then, replacement is not an experience unique to infertile women. The fact that a larger proportion of fertile women than infertile ones are replaced by their husbands or fear impending replacement stands as proof that children are *not* necessarily the source of marital security that poor urban Egyptians expect them to be. Rather, in an attempt to deconstruct the Egyptian adage that "children tie a man to his wife," we have examined the multifarious forces, including infertility, that impinge upon the marital relationship. As seen here, depending upon individuals' reactions to these forces, some marital relationships are relatively secure and characterized by a dynamic that can only be termed "egalitarian." Others are not, and, in these marriages, men may dominate their wives through physical, financial, and emotional means.

Yet, if there is one overarching conclusion that can be reached, it is that, among the urban Egyptian poor, "companionate" marriages—characterized by love, mutual respect, sharing of problems, decency of treatment, and the absence of overt forms of male domination—are characteristic of the majority of both infertile and fertile unions. Although movement toward the companionate ideal has been recognized for the Egyptian middle and upper classes (Baron 1991; Brink 1987), it is still considered an anomaly among the urban poor, who are usually ignored in scholarly discussions of marital democratization, a shift that is being observed throughout the Middle East (Barakat 1985; Boddy 1989; Mernissi 1985, 1989) and perhaps throughout the world at large (Moore 1988). Furthermore, movement toward "coupling" and the "conjugal family" among the uneducated lower classes in the Middle East is often portrayed as inherently dangerous for women, because it may increase women's financial and emotional dependence upon a solitary patriarch and "unyielding other"—namely, one's husband (Abu-Lughod 1990; Boddy 1989; Hoodfar 1988; Nader 1989).

However, as argued by Hatem (1986b) for Egypt and as evident in the foregoing discussion of marriage among the urban Egyptian poor, increasing heterosexual intimacy has the potential for subverting systems of segregated patriarchy throughout the Middle East. As men and women, including poor men and women, attempt to negotiate new kinds of marital relationships—relationships based on the kind of loving connectivity experienced and expected in families of origin but that heretofore has not necessarily been transferred to the conjugal unit—the politics of marriage are bound to undergo metamorphosis, especially under the influence of increasing nuclearization and the separation of marital partners from their extended families. Alone under one roof, young Egyptian couples, including poor couples, have come to see their marital relationships as primary and to defend their spouses and their marriages from outside interference. For poor women, whose lives are now deeply enmeshed in the dynamics of marriage, this has meant attempting to create, with limited means, happy, comfortable home lives for their hardworking husbands and to promote understanding of mutual needs and desires. In return, "good" husbands, who represent the majority of poor urban men, reciprocate such favorable influence through warmth, affection, love, and loyalty, even when they can provide little in the way of material resources to the household. Although money is a constant struggle for many poor couples, the majority of husbands and wives can be seen to form true partnerships—not only in financial matters, but in matters of the heart. That this is true even among many infertile couples—who are expected by almost everyone, including the infertile themselves, to experience marital collapse—attests to shifting marital praxis and particularly to the emergence of the committed, connected "couple" in a society where no such dyad has heretofore been recognized. Although marital ideals, as well as expectations, have yet to catch up with marital realities, it can be assumed that over time the ideology of marriage among the urban Egyptian poor, too, will change, presumably in the direction of increasing tolerance for love, companionship, connectivity, and coupling *before* marriage.[15]

That marital praxis among the urban Egyptian poor is undergoing significant transition frankly has much to do with the changing attitudes of men. Although women may influence the course of their marriages through pleasing behaviors and affection toward their spouses, they also realize that the tenor and success of any marriage is determined largely by the character of one's husband. Men who are "good"—who provide for their wives and children and treat them with kindness and decency—are, in fact, everyday resisters. They refuse to submit to the culturally embedded patriarchal scripts that allow them to exert their power and authority over their wives and children in ways that are detrimental to their families' well-being and security. Instead, these "new generation" poor urban Egyptian men appear to seize upon their connective claims to their wives and children—looking to and needing these significant others for the completion of their relational selves—while dispensing with the overtly patriarchal behavior that is widely expected in family life throughout the Middle East.

Indeed, the success of so many infertile marriages bespeaks the strengthening of conjugal connectivity in Egypt at the expense of patriarchy, which is being undermined. Although patriarchal religious, legal, and cultural norms allow men to replace their infertile wives, many men refuse this option out of feelings of love, loyalty, and commitment. That such connective relations can be developed, nurtured, and sustained between spouses even in the absence of highly valued children is indicative of the ways in which Egyptian families are effective in socializing their members into connectivity—socialization that carries over in unexpectedly positive ways in infertile unions. It would seem that when children are unavailable to provide a kind of indirect connection, or tie, between a husband and wife in an arranged marriage, husbands and wives turn to each other for the direct sense of connection and personal completion that would be expected of individuals in connective systems. In fact, the absence of children may well fortify conjugal connectivity in infertile marriages by eliminating the external object upon which both partners can project their love away from each other. Perhaps this is why infertile marriages are equally, if not more, successful than fertile ones: in infertile marriages, a couple's lack of incessant focus on the children and their needs may shift the focus onto the connection with one's partner.

In summary, then, among the urban Egyptian poor, conjugal connectivity seems to be growing at the expense of patriarchy, given that connectivity and patriarchy can exist independently (Joseph 1993). However, this is not to say that patriarchy (or patriarchal connectivity) has been eliminated in Egypt or that its eventual breakdown will be easy or rapid. On an ideological level and in the lived experiences of many poor urban women, men still have the upper hand in marriage and prefer it that way, exerting their power and authority through a variety of official and unofficial means. As a result, about half of all marriages among the urban Egyptian poor, both infertile and fertile, are unstable (although the degree of instability varies greatly) and are clearly dominated by men, who, in using their socially sanctioned power, tend to abuse it and the wives whose marital lives and destinies they ultimately control. This is perhaps especially true in marriages plagued by "outside interference." Men who are under the influence of their families of origin are often the ones who view their relationships to their wives as secondary and who treat them as subordinate. The role of extended families in helping husbands to realize their power and control over wives—particularly when children are not forthcoming in the marriage—cannot be underestimated and is the subject to which we now turn.

4. Relatives' Responses

A constant buzzing in the ears gets the message across better than magic.

—An Egyptian proverb

Nafisa's Story

If Nafisa could point to her biggest problem in life, it would be neither her childlessness nor her relative poverty, but rather her treatment by kinfolk, who have made her life and her marriage difficult from the start. Unlike so many other Egyptian women who consider their mothers to be their closest friends and allies, Nafisa was denied maternal affection, a problem that started in childhood and seemed to increase over time. Nafisa was one of five sisters, a younger brother having died in infancy. Although Nafisa's educated but impoverished shoemaker father loved all of his children equally, Nafisa's mother was "difficult" and differed radically in the treatment of her daughters. To three of her daughters, Nafisa's mother showed love and concern. But Nafisa and her sister Ibtisam could do nothing right in the eyes of their mother, although they never understood why their mother resented them or why she attempted to turn their father against them.

Because Nafisa's discomfort with her mother increased as she finished elementary school and neared adolescence, she went to live with her mother's sister, who had always treated Nafisa lovingly. In order to lighten her impoverished aunt's load, Nafisa went to work at the age of fifteen, starting in a toothpaste factory, but moving soon thereafter to a printing press. Although the work was physically grueling and required Nafisa to stand for hours on end amid the overwhelming fumes of ink and paint, Nafisa often ate only one meal a day, usually the free breakfast or lunch provided at the company. As Nafisa recalls, "There were many days when I went to bed with no lunch or dinner. I wasn't eating. I had no money, and when someone told me, 'Go ahead and eat,' I was too shy. I wouldn't eat. I say, 'I ate, praise be to God.' I don't accept so as not to be too heavy for my aunt."

It was during this period at her aunt's house that Nafisa came to know Usama, the eldest son of her aunt's neighbors. Finding him "beautiful," Nafisa fell in love with Usama from a distance, but told no one of her secret desire for him. One day when Nafisa was waiting to take the tram to work, she turned to find Usama behind her, and, in her excitement, handed the ticket money to him instead of the conductor. Usama paid for both of them, then started talking to her. Before they knew it, they had both skipped work and were spending the day at a casino along the shores of the Mediterranean, where they talked for hours on end. Although Usama was attracted to Nafisa, he was already engaged to a neighbor girl and thus "did not have marriage in mind" with Nafisa. But, when another suitor came to ask for Nafisa's hand, Usama broke off his engagement immediately and told Nafisa he would propose to her instead. He and his parents came to Nafisa's parents' home, but the marital negotiations went badly, with neither set of parents wanting the prospective "love marriage" to occur between their children. Thus, in defiance of her parents' wishes, Nafisa enlisted the help of her older sister, her sister's husband, the aunt with whom she had been living, and her aunt's husband, who signed the *katb il-kitāb*, or marriage contract, on behalf of Nafisa instead of Nafisa's own father.

"After this, lots of problems happened," Nafisa recalls. For one, Usama was very jealous and doubtful of Nafisa, to the extent that sometimes he beat her in front of others in the street. Part of his jealousy stemmed from his uncertainty regarding Nafisa's virginity. Although Nafisa had never been with another man, she and Usama began having sex with one another in hotel rooms, before an official wedding party had taken place.[1] At first, their lovemaking did not involve intercourse, but, during this period, Usama still accused Nafisa of having already lost her virginity. There were tearful trips to doctors and hospitals to prove that, Nafisa did, indeed, retain an intact hymenal membrane. But, as Nafisa recalls, "Bit by bit, I found myself a woman [nonvirgin]. With practice, it increased [in size]. I became a woman. So, when I got examined again, the doctor told me, 'You are a woman.' I told Usama, 'It's over for me. You got me lost. And I've become a woman.'" Usama shouted at Nafisa and "did strong things to her." But, later that day, he decided to marry her "officially." He bought Nafisa a gold wedding band, took her to a hotel, and slept with her until what was left of her "honor" (hymenal blood) came down from inside.

This act sealed their marriage, but Nafisa and Usama still had no place to live, given the expense of procuring an apartment. Because Usama was the eldest of nine siblings (three boys and six girls), he was expected by his parents to apply his salary as a plastics factory laborer to the needs of the household. Thus, most of the time, he himself was penniless and was in no position to create a new home for himself and his bride. Instead, they went to live in the cramped apartment of his family, where Nafisa was forced to sleep with Usama's younger sisters and was made to feel unwanted. Because their marital life was so constrained by these circumstances, Usama decided that the best way for him to improve their situation was to travel to Jordan or Iraq as a labor migrant.

Over a period of six years, Usama migrated four times for a year at a time, leaving Nafisa to fend for herself among his family. Because Nafisa was not working at Usama's request, she was forced to live off his parents, who frankly wished that she were not part of their family. Just as with her own mother, Nafisa's mother-in-law was cruel and incited the family to be unkind toward Nafisa—even after Nafisa obtained a textile factory job and began making her own wages. On several occasions while Usama was away, Nafisa's mother-in-law kicked her out of the household, forcing her to return to her mother's, where she was also unwelcome. Indeed, when she would return to her natal home, her mother would taunt her, saying, "Go on, go out! Isn't your marriage contract written? Go there to your husband. Don't sit here for me." As Nafisa explains:

Circumstances were bad in our house, and circumstances were bad in his house. In his house, [his family members] were also bad. Their treatment was bad. . . . When we lived at their place, I was uncomfortable. They used to make tongues on me. They said, "We increased water on the mud when we brought you into our family." I worked all day, and they kept on mumbling. And the woman [his mother] was bad. His brother got engaged. And, as you may say, he was too ashamed to introduce me to his wife. I was sitting there; he closed the door. His wife was in the other room. I didn't see her except on the wedding day. . . . They were ashamed of me. They made me feel less than they are. And his sister—he was away, and she got engaged, and they said, "No, we'll make it family-like." And they had a wedding and a fuss, and they got her to wear her *shabka* [bridal gold], and I didn't attend. They're bad people. They have many things [wrong with them]. They were not good with me. . . . If it weren't for Usama, I wouldn't have tolerated such a life, but I tolerated it for Usama's sake.

Part of the problem was that Nafisa, as the wife of the eldest son, had failed to produce any offspring for her husband's family. Frankly, given Usama's extended absences and the crowded circumstances in his house-

hold, it was virtually impossible for Usama and Nafisa to attempt to procreate, unless they went to a hotel to have sexual relations. Nonetheless,
Usama's family began "buzzing around Usama's ears," and on a return trip
from Jordan, Usama, more frustrated about their difficult living situation
than about the lack of children, told Nafisa that it might be better for both
of them if he divorced her. But Nafisa, who still loved Usama very much,
told him, "Why divorce me? I work and you work. We help each other and
find ourselves housing outside. And after these long years, thank God that
you're back safely."

Thus began Nafisa and Usama's period of "cooperation" as a couple.
Although Usama had saved only £E 300 ($120) following four rounds of
labor migration, Nafisa had managed to save £E 1,200 ($480), which she
turned over completely to Usama. By this time, Usama had returned to his
former job in an Alexandrian plastics factory and had applied for company
housing as was his right. Luckily for them, a two-room, basement-level
apartment that other workers had not wanted because of its tendency to
flood became available on short notice. Usama applied their savings to the
down payment and was able to secure a few pieces of furniture to place in
the two rooms. Flooding or no flooding, furniture or no furniture, Nafisa
felt nothing but joy, for without their new apartment, they were certain to
remain without housing.

Since that time four years ago, Nafisa has been happier than at any
time in her life. Now that they are together alone under one roof, her marriage to Usama has improved tremendously. Their love, which was ever
present but confounded by untoward circumstances, has been able to blos-
som into true passion and understanding. Usama is kind—very kind—to
Nafisa, and tells her he doesn't care much whether they ever have children,
as long as they can be together without the interference of their families.
As Nafisa explains:

> Children don't affect our love. There are people, children become an obstacle
> in their way. But us, no. Children don't affect our love ever. Never. No. They
> don't affect our marital life. As long as there is love and understanding, it's
> not possible. This story of children is something from God the Almighty.
> Okay, he could marry another woman and have no children from her. And
> I could marry another man and have no children from him. And maybe if
> I marry another one, he would not treat me as Usama does. He won't love
> me as Usama loves me. And maybe I wouldn't love him like I love Usama.
> We spent our life like this together. We are frankly, thank God, happy—very
> happy—together. . . . . Usama is a very, very kind person. If I went around the
> whole world, I won't get someone like him.

Although Usama does not pressure Nafisa to have children or to seek treatment for what doctors tell her is a complicated infertility problem involving her ovaries, fallopian tubes, and cervix and Usama's sperm, Nafisa herself ardently desires a child to keep her company when Usama is at work and to "complete her motherhood." As Nafisa explains, "A child, I mean, as you may say, the woman has the kind of love of motherhood. The love of motherhood is in every woman. When I see a child, I yearn for it. What would it be like, then, if I have my own son to fill the world for me?"

On two occasions, Nafisa has had the opportunity to accept abandoned infants—one the illegitimate child of a neighbor's married daughter (who had an affair with a neighbor man while her husband was away as a labor migrant) and the other an abandoned newborn whom Usama found wrapped but "thrown away" on the street. Although Nafisa would have been willing to take either child and told Usama so, his reply was, "No, it's a responsibility," even though he felt genuine pity for both infants. As Nafisa explains, "There are lots of [infertile] people who take children like this. But we don't want somebody else's child. This subject of adoption doesn't work among us here. Sometimes this child, I want to tell you . . . the child inherits from his parents. If his parents are not good, he grows up to be like them. The blood inherits this thing, also."

Thus, for Nafisa, her only hope of having a child is to bear one biologically. But Nafisa, who is approaching forty, is concerned that her opportunity to achieve motherhood has ended. As she laments:

> I have been coming and going now for three years to the hospital—for children—and no result. I don't know whether I will have children or not. God knows. So we'll see. *I wish*. The transportation tires me a lot. And sometimes Usama, he doesn't have money. The injections [fertility drugs], I would have bought them by now, but the injections are too expensive for us. There is no money for injections. If I were working, I would have bought them by now. But I don't work [at Usama's request]. The injections are £E 220 [$88]. If only they were a little cheaper, I would have bought them. And now my life has gone by. I would have liked to have had a child. But life has gone by.

Infertility as a Family Matter

In addition to their fears about their reproductive health and, in some cases, the future of their marriages, infertile Egyptian women such as Nafisa may be haunted by another fear: that of *ṭanīn*, the "buzzing" into the ears of husbands on the part of concerned relatives, who attempt to affect change in the infertile marriage through the pressure of negative familial opinion. Such external pressure on a marriage may have countervailing effects. In some cases such as that of Nafisa and Usama, it may cause a sort of marital entrenchment, with husbands and wives renewing their commitment to each other in an attempt to stave off hostile family forces. In these marriages, the marital bond is stronger than the forces attempting to sever it, for reasons having to do with the marital partners themselves, various structural factors in the marriage, and conjugal connectivity that seems to be intensifying in the urban Egyptian setting. On the other hand, external pressure on an infertile marriage may drive an even deeper wedge between a husband and wife whose marital bond has already been weakened by the problem of infertility. In these marriages, as illustrated by the case of Aida in the last chapter, relatives may be successful in staking their connective claims to a husband or wife whose marriage is already faltering and who may link the need for biological reproduction to the social reproduction of the family.

In the vast majority of cases, any pressure experienced by the partners in an infertile marriage comes from kin—those who are closest to the infertile pair and whose interests they presumably share. However, the interests of husbands' and wives' relatives tend to be remarkably different.

With respect to husbands' kin, issues of classic patriarchy and patriarchal connectivity come to the fore when a husband and his wife fail to produce offspring. As argued by Kandiyoti (1988; 1991), the key to the reproduction of classic patriarchy lies in the operations of the patrilineal, patrilocally extended, three-generation household, where, ideally, the husband brings his young bride upon marriage. The bride establishes her place in this household only by bearing the children (and especially the sons) of her husband, who ensures the perpetuation of his patriline through the procreation of offspring. When, for some reason, children are not forthcoming in the marriage, such familial perpetuity is threatened; thus, the husband's extended family is likely to activate their connective claims on him, encouraging him to replace his unreproductive wife for a fertile partner.

Not surprisingly, no party is more influential in affecting a husband's decision to replace his infertile wife than the husband's extended family—particularly his natal nuclear family and especially his mother and sisters. Among husbands' kin, their concerns tend to rest with the husband alone and to revolve around the most essential demonstration of his patriarchal power: that is, his ability to produce children and thereby to reproduce the family in a new generation. If a husband is married to a woman who is seen as thwarting these goals, then the husband's kin will act in what they see as their own best interests and those of the husband: namely, by attempting to stigmatize the wife for her inability to bear children, thus prompting her husband to assert his rightful control over the marriage by replacing her with a fertile wife. Thus, it is the husband's extended family members who, by virtue of their connective claims on him as son/brother/nephew/cousin, tend to apply consistent pressure on the husband to cast off his barren wife and to find a fertile woman with whom he can produce heirs. Given this powerful, familial reproductive agenda, it is not surprising that the relationship between infertile women and their affines—especially those occupying the same household—may be extremely strained and may be marked by a dynamic of escalating tension and hostility.

In response, the extended family of the infertile wife may act protectively, for their interests tend to lie with the wife alone, whom they pity because of her mistreatment at the hands of her in-laws and sometimes her husband. Fearful of her replacement through divorce or polygyny, they may intervene in her marriage, attempting to "manage" her stigma through the control of information about her to her affines (Goffman 1963). Additionally, a wife's family members may help her to seek treatment for her infertility, and, if they have access to her husband, they may urge marital forbearance in the hopes that impending pregnancy will be achieved. However, because wives tend to live apart from their families of origin—even if they are not residing patrilocally—their relatives may have little actual influence over the course of their marriages. This is especially true in relation to husbands' families, whose access to the couple tends to be better because of the increased likelihood of co-residence.

Thus, among poor urban Egyptian couples who happen to experience infertility, familial intervention is the rule, for reasons to be explored in this chapter. And despite occasional exceptions, husbands' and wives' kin play diametrically opposed interventional roles in the infertile marriage.

Moreover, family politics are closely allied to gender politics in this setting. As we shall see, relationships between husbands and wives that would thrive if left alone are often significantly disrupted by the political maneuvering, much of it behind the scenes, of concerned family members. These "unofficial politics" often pit families against one another. But, perhaps more important, they pit Egyptian *women* against one another. Namely, it is women, and particularly mothers and sisters, who are disproportionately involved in influencing the outcomes of infertile marriages. By virtue of their continuing ties to sons and brothers, women of the husband's extended family tend to identify their interests as being with the husband alone rather than with his wife, and they often become a husband's greatest allies and a wife's worst enemies in the familial maneuvering surrounding infertile marriage. Instead of challenging the oppressive, patriarchal norms that make motherhood imperative for every Egyptian woman, women serve as the greatest upholders of these norms and, in so doing, make life exceedingly difficult for women who are barred against their will from joining this cult of motherhood. Interestingly, however, it is not motherhood itself that is usually upheld as the normative ideal against which infertile women are judged so harshly by their female affines. Rather, it is patriarchy that women uphold. Perhaps unwittingly, Egyptian women participate wholeheartedly in the reproduction of patriarchy by defending the rights of men as fathers and by challenging, often viciously, women who, by no fault of their own, are unable to facilitate men's achievement of patriarchal authority through fatherhood. In other words, when husbands' female family members, and especially their mothers, harass the infertile wife, they are less concerned with her failed motherhood (although this, too, may be important) than with her failure to allow her husband to become a familial patriarch—a role that he must be allowed to achieve if he is to add to the strength and scope of the extended family itself.

To understand the rather complex patriarchal politics of infertility within the Egyptian family, it is first necessary to define what is meant by "family" and then to explicate the various reasons why infertility poses such a threat to family life.

The Egyptian Family

On a scholarly level, the nature of Middle Eastern family life is poorly understood, in terms of both the structure of the family and its internal dynamics (Tucker 1993; Joseph 1994). As the feminist historian Judith Tucker (1993) has argued, the essential "otherness" of the Arab family has been conveyed through monolithic portrayals in which the elements of endogamy, arranged marriage, patrilineality, family honor, and the powerlessness of women (as evident through polygyny) have been highlighted. As a result of this hegemonic typification, little scholarship has been conducted to unearth the realities of family history in the Middle East, or to explore variations in family life across classes and through time (Tucker 1993).

Fortunately for scholars of Egypt, one of the best analyses of the nature of family life—one that contrasts the situation of the urban poor with that of the middle class—can be found in anthropologist Andrea Rugh's masterful ethnography, *Family in Contemporary Egypt* (1984). In this book, Rugh engages in an ongoing debate about the individualist versus corporatist nature of Arab society, applying her distinctly corporatist position to the examination of the Egyptian family.

Essentially, Rugh argues that Egyptian society valorizes "corporateness" at the expense of "individualism." By corporateness, she means the sense the Egyptian has of the inviolability of his or her social group—of an indivisible unity that persists regardless of its constituent members. Thus, in corporate societies such as Egypt, the social group comes first, and individuals are expected to sacrifice their own needs for the greater good of the group. Furthermore, the personal status of the individual is defined by group membership rather than by individual achievement. As a result, individual behaviors are evaluated primarily by how they reflect upon the group, the group taking the blame or reward for such behaviors.

In individualist societies such as the United States, on the other hand, groups are seen as mere collectivities of individuals joining to achieve the common interests of individual members. Within collectivities, individual rights supersede group rights, and individuals are evaluated on their own merits, achievements, and potentialities, rather than on how they reflect upon the group as a whole. According to Rugh, individualism of this sort has little positive recognition in Egyptian society and, in fact, is equated with a number of negative outcomes. She argues that Egyptians rarely think of themselves as individuals with potentials to develop or needs to satisfy. Thus, an individual in Egypt is significant only as a social being, and not as a unique person.

Rugh goes on to argue that family is the "most intense" of all corporate groups in Egyptian society and is the "ideal by which other social groupings are measured" (Rugh 1984:43). Not only are family idioms (for example, kinship terms) used to reinforce other social, political, and economic relations within Egyptian society, but these other relations are constructed on the model of the family. Thus, businesses, even large ones, operate on a kind of authoritarian familialism, and Egyptian politicians, from the president on down, emphasize their position as "father figures" to the masses. As Rugh notes, this tendency toward familialism can be seen throughout Egyptian society, but the patterns upon which it is based first receive their expression in the Egyptian family itself—the family being the fundamental building block of Egyptian society at large. As she concludes:

"Egyptians see their happiness as resting in the realization of certain corporate activities in marriage, in having children, in experiencing a satisfying family life, in exerting efforts to strengthen and coalesce their family ties. By the very act of believing that family, however it is defined, is the most significant institution of society, it becomes so" (Rugh 1984: 218).

Although the corporatist position adopted by Rugh for Egypt has attracted a large following among scholars of Middle Eastern family and gender organization, Joseph (1993) argues that the position is problematic on three grounds. First, the corporatist position, like the individualist one, can lead to a focus on the dysfunction of Arab societies, depending upon the viewpoint and position of the author. For example, "relational selfhood," characteristic of individuals in corporate Arab societies, may be viewed as highly dysfunctional from the standpoint of Western psychology, which regards self-actualization and individual autonomy as essential for the realization of psychologically healthy persons. Second, the corporatist position is inadequate to understand the intricacies of Middle Eastern gender organization, for patriarchy is left out of corporatist discussions of constraints on individual autonomy, particularly among women. Finally, the corporatist position seems to exaggerate relational selfhood at the expense of individual initiative and agency. Certainly, not all behavior among Egyptians or other Middle Easterners is "corporate," and hence relational, in nature. In many cases—and perhaps increasingly so with the breakdown of the traditional family—Egyptians *do* think first about their own needs, interests, and desires, allowing them to behave in self-interested ways that may actually conflict with the needs, interests, and desires of the group, including family members. Such is the case, for example, among poor urban Egyptian couples who marry for love, or who refuse to abide by family injunctions to divorce when the wife (or husband, for that matter) proves to be infertile.

Thus, the corporatist position is not completely adequate for analyzing present-day social realities in the Middle East, and may be more accurately seen as a kind of "ideal type" model. Nonetheless, the corporatist position applied by Rugh to the analysis of Egyptian family life is highly suggestive of the ways in which families actually operate, particularly when group interests are threatened. It is this sense of corporateness—the good of the social group—that compels husbands' family members to emphasize group interests when a husband's procreativity is threatened by his wife's infecundity. And, from the vantage point of corporateness, it seems reasonable for a husband's family members to expect him to sacrifice his marriage and his wife for the sake of the family. That many husbands refuse to do this, as we have seen, bespeaks the breakdown of traditional corporate family ties and the valorization of marital ones in an increasingly nuclear-izing urban setting. Yet, as will also be seen in this chapter, it is true that Egyptians are extremely group conscious and aware of the ways in which their individual actions and life situations reverberate within the family.

In the lives of most poor urban Egyptian women, the "family," both broadly and narrowly defined, is by far the most important social group-ing. In the broader sense, "family" is defined by women as the *'a'ila* (plural: *'a'ilāt*), or the extended family. By formal definition, the *'a'ila* includes all of the patrilineal relatives, because, theoretically at least, Egyptian society is patrilineally organized. However, as Egyptian women make clear, on both the practical and affective levels (e.g., during marriage arrangements), an individual's *'a'ila* takes the form of an ego-centered kindred; in other words, it includes both mother's and father's relatives and comprises an inclusive, bilateral set of kinship relations, which the individual may draw upon for support (Rugh 1984). Most important to this discussion, when two individuals come together in marriage, their separate *'a'ilāt*—their kin-dreds—do not merge to form some larger structure. Rather, even when husbands and wives are related, they still think of themselves as having their own *'a'ilāt*, which, in the case of cousins, are partially shared. Thus, in times of trouble, husbands and wives turn to their own *'a'ilāt* for sup-port, for it is within the *'a'ila* that mutual obligations, jural in nature, are primarily enacted (Rugh 1984).

In the narrower sense, "family" is defined by women as the *usra* (plu-ral: *usrāt*), or nuclear family. Although *usra* is an Islamic scriptural term that, until the last two decades, was rarely employed by the urban and rural poor in quotidian discourse on the family (Gadalla 1978; Rugh 1984),[2] international family planning initiatives in Egypt have used the term *usra* to refer to the nuclear family in their widely publicized messages about birth control and spacing. Through media exposure, the term has become synonymous with "nuclear family," and today it is widely used by the urban poor to refer to this family form.

Given these dual definitions of family, a number of points must be made. First, these definitions are nested, in that *'a'ilāt* are seen by Egyp-tian women as consisting of a number of related *usrāt*. As such, the *'a'ila* is viewed as an overarching structure, which links together a number of atomized but related *usrāt* and which forms a network of social relations with the power to influence its component parts. Consequently, *usrāt*, even when spatially isolated from the rest of the *'a'ila*, rarely stand alone and are usually closely tied to a broader, bilaterally linked kin network with direct influence over member families. Indeed, the power of the *'a'ila* to exert social control over its constituent members—even after dislocation in the urban setting—may be profound, as we shall see.

Furthermore, breakdown of the *'a'ila* does not necessarily ensue with urbanization. Because of the severe shortage of housing space in urban Egyptian centers and the consequent difficulties of securing an affordable room or apartment, many young couples are forced to live with other family members, as seen in the case of Nafisa and Usama. Generally, young couples who must share accommodations with relatives co-reside with husbands' family members. In most cases, this means moving into a husband's parents' household, where other married siblings and their children may also reside if the apartment is capacious enough. Additionally, a fairly common residential pattern among the urban poor involves co-residence of a number of related *usrāt* each in their own small room or apartment within the same urban apartment building. In the vast majority of these cases, this urban form of the nucleated extended family household—or what has been called the "contracted extended household" (Brydon and Chant 1989)—is patrilocally constituted and may involve actual ownership of the building by one or more *'a'ila* members. Moreover, even when *usrāt* live alone, other members of the husbands' or wives' *'a'ilāt* may live on the same street or in the same urban neighborhood, due to attempts to keep family members close by when a husband and wife marry and set up a new residence. Thus, for many young Egyptian couples, relatives are never far away due to such "social extension" (Omran and Roudi 1993), and visiting between—and interference from—members of the *'a'ila* is common.

Yet, given that urban *'a'ilāt* are much less likely than rural ones to cohabit, the *'a'ila* has lost some of its significance as a meaningful social unit in the lives of poor urban Egyptians. As the result of the lack of spacious, *'a'ila*-sized housing in the cities, nuclearization of the urban Egyptian family has occurred rather rapidly during the past four decades, and particularly since the 1970s. The effect of this extended-family breakdown has been the elevation, both ideologically and practically, of the once rather inconsequential *usra* as a functioning social unit. These changes in family organization and the growing ideological acceptance among urban Egyptians of the nuclear family as the ideal form cannot be underestimated and are reflected in the yearning of husbands and wives for their own nuclear-family-sized apartments. Furthermore, as most poor urban women note,

Photograph 7. A nuclear family. (Photograph by Marcia Inhorn)

their loyalties—and their obligations—lie first with their *usrāt* and then with their *'a'ilāt*, because, after marriage, the members of their *usrāt* are their preoccupation and the focus of their daily activities. Despite continuing relations between *'a'ila* members in the cities, the *usra* has become by far the most important social unit in the daily lives of poor urban Egyptian women.

This ideological and practical shift in emphasis away from the *'a'ila* and toward the *usra* is apparent in poor urban Egyptian women's rather impassioned discourse on their own shifting views of "family" and family loyalty, as well as their ideas about why such a shift has occurred.

As one woman explained: "The *usra*, of course, is more important than the *'a'ila* because love, being close is important. Because the *'a'ila* is far away nowadays. Since thirty years ago, in my mother's generation, everyone married in[to] the same house and it was considered a shame if a young man married outside. They married and stayed in the same house.

But now, no one accepts living with his parents. And even if a young man would, his wife would object, because there are many problems between mothers-in-law and wives. Since the 1970s, the times have changed. It's partly due to imitation. You see someone with their own apartment, and you want one, too."

Another woman opined: "In my [natal] village, a long time ago, the *'a'ila* used to share clothes, food, problems. They felt each others' problems. They were compassionate. But now you'd use an old dress for cleaning rather than give it to a poor person in the *'a'ila*. Because there is not enough money, what a man earns, he gives to his wife and children. He can't afford to give to his sister and mother. So now, the *usra* is the support. The *usra* is something important. If someone is happy, it's said, 'They have money, a man and children.' The *usra* is more important, because the fewer they are, the stronger the love is. When people are too many and live together, they step on each other."

"The *usra* is more important than *any* life she had before, because she has her own family and she will live for herself and the family *she* made, which will be more precious than anything else," another woman remarked. "This is true for men, too. Now, we are *making* our own family, isolating ourselves. The big *'a'ila* is still important. You can never do away with it. You still have to be there on the first day of the feast [e.g., during Ramadan]. But the small *usra* is where a person spends his whole life every day. So it's more important to a person."

Although poor urban Egyptian women extol the virtues of the nuclear family for the reasons described by them above, this valorization of the nuclear unit has been problematic on purely conceptual grounds for the infertile. Namely, by definition, a husband and wife living alone do not constitute an *usra*, because an *usra* consists of a husband, a wife, *and their children*. This, coupled with the fact that the term "couple" does not exist in Egypt, means that a childless husband and wife constitute a truly aberrant, structurally liminal dyad, for which Egyptians themselves can find no term. Even infertile women are reluctant to call a childless husband and wife an *usra*, because a man and woman without children cannot be considered a true "family" in their view. Although some women concede that a childless, "*usra* of two" is theoretically possible, all acknowledge that the term is rarely applied this way.

For infertile women, then, part of the threat of infertility involves the frustration of their desires to build an *usra* and to achieve structural parity with other married members of their own *'a'ilāt* and married persons in

Photograph 8. A nuclear family. (Photograph by Marcia Inhorn)

general. Comparisons between self and others are frequent among infertile women and their husbands. But, more important, such comparisons are sometimes made by members of their *'a'ilāt*, who remind the childless husband and wife that they have failed to achieve structural parity with other married members of the same generation and age group within the *'a'ila*. In fact, infertile women with kin nearby may be compelled to spend most of their time in the homes of other members of their own or their husband's *'a'ilāt*, because they are considered by *'a'ila* members to be "*usra*-less" and thus lacking a purposeful existence in their own homes.

Infertility and the Husband's *'A'ila*

It is not only the couple's building of an *usra* that is threatened by infertility. For members of the husband's *'a'ila*, infertility may be perceived as a threat to the structural integrity of the 'a'ila itself. Namely, in order for an 'a'ila—and, by extension, its patriliny—to be perpetuated, each generation must reproduce itself by producing children, and especially male children, who will inherit and carry on the family surname. Thus, the biological reproduction of 'a'ila members is critically linked to the social reproduction of group structures. Infertility, when it strikes individual family members, is a threat to the structural integrity of the 'a'ila as a corporate entity.

The Patrilineal Reproductive Agenda

As a result, patrilineally linked 'a'ilāt in Egypt can be said to have their own reproductive agendas, which are imposed on family members in a number of ways. First, members of the 'a'ila are implored by other members, and particularly close relatives, to have children and to thereby "strengthen the 'a'ila." The perceived importance of children to the social empowerment of the 'a'ila cannot be underestimated and is reflected directly in the oft-repeated sayings that "children are power" and that "children create a gathering." Members of the 'a'ila inculcate other members with the desire for children by reminding them that their children will carry the name of the 'a'ila into the future, will prevent the dispersal of the 'a'ila's patrimony, and will ensure that shared ventures of the 'a'ila (e.g., family businesses) continue. Furthermore, members of the 'a'ila are often reminded that children provide a "memory" of them—and of the 'a'ila—after death and that individuals who die childless also die a social death, since they, and potentially their 'a'ila, will be forgotten. Such fears of social death are reflected in shared perceptions among Egyptians that individuals who die childless "might as well have never lived" and that such individuals "made no difference in the world."

Second, because of these fears, members of the patrilineally linked 'a'ila often work diligently to break up infertile marriages of family members, marriages they view as pointless at best and dangerous at worst. As we shall see, a husband's parents and siblings, who are concerned about patrilineal continuity, often form an aggressive social unit, reminding their son/brother of their desires to "see his children" and attempting to convince him that his own happiness and future are directly tied to fathering offspring. This familial pressure on the husband often becomes very intense and, in most cases, also involves his wife, who is stigmatized as "unproductive" and "undeserving" of him as a marriage partner by his family.

In most instances, members of the husband's 'a'ila assume his wife is to blame for the infertility, unless they have convincing proof otherwise.

Indeed, unless or until proof of male infertility is forthcoming, they tend to apply relentless pressure on the husband to replace his wife, while, at the same time, making life miserable for the infertile woman in ways that will be described shortly.

Part of this family reaction is certainly tied directly to the issue of "courtesy stigmas" (Goffman 1963). Namely, individuals who are related through ties of kinship to a stigmatized individual may also be stigmatized "by association." As Goffman (1963:30) explains: "The problems faced by stigmatized persons spread out in waves, but of diminishing intensity. . . . In general, the tendency for a stigma to spread from the stigmatized individual to his close connections provides a reason why such relations tend either to be avoided or to be terminated, where existing."

In the case of the husband's *'a'ila*, efforts are usually directed at purging the *'a'ila* of its courtesy stigma by removing the infertile woman from its midst. In so doing, the husband's *'a'ila* attempts to insure through remarriage of the husband that its own family member is not held responsible for the stigmatizing reproductive failure. Male infertility is not only potentially stigmatizing for a man, but it is also socially embarrassing for his *'a'ila* (Inhorn n.d.b). Therefore, a husband's *'a'ila* will often go to great lengths to help prove a husband's fertility to the community by insisting that he "remarry for children." If, on the other hand, male infertility is determined through semen analysis and the results are made known to other members of his *'a'ila*, they may either deny assiduously the veracity of the results, or, more commonly, they may "keep quiet" about the infertility and even cease their social pressure. According to Egyptian women, when male infertility can be proven beyond a reasonable doubt, members of the husband's *'a'ila* usually "shut up," "go mute," or "become silent" in terms of marital intervention, although they often continue to imply to the outside world that the problem stems from the wife and not the husband.

For all of these reasons, the reaction to infertility on the part of the husband's *'a'ila* tends to be strong, swift, and severe and usually consists of the enactment of a "social drama" (Turner 1974), which draws in not only the husband, but his wife and her concerned family members. Victor Turner has defined a social drama as a series of events in which social divisions are revealed, when "people have to take sides, in terms of deeply entrenched moral imperatives and constraints" (Turner 1974:35). In Egypt, the social drama surrounding infertility involves a sort of "non-event": the failure of children to emerge from an infertile marriage. Yet, the drama that unfolds over such failure to conceive often forces families to take sides in an extended conflict that involves five typical phases described by Turner. These phases include: (1) *breach of norms*, which occurs when a married Egyptian couple fails to achieve parenthood; (2) *crisis*, which involves open recognition of, blame for, and stigmatization of one or more of the infertile partners; (3) *redressive action*, when treatment attempts and stigma management are tried; (4) *regression to crisis*, which involves recognition of treatment failures, further blaming and stigmatization, and pressures on the husband to replace his infertile wife; and (5) either *reintegration of the social group* through birth of a child or refusal of a husband to replace his wife, or a *lasting schism between contesting parties* when a wife is eventually replaced through divorce or polygynous remarriage. As we shall see, the enactment of these phases in the family drama surrounding infertility tends to be devastating for infertile women, whose experience of this social drama vis-à-vis their in-laws is one of the major shared features of their lives.

Generally speaking, forging cordial relations with one's in-laws is considered to be both a marital ideal and a wise strategy; peaceable relations with a husband's family members, especially those living under the same roof, can help to promote one's own conjugal connectivity to a husband who is not pressured by divergent loyalties to his wife and family of origin. However, in-laws are widely perceived by women to be the greatest source of interference in a marriage; for it is they who continue to claim the time, money, energy, love, and allegiance of the husband, whose connective ties to his family of origin may lead him to subordinate his own wishes and needs, as well as those of his wife, in favor of those of his natal family.

Such familial interference stems from the connectivity characteristic of Middle Eastern family life in general (Joseph 1993; 1994). As described in Chapter 1, Middle Eastern families, including Egyptian families, place a premium on connectivity—expecting love and involvement between family members, influencing each others' lives, prioritizing family solidarity, and encouraging the subordination of members' needs to collective ones. Not surprisingly, such connectivity, nurtured through socialization practices within the family, is not severed upon the marriage of family members. Rather, husbands and wives often feel significant pressure to continue pleasing their families of origin, even when such familial accommodation militates against the nurturance of one's own conjugal ties.

Given this scenario, natal family members, and especially senior ones, tend to feel highly justified in continuing to direct the lives of young husbands and wives following their marriages. This is especially true in situations of continuing co-residence, which tends to be patrilocally based.

Photograph 9. Members of an extended family. (Photograph by Marcia Inhorn)

However, even in cases of postmarital neolocality, natal family members may use every opportunity to advise a husband and wife, influence their decision-making, criticize decisions and behaviors of which they do not approve, and generally direct the lives of the couple to their own advantage.

Such interference in a marriage is expected to be intensified when a husband and wife are unable to have children. In these cases, the interference is expected to derive almost exclusively from the husband's *ʿaʾila*, whose aforementioned reproductive agenda incites them to "buzz around the husband's ears." Such "buzzing," or influence, on the part of husbands' *ʿaʾila* members is rarely benign and is deemed the cause of significant problems in many infertile marriages.

One woman explained: "A man and his wife alone can help each other to be patient [over children]. But never with his *ʿaʾila*. They want him to marry another. Some attempt to incite him. They're the cause of all the problems, of divorces, even of the loss of children."

"The husband's *ʿaʾila* pressures him to remarry," another woman lamented. "Even if he loves her, they keep on nagging and want to marry him off to see his children, to see the family continue. If he's strong enough and has his own opinion, he won't listen. [The infertility] could even be his fault, but his *'a'ila* won't admit it, even if he said so, because they would think he's protecting her."

Another woman put it this way: "If there is no family, there is no problem. *All* the problems are from the buzzing. Of course, he's influenced by his *'a'ila*. Will he get out of his *'a'ila* just to hold onto the woman?"

Despite women's expectations of such "buzzing," not all husbands' families are as meddlesome in real life.[3] First, a husband who is in love with his wife may make it abundantly clear to his family that he is beyond their influence, as seen in the last chapter. Second, some husband's family members are religiously devout, accepting infertility (even when it stems from the wife) as God's will and hence beyond human control. Third, an infertile woman may be related to her husband and hence his *'a'ila*, making *'a'ila* members more sympathetic to her plight and less likely to interfere in her marriage. This is also true when other female members of the husband's *'a'ila* are experiencing infertility problems of their own, serving to raise familial consciousness about the problem of infertility and the suffering of women who experience it. In such cases, *'a'ila* members are more likely to have empathy for the infertile wife of a male family member. Fourth, in rare cases, a husband's family members may grow exceedingly fond of an infertile wife and decide that retaining her goodwill and her membership in the family are more important than "seeing grandchildren." Finally, lack of such familial interference may stem from neolocal isolation—from the fact that husbands' family members live too far from the infertile couple to influence their daily existence or the dynamics of their marriage.

Without a doubt, it is this last factor—neolocal nuclear family residence—that has most significantly loosened the ties of husbands to their *'a'ilāt* and consequently prevented the interference of husbands' family members in infertile marriages. Poor urban infertile women often "thank God" that they live in their own small apartments and consider themselves especially lucky if the husband's family continues to reside in a rural area or in a distant part of the city. Although nuclearization may shift the balance of power from a woman's in-laws onto her husband, most infertile women prefer it this way, since even a bad husband may be a better roommate than a horde of harassing in-laws. Not surprisingly, infertile women whose impoverished economic circumstances force them and their husbands to live with the husband's family are generally pitied for their inability to escape from their in-laws, who are likely to mistreat them and to cajole their husbands into remarriage.

Indeed, the emancipatory effects on poor urban infertile Egyptian women of the breakdown of the patrilocal extended family and the subsequent rise of the nuclear family cannot be underestimated. Although nuclearization brings with it the kinds of social isolation for infertile women described in Chapter 2, increasing freedom from in-laws is viewed by many women as a major form of consolation and is often deemed a significant factor in marital success in both fertile and infertile marriages. It is not surprising, therefore, that more and more urban Egyptian newlyweds, including poor couples, are delaying marriage for the purposes of acquiring their own residences. And, as a result of these changing preferences, the neolocal, nuclear family pattern is emerging as the most common household type in both urban and rural Egypt (Brink 1987; Gadalla 1978; Ibrahim 1985b; Nadim 1985; Rugh 1984), (as well as in other parts of the Middle East, where its liberating effects on women are also being documented [Bowen and Early 1993; Brydon and Chant 1989; Kiray 1976; Moghadam 1993; Omran and Roudi 1993]).

WOMEN'S IN-LAW PROBLEMS

Even though growing numbers of poor infertile Egyptian women are eluding significant in-law interference by virtue of neolocal isolation, nuclearization of the family alone does not necessarily diminish the influence of extended family members.

As Halim Barakat describes in his review essay on "The Arab Family and the Challenge of Social Transformation": "Despite the reduced prevalence of the extended family, relatives generally remain closely interlocked in a web of intimate relationships that leaves limited room for independence and privacy. They continue to live in the same neighborhood, to intermarry, to group on a kinship basis, and to expect a great deal from one another" (Barakat 1985:37).

That this is true of Egyptian families is reflected in the significant "in-law problem," or the disruption of women's lives and marriages by members of the husband's 'a'ila, who may or may not be co-residents. For most infertile women, who generally experience such problems more intensely, the interference of in-laws tends to be overt and to consist of direct social pressure on the wife to conceive, as well as attempts to discredit and stigmatize her in the eyes of her husband.

Generally, it is the women of the husband's 'a'ila—particularly the mother and sisters and occasionally sisters-in-law, aunts, and female cousins —who are the major perpetrators of the initial crisis reaction in the social drama surrounding infertility. Mothers-in-law in particular are apt to ruthlessly insult and stigmatize their infertile daughters-in-law and are viewed by many infertile women as their major foes in life and even the true banes of their existence. Furthermore, when a mother-in-law is no longer living, it is not unusual for "substitutional practices" (Rugh 1984) to take place, with husbands' sisters becoming "second mothers" (Bowen and Early 1993) to their brothers and assuming the mother-in-law's negative position vis-à-vis the infertile woman.

As one infertile woman whose mother-in-law was dead summed up her own situation: "His sister did *all* the work for my mother-in-law. Even now, I don't go to visit her, because every time I used to visit her, she would ask me, 'What's the reason you can't get pregnant? Did you go to that doctor?' And so on."

Typically, such female affines attempt to make an infertile wife as miserable as possible by reminding her of her reproductive failing, by verbally defeminizing her through insults about her womanhood, and, in some cases, by accusing her of giving the "evil eye," a topic to be taken up in the next chapter. Thus, it is women—specifically the female relatives of husbands—who most often serve as the standard-bearers of the norms regarding motherhood and who are usually the first to castigate and stigmatize fellow women who fail to achieve "normal womanhood" by becoming mothers after marriage. Furthermore, their reasons for setting this crisis reaction in motion often revolve around protective concerns for their male relatives, whom they see as being "deprived" of their ultimate right: that of creating life, of producing living offspring, thereby demonstrating the legitimacy of their claims to patriarchal power on both a familial and societal level.

Although it may seem ironic that infertile women are pitted against other women in a struggle over the preservation of patriarchy and patrilineal continuity, these intragender dynamics become illuminable if viewed from the perspective of classic patriarchy in the Middle East (Kandiyoti 1988; 1991). Namely, under such conditions, men's power is assumed, but women must negotiate any access to power resources. Because women are usually loath to claim power (at least directly) in their interactions with men, women's claims to power and their competitions over power tend to occur in same-sex interactions. Because women's power increases with seniority under conditions of classic patriarchy, it is older women who tend to assert their power over younger women, and particularly younger women who have married into the family. Translated into real-life settings throughout the Middle East, this means that a young woman's mother-in-law and her husband's sisters (especially older ones) may become bullies and tyrants, making her life miserable, even unbearable, especially if she has married into the husband's family's household.

The reasons for this untoward, intergenerational, intragender affinal dynamic can be traced back to the conditions existing under classic patriarchy. With respect to the intergenerational component, women of the senior generation have themselves been forced to suffer the indignities of disempowerment at the hands of their own mothers-in-law and sisters-in-law. Unable to resist this power, they nonetheless internalize it—looking forward to the day when they will be able to reproduce such power relations vis-à-vis the wives of their own sons and younger brothers. In effect, then, the "oppressed" woman becomes the "oppressor" under conditions of classic patriarchy, using the power accruing with age to control the lives of her own set of junior female "victims."

That such victims are usually not "blood" relatives, but rather affinal women who have married into the family, is not at all surprising. Under conditions of classic patriarchy, women are generally reliant on men for continuing economic support and must turn to their married sons and brothers in the event that they become widowed or divorced. Therefore, it is not enough for a woman to rely solely on her husband; she also needs the continuing allegiance of her male blood relatives—namely, married sons and brothers—in order to insure her own security, especially in old age. Because the wives of sons and brothers threaten such allegiance and security by "making them forget" the needs of their mothers and sisters, women who are mothers and sisters to these men see their own best interests as existing in virtual opposition to those of in-marrying women. To reduce the threat posed by their female affines, mothers and sisters may engage in various interpersonal strategies, or patriarchal bargains (Kandiyoti 1991), designed to maximize their own security. In many cases, this involves efforts to diminish the strength of the conjugal bond by playing sons and brothers off against their wives, who, from a structural standpoint, may be viewed by mothers and sisters as virtual enemies.

Additionally, mothers and sisters are committed to preserving the strength of their own patrilineage by investing in the reproductive lives of the patrilineage's male members. By virtue of their fecundity or infecundity, wives of male patrilineage members may either facilitate or threaten the reproductive lives of these men. Thus, a husband's mother and sisters, who share a stake in the future of the patrilineage, will be exceedingly interested in insuring a husband's production of offspring. This will typically involve monitoring his wife's fertility and recommending against a woman whose infertility is seen as threatening patrilineal continuity.

When a woman is unable to produce offspring for her husband and his patrilineage, her oppression by the women of the husband's *'a'ila* typically takes two forms. First, the husband's female relatives are usually the ones who immediately notice that the wife is not becoming pregnant. Not only do they remind her that "we want children," but they begin to pressure her to seek treatment in an effort to conceive (Inhorn 1994). In many cases, this pressure on the wife to seek treatment begins within the first year of marriage and becomes relentless—even in the face of convincing evidence that the infertility problem stems from the husband. Many women whose husbands are infertile continue to be blamed for the infertility because of absolute denial on the part of their husbands' relatives to believe that the husband might be at fault. Continuing pressure on the wife to seek treatment is an integral part of this process of familial denial and also occurs in cases in which the wife's own infertility problem has been proven beyond a doubt and is known to a husband's relatives.

Second, the women of the husband's *'a'ila* are often the most vicious commentators on the wife's failure to become pregnant, openly disparaging her in an attempt to "hurt her with words." In many cases, this verbal abuse is undertaken in front of the husband in an effort to devalue the infertile wife in his eyes. For example, many infertile women are constantly reminded by their husbands' female relatives that they are "still not pregnant" and are "unlikely to become pregnant." As wives, they are deemed undeserving of the attentions of their "poor husbands," who are seen as "all alone in life" without children and whose rights to children are seen as being denied by a wife's failure to conceive. An infertile woman's female in-laws may inform her that she is unworthy of even the food provided to her by her husband, since she has produced "nothing in return." In many cases, women's insults also involve a questioning of the infertile woman's femininity and womanhood; commonly, she may be compared to a male or her unwomanly barrenness may be indexed metaphorically.

As one infertile woman, whose husband was eventually able to extricate her from a patrilocal residence, described her situation: "[My mother-in-law] wanted a baby, and I was getting treated a lot. And there was no baby. What do I do? She always used to tell me, 'This person became yellowish because she's pregnant. This woman gained weight because she's pregnant. And this other woman is tired because she delivered a baby. But you, you are like a house that is standing. You are like a man. You don't have children. You are like a tree that doesn't bear fruit.' And she always used to speak. She mocks me, and things like that. I was upset, and I cried a lot. . . . All mothers-in-law are bad, not good."

As indexed by this woman's last comment, it is mothers-in-law in particular who tend to generate feelings of ambivalence and even hatred among infertile women, who may refer to their mothers-in-law as "scorpions" or "old hags." Generally speaking, the interfering mother-in-law—who considers it her right to insert herself "triadically" in the midst of the conjugal dyad—is a problematic figure in the lives of Egyptian and other Middle Eastern women (Brink 1987; Brydon and Chant 1989; Dwyer 1978b; Hatem 1987b; Mernissi 1985; Taylor 1984). However, the mother-in-law of an infertile daughter-in-law is deemed by Egyptian women to be a particularly aggressive and ruthless character.

As one infertile woman who experienced the "mother-in-law problem" explained: "It's the mother-in-law who most of the time tells you that you're not getting pregnant and who begins to create problems at home. For example, my mother-in-law tells me most of the time, 'I want my son to have children.' If she sees a baby on TV, she says, 'Oh, I wish that my son had a child like that.' Or, if someone comes to visit and has a child, she carries it and says, 'My poor son doesn't have any children.' She causes me to be *very* upset. She wants to make me cry."

Another woman described her situation this way: "My mother-in-law said *a lot* of bad things [to me]. 'You're a man. You're useless. You're just sitting and eating. You're not getting children.' She was a *real* mother-in-law. She used to tell my husband, 'Remarry! It's a pity you're feeding [your wife] and she's not getting you children.' She was a strong [i.e., aggressive] woman. She died two years after our marriage, but in these two years, she showed me all the stars in the morning [i.e., she gave me a hard time]. If she were still alive, who knows how many times she would have remarried her son? I was *very* happy when she died."

Although few infertile women escape having feelings of animosity, bitterness, and contempt toward mothers-in-law who interfere in their lives and marriages, they rarely openly express these feelings because of culturally prescribed notions of "respect" and "service" to be shown by women to both their in-laws and their elders, as well as fears that a retaliatory response will promote further disharmony and cause their husbands to divorce them. Reluctance to resist such abuse is usually more intense among women living in patrilocal residences. Because of the cramped conditions of most poor urban households, infertile women living with other members of their husband's *'a'ila* are often juxtaposed continuously to their tormenting mothers-in-law and other female affines, and are literally unable to escape social scrutiny and negative appraisal. Yet, because of their weak structural position as in-marrying daughters-in-law and their relative lack of social power as "strangers" to the husband's *'a'ila*, most infertile women who want to remain in their marriages are fearful of fighting back and are forced to tolerate and accommodate various forms of social devaluation and censure.

HUSBANDS UNDER PRESSURE

In addition to their poor treatment of infertile wives, husbands' family members often exert considerable direct pressure on the husband to replace his infertile wife with a fertile woman. In fact, overt strategies undertaken by the women of the husband's *'a'ila* to denigrate and stigmatize the infertile wife are less common than covert efforts on the part of *both* men and women in the husband's *'a'ila* to undermine infertile marriages. Although male members of the husband's *'a'ila*, including fathers, brothers, uncles, and male cousins, only rarely engage in the overt strategies described above, their covert leverage in an infertile marriage may be considerable and may involve the encouragement of the more direct means of interference employed by women against other women.[4]

Specifically, members of the husband's *'a'ila*, and particularly his parents and male and female siblings and their spouses, may secretly encourage the husband to replace his infertile wife. Although these replacement suggestions are occasionally made in the presence of the infertile woman, more often the "buzzing around the husband's ears" occurs behind the infertile woman's back, especially when her husband is spending time alone with members of his *'a'ila*. Not surprisingly, infertile women tend to worry incessantly about what the relatives might be saying to their husbands in private, and this is a source of fear and paranoia not generally shared by fertile women. Yet, these concerns on the part of infertile women are legitimate, given that husbands sometimes report to their wives that they are being encouraged by their family members to remarry.

As one woman described her own situation: "My husband's good with me. It's only this problem [of not having children] that we have. But his uncles, whenever he visits them, they have to tell him, 'Why don't you do something about it?' My husband tells them, 'She's getting treated. Whenever she goes to the doctor I don't mind.' A year ago, his father came to visit us, and he told his son he should remarry. My husband got upset and told him, 'I can't, and that's not your problem.' The day I heard this from my husband, I faced my father-in-law. 'Why would you say such a thing? There is nothing in my hand. It's up to God.' When he visited again six months later, he didn't say anything. But I'm sure that when my husband goes alone to visit them, they talk to him and get him upset. After he travels to his relatives and returns, he becomes upset and when I ask him why, he says, 'They are talkative. They try to fill my mind with the importance of having children.'"

Familial pressure on the husband to replace his infertile wife is particularly pronounced in cases in which the husband is the eldest and/or the only son in his natal family. Eldest and only sons hold privileged roles in their families of origin, not only as protectors of the patriline's continuity, but as parents' favorites by virtue of their maleness and birth order.[5] As role models for their younger siblings, eldest and/or only sons are absolutely expected by their families to produce heirs—and, in the case of the eldest, to set the procreative example for other siblings (especially younger brothers) who marry later.

As an infertile woman married to an eldest son explained: "My mother-in-law bothers me. . . . She's not bad all of the time, but because her daughter and another daughter-in-law are both pregnant, and I'm the wife of the eldest, she gets upset. Being the wife of the eldest son makes a *big* difference. The eldest is the first joy and usually the favorite, and he must be the first to marry and, of course, he must have many children. So, naturally, the mother prefers him to all the others, and when a woman comes to take him from her [through marriage], she's taking all her life from her."[6]

When children are not forthcoming immediately from the marriage of an eldest and/or only son and his wife, familial pressure on the favored son to try again through a new marriage is generally intense. And, as might be expected, wives in these marriages tend to suffer immensely at the hands of their husbands' relatives, who remind them continuously that they have failed in their privileged position as the wife of a special man. Not surprisingly, familial pressure on the eldest and/or only son to replace his infertile wife is more likely to take its toll on a marriage, leading to significant instability and even divorce in some cases.[7]

Yet, familial pressure on husbands to replace their infertile wives is not always so effective. Namely, some men, including even eldest/only sons, withstand such pressure and remain firm in their conviction that their wives are more important to them than children. As seen in the last chapter, such men work to promote marital stability and to minimize their wives' re-

Photograph 10. A mother and her eldest son. (Photograph by Marcia Inhorn)

placement anxieties. Women married to such men are often told by their husbands that familial pressure will have no effect upon their marriages; as these men explain to their wives, they have committed themselves to their marriages and, for them, that commitment is inviolable. As a result, women in these marriages live with less fear about the future and with some assurance that their marital relationships will not change as a result of familial intervention.

Women who believe that their husbands are being unduly influenced by their families, on the other hand, are much more likely to be insecure. Not surprisingly, these men are more likely to have actively destabilized their marriages, so that their wives begin to notice various changes, sometimes subtle, in their marital relationships and to predict that continuing pressure will induce further changes, including the possibility of divorce or polygyny. Although the reasons for the differences in the success rate of infertile marriages have been analyzed in the preceding chapter, it is important to reiterate that familial intervention on the part of the husband's *'a'ila* is one of the major precipitating factors in marital instability.

Moreover, when members of the husband's *'a'ila* are successful in influencing the husband to replace his infertile wife, they are usually enthusiastic participants in the process of aiding and abetting his remarriage. For example, male family members may loan the husband money to remarry or help him to secure a second apartment. In many cases, the female members of the husband's *'a'ila* participate actively in the search for a new wife.

The following tragic story, recounted by an infertile woman's fertile sister-in-law, illustrates the power of familial involvement to shape the course of an infertile woman's marriage and, ultimately, her life and death. As the woman's sister-in-law recalls: "The brother of my husband, he was engaged for two years and married for three years and he had no children. He was getting pressured to remarry by his mother and his neighbors, but mainly by his mother, because he was the oldest boy and [his mother] wanted children by him. He's religious and he went on the pilgrimage, but he thinks too much of children, so he decided to remarry. His wife, she was twenty-three-years old, and the doctor told her there was no hope [for her to become pregnant]. When she heard [her husband] was going to remarry and that he got engaged, she went to the bathroom and covered herself with gas and then lit herself from the feet.[8] She died after two or three hours. This was two years ago, and forty days after her death, he remarried. He was sad for awhile, but he married right away, so he must have forgotten. My mother-in-law, she was sad for just a few days and she cried for just a few days. No one felt as sorry as the girl's own parents and family. I had lived together with [the infertile woman in the same patrilocal, extended-family household], and I never thought this would happen. She was in love with him too much, and I thought that, with all the love this woman gives to this man, he would maybe settle for a life without children. But it was all the 'buzzing' around him. The devil is evil."

Infertility and the Wife's *'A'ila*

This woman's comment that "no one felt as sorry as the girl's own parents and family" is an apt assessment of the attitude of women's *'a'ilat* toward the many problems encountered by their infertile daughters, sisters, nieces, and cousins. When asked about the attitudes and reactions of women's *'a'ilat* to the problem of infertility, both fertile and infertile women commonly respond with the word "sadness," noting that parents in particular feel profoundly sorry for their infertile daughters.

In describing their relationships with members of their own *'a'ilāt*, infertile women most often note that their family members, and particularly their mothers and sisters (if they are alive and in close proximity), are extremely sympathetic toward their plight—suffering with them, listening to the details of their problems, consoling them, emotionally and financially supporting their quests for therapy, and praying for their futures. In fact, for women whose relationships with their husbands are floundering, mothers and sisters are most often their closest confidantes,[9] and this may even be true among women in stable marriages who are quite intimate with their husbands. Secrets and fears that have no other outlet for expression often find their way into the ears of kind mothers or siblings, whose empathy and compassion are a source of solace to women in sometimes desperate situations. Indeed, in many infertile Egyptian women's lives—especially those characterized by marital duress—women's own family members, and especially their mothers and sisters, are the major providers of social support and sympathy, playing the role of "wise normals," or "persons who are normal but whose special situation has made them intimately privy to the secret life of the stigmatized individual and sympathetic with it" (Goffman 1963:28). Furthermore, in the family battles that erupt over infertility—in which the women of the husband's *'a'ila* are usually perceived as foes who are out to "defeat" the infertile woman and "destroy" her marriage—the women of the wife's own *'a'ila* are often her greatest allies, who offer friendship, counsel, and a variety of other social support services, as we shall see.

The Mother-Daughter Bond

Whereas infertile women tend to view their mothers-in-law as their major enemies, they tend to see their own mothers as "best friends." Mothers are often crucial figures in infertile women's lives, providing unconditional love, religious solace, and psychological support to their infertile daughters and attempting to help them overcome their misery through a variety of instrumental means. In fact, in general terms, the mother-daughter bond within poor urban Egyptian families is among the strongest of all affective relationships—often surpassing in intensity the relationship between husband and wife, father and son, or mother and son. Although poor urban Egyptian women *need* sons for the reasons already described, they *want* daughters for reasons that ramify throughout the many areas of their lives. Despite the overarching patriarchal valorization of sons in Egypt, especially in culturally conservative rural areas of the Nile Delta and *Ṣaʿid*, daughters are strongly preferred by most women, even infertile ones who have yet to deliver a child.

Although this preference for daughters over sons among women is rarely described in the scholarly literature on Egypt,[10] it redounds throughout Egyptian popular culture and in women's own discourse on the superiority of girls over boys. A popular song that extols the virtues of the daughter as "the love of the mother" accurately summarizes the intense love and identification that mothers and daughters often feel for each other among the urban Egyptian poor, with mothers often describing their daughters rather than their own husbands as their "sweethearts" and "darlings." Despite occasional exceptions (for example, as seen in the story of Nafisa at the opening of this chapter), expectations for lifelong emotional intimacy between mothers and daughters run high among poor urban Egyptian women, who often describe their adult relationship to one another as one of sisterly friendship with the expectation of continuing disclosure of secrets and a sharing of life's problems.

Furthermore, gender role socialization within poor urban Egyptian households and the expectation that completion of schooling is not imperative for girls means that daughters still young enough to be living in the household are often a mother's greatest source of domestic labor as well as emotional support. Although girls are considered to be naturally more affectionate, loving, calm, obedient, quiet, polite, honest, and dependable than boys, daughters are actually socialized by their parents to be more compliant and emotionally nurturant than their brothers. Mothers train their daughters to be their major helpers, and, when they are successful, their daughters invariably reciprocate—willingly learning the domestic routine, assuming household responsibilities, babysitting, and caring for their parents when they are sick. On the contrary, boys are often seen by women as exhibiting the opposite tendencies, including coldness (even cruelty), naughtiness and disobedience, selfishness, and lack of concern for their parents or for tangible contributions to the household. For these reasons, many women argue that daughters are much closer to their mothers than sons, who, when they grow up, "forget their mothers" much too easily.

Indeed, girls' and boys' opposing natures are thought to extend into adulthood, with daughters continuing to attend to their parents and other family members, but sons being easily "lost" to their wives and friends. Among many women, daughters are now cited as being a more reliable source of old-age security than sons, a belief that some fathers have come to share. The popular expression "Nowadays, a girl is just as good as a boy" reflects the growing appreciation among both men and women of their daughters and their daughters' contributions to family life. Particularly among a new generation of poor families who have chosen to educate their daughters against all odds, girls are seen as an investment—as future workers who will be more willing than sons to help their families economically and to take care of the financial and nurturance needs of aging parents. Furthermore, daughters who are able to work are less of an economic liability to parents, who are otherwise expected to provision their daughters until marriage and upon divorce.

These increasingly widespread beliefs about the particular assets of daughters in relation to sons receive empirical support by virtue of the fact that more and more poor urban couples are limiting their family size to two children, no matter what the sex of the offspring. Similarly, many infertile women state that they and their husbands will be satisfied with just one child—a boy *or* a girl.

This shift in the deeply rooted, historical preference for sons in Egypt probably reflects the recent changes in urban family structure described in this chapter. Perhaps most important, whereas in agrarian communities throughout rural Egypt sons are desperately needed to assist their fathers in agricultural production, this need for an offspring-based male labor force is largely attenuated in urban settings. Thus, from the perspective of poor urban women, only two major reasons remain for parents to prefer their sons over their daughters.

First, parents needn't worry as much about their sons, primarily in terms of their whereabouts and virginity before marriage and their happiness and security after marriage. With daughters, the responsibilities incumbent upon raising them are issues of major concern for parents—especially given that a family's *sharaf*, or honor, rests on the premarital conduct of its female members. In other words, a girl who loses her virginity before marriage—or is even suspected of this if caught in an illicit rendezvous—destroys her own honor and that of her family, causing scandal and shame. For these reasons, a daughter's whereabouts are closely monitored, and parents are prone to worry about a daughter's movements outside the home and her safety from corrupting influences, especially in the more threatening and anonymous urban environment.

A son's premarital loss of virginity, on the other hand, does not constitute a disgrace for his family and may, in fact, be expected. The expres-

Photograph 11. A mother and her daughter. (Photograph by Marcia Inhorn)

sion "A son can never bring shame to his family" is a reflection of the double standard of marital virginity for males and females in Egypt. This lack of concern over a son's sexual behavior means that parents needn't worry about a son's whereabouts—"even if he stays out all night"—and is what allows parents to let their unmarried sons live alone for the purposes of schooling or work, including, increasingly, labor migration abroad.

Daughters, on the other hand, are seen as unable to live on their own or to adequately protect themselves, given their sexual vulnerability. Thus, unmarried daughters continue to live at home and, in the vast majority of cases (at least among the urban poor), virginity expectations for unmarried daughters are realized. In large part, this may be due to the repercussions of a woman's lack of premarital chastity, even if she is engaged to the man who has "made her a woman" through sexual intercourse. These repercussions include major battles between the families of the deflowerer and the deflowered, social ostracism of the girl and her family by the community upon discovery of the behavioral breach, and even murder of the "lost virgin"—often glossed as "honor killing"[11]—by her own disgraced family members. Because of these rather significant ramifications, parents are said to "fear for their daughters."

Likewise, parents fear for their daughters during and after marriage. *If* a worthy bridegroom can be found (and there is no guarantee of this, given the plethora of "bad" men), marital negotiations may still go poorly, and the bride's wedding expenses not covered by the groom may further impoverish a poor family. Furthermore, given the assorted marital problems expected to occur among poor urban couples (detailed in the preceding chapter), parents tend to worry much more about their daughters after marriage than about their sons, the latter of whom are seen as being in control of marital outcomes and able to take care of their own problems in life.

Such parental worry is particularly exacerbated when a married daughter is unable to become pregnant. Parents fret not only about their daughters' emotional and physical well-being, but also about their futures—given that parents generally assume responsibility for a divorced daughter and, ultimately, her remarriage to another man. Because of the difficulties of marrying off a stigmatized, infertile divorcée, the prospects of a daughter returning home after a divorce are not joyous ones for infertile women's parents. Yet, many parents—including some fathers, who may remain extremely close to their infertile daughters—make it known to these women that they can expect to receive their parents' undivided support and attention throughout the processes of divorce, homecoming, and potential remarriage. Although most women are much closer to their mothers than to their fathers for the reasons described above, women's fathers may occasionally foster extremely loving relationships with their daughters and promise to support them against their husbands or husbands' families if problems arise in the marriage.

On the other hand, it is also common for poor women to have extremely antagonistic relationships with their fathers, who view daughters as "useless" and as "ruining their parents with problems." Women with "bad" fathers are apt to feel particularly trapped in their marriages, given that they dread returning home to fathers whom they may fear and even hate and who will reassume positions of authority and control over their lives.

According to women with difficult fathers, their fathers resent them for various reasons—but perhaps most important, for being daughters rather than sons. Herein lies the second major reason for a lasting son preference in Egypt—namely, the continuing attitudes of men, especially of the older generations, about the superiority of male children. Whereas most women prefer daughters, most men continue to prefer sons—as companions, coworkers, potential heirs, a source of lineage continuity, and a father's "memory" after death. Having sons to "carry one's name" is the primary way in which men reproduce themselves socially; it is, in fact, a form of male reproductive success. Put another way, when men have sons, they feel proud not only of their children, who may become accomplished through education, work, or travel, but also of themselves, in part because they have made a "memory" of themselves to be carried to future generations. Although daughters, too, are seen as "preserving their father's memory" through the carriage of the father's and his family's name, they do not "rebuild the family," since their own children will be members and carry the name of another patrilineage. Moreover, daughters do not provide (or at least are not expected to provide) their fathers with the other attributes of sons. These include: (1) adult companionship through co-residence, since a daughter generally leaves her natal home upon marriage; (2) major inheritance rights to the father's patrimony; (3) independent economic contributions to the family; (4) support of the father and his economic endeavors during his lifetime; and (5) economic support of other family members, especially mothers and daughters, following the father's death. Thus, according to most women, fathers are less likely to be emotionally invested in their daughters, whom they see as useful, structurally and affectively speaking, only to their mothers.

Yet, as noted earlier, the sense of investment in daughters, even by fathers, appears to be increasing in urban areas as attitudes about and expectations for young women of the lower classes change regarding education, employment, and economic independence. Even in the absence of such changes in young women's lives, many women describe loving, emotionally supportive relationships with *both* their fathers and mothers, which, among infertile women at least, enable them to cope with their childlessness because of the knowledge that their parents are behind them.

Indeed, as "wise normals," whose primary affinities lie with their daughters, infertile women's parents, as well as other members of their *'a'ilāt*, serve a number of important roles in the lives of these women. Whereas husbands' family members are most likely to instigate crisis reactions in the social drama surrounding infertility, women's family members are most likely to undertake redressive measures designed to minimize a woman's suffering and the potential of her replacement through polygyny and divorce. In other words, while husbands' family members typically promote problems in an infertile marriage, women's family members commonly search for solutions, be they attempts at stigma management, marital mediation, or fostering arrangements, to be described now.

STIGMA MANAGEMENT

The diametrically opposing roles of husbands' and wives' *'a'ilāt*—and especially female members—can be seen in the production and management of social stigma (Goffman 1963). Whereas the women of the husband's *'a'ila* are often willing to stigmatize a wife with or without definitive proof of the source of the infertility problem, the women of the wife's *'a'ila* serve as her advocates and defenders, attempting to help their infertile family member to "manage" this stigma through the control of vital personal information.

Most commonly, such stigma management revolves around the artful conveyance of medical knowledge. Following visits to doctors, mothers and sisters often become actively engaged in helping the infertile wife to disclose information about herself to her husband and his family in ways that will serve to decrease their skepticism about her reproductive potential and shift some of the burden of responsibility for the failure to conceive from the woman onto her husband. Thus, following appointments with physicians, which tend to be frequent (Inhorn 1994), infertile women may be encouraged by their family members to leave out the bad news and report only the good news. Or, if there is no bad news to report, women are often encouraged to disseminate to husbands' family members that "the doctor tells me that there's nothing wrong with me"—the implication being that the infertility problem rests with the husband.

Likewise, women with menstrual irregularities are often encouraged to impute their menstrual delays to early miscarriages. In a few cases, women are even encouraged by their female relatives to manage social information through outright lying or fabrication. For example, women with ovarian or other hormonal problems that cause them not to menstruate at all or for long periods of time may be encouraged to "fake" their menstrual periods, even before their husbands (primarily by not having sexual intercourse during the supposed period of menstruation). Such dishonest strategies are sometimes recommended by women's family members for fear that the truth about such a grave and recalcitrant reproductive problem will lead to certain dissolution of the infertile marriage.

Photograph 12. The author with female members of an extended family. (Photographer unknown)

MARITAL MEDIATION

The diametrically opposing roles of husbands' and wives' *'a'ilāt* can also be seen in the realm of marital intervention. Whereas members of the husband's *'a'ila* are often aggressive in their efforts to tear asunder the childless marriage, members of the wife's *'a'ila* tend to play a mediational, supportive role. In fact, it is widely acknowledged by both fertile and infertile women that wives' families rarely "make problems" for the infertile husband and wife,[12] even when male infertility is the clear-cut and widely acknowledged cause of the childlessness. As long as the husband accepts his responsibility for the childlessness and treats his wife lovingly, then members of the wife's *'a'ila* will typically argue that a childless marriage to a kind, appreciative, infertile husband—who will "treat his wife like a queen"—is far preferable to a divorce and remarriage to a fertile man of "unknown character." In their minds, the exceptional happiness of a marriage to a dedicated (although somewhat emasculated) infertile husband should serve to outweigh the happiness of having children with a potentially unsuitable mate.

Furthermore, among the urban poor, many people consider it shameful for a woman to initiate a divorce, even if her husband is unable to impregnate her. Moreover, if a wife's family urges her to divorce her infertile husband, then they are responsible for remarrying their daughter, which presents its own set of problems. In addition, since the children of a woman are seen as being hereditarily and jurally linked to her husband, the wife's family does not usually see her children as "strengthening" their own *'a'ila*, given that the children are not part of their patrilineage. In other words, infertility does not threaten the perpetuation of the wife's *'a'ila* in the same way that it threatens the husband's *'a'ila*.

For all of these reasons, the interests of wives' family members revolve around securing the infertile marriage—a goal quite different from that of husbands' families. Among the wife's *'a'ila*, their overriding objective is usually ensuring marital preservation and only secondarily the marital happiness of their family member. Although many parents tell their infertile daughters that they are willing to take them back should their marriages disintegrate, they are also clear that this option is to be viewed as a last resort—to be used only under conditions of relentless marital misery. In fact, wives' relatives are likely to urge forbearance even in unstable marriages in which the wife is suffering at the hands of her husband or his relatives. In such cases, members of the wife's *'a'ila* are likely to point out to both the husband and the wife that, with patience and perseverance, the infertility problem will probably be overcome in due course. Furthermore, they may attempt to convince the wife that a divorce and its aftermath are worse than an unhappy marriage itself; this argument is certainly motivated in part by their own desires to avoid the familial shame consequent upon a woman's request for divorce, as well as the responsibility for a woman whose chances of remarriage are less than normal.

Thus, in the vast majority of cases, wives' family members serve as the major supporters of the infertile marriage, playing either a direct interventional role in placating disgruntled husbands and thereby mediating marital conflicts, or a less direct conciliatory role in pointing out the many benefits to the infertile couple of staying together, no matter which partner is to blame for the infertility problem.

FOSTERING ARRANGEMENTS

In addition to the social safety net they provide, members of infertile women's *'a'ilāt*, particularly siblings, serve another crucial function—namely, providing their own children for more or less permanent fostering arrangements. Fostering a relative's child is viewed by some infertile couples as an acceptable solution to their childlessness and is employed in a small but not insignificant percentage of cases.[13] When family members offer their children for fostering (whether or not their offers are accepted), women's siblings, and sisters in particular, are usually the ones to suggest this idea.[14] When infertile women and their husbands agree to such arrangements, fostering of a niece or nephew may be undertaken on either an informal, day-by-day basis or on a more permanent, quasi-adoptive one.

Informal fostering is the rule, with infertile women caring for their siblings' children during the day (and sometimes overnight), but returning them regularly to their real parents. Through such daycare, infertile women are able to forge and maintain relationships of extreme affection toward their siblings' children—relationships so close that their nieces and nephews may call them "Mama" and may consider them to be the primary maternal figure in their lives. In this way, infertile women are also able to express their thwarted "maternal instinct" and to prove their abilities in the domain of motherhood, especially in the eyes of their doubtful in-laws and neighbors.

Less commonly, fostering a sibling's child may occur on a permanent, quasi-adoptive basis. In these cases, a sibling's child is usually offered at the time of its birth, and the family may maintain the fiction (especially to the child itself) that the infertile husband and wife are the real parents. Sometimes such fostering continues throughout the child's lifetime. But in most cases, the child is eventually apprised of its quasi-adoptive status and may choose to return to or may be taken back by its biological parents. In fact, most infertile couples eventually return their foster charges, usually in accordance with their siblings' requests.[15] In most of these cases, couples have fostered children for two to four years before the requests for return are made, and, by then, severing the emotional ties that have formed causes great difficulty for both the foster parents and children. Occasionally, third parties from the women's *'a'ilāt* intervene, and foster children are eventually returned to their foster parents. However, in the majority of cases, foster children are "lost" at some point by the infertile couple when the biological parents renege on their original, altruistic offer and request that the child be returned permanently.

Because this potential outcome of familial fosterage is well known among poor urban Egyptians, many infertile women, and especially their husbands, refuse well-meaning siblings' offers of children. According to them, a sympathetic and overburdened fertile sister may offer to her infertile sister one of her several children at the time of its birth; but, as she and her husband see the child grow, they cannot resist recalling it as one of their own.

As one infertile woman explained: "My sister wanted to give us her daughter. She said, 'Give her your name, and she'll be your daughter.' But [my husband] refused, saying 'Unless a child is from my own nerve, it's no good.' They didn't write the girl's birth certificate until she was two years old to push us to take her. But I refused, too. The saying goes, 'You who raise other than your own children are building a house on other than your own land.' The girl is bound to know who her real parents are and go back to them. It's as if I'm borrowing a dress that's not mine and one day I'll have to return it to its owner."

Furthermore, fertile women—even those with many children—support this view that their own children are ultimately indispensable to them. Therefore, they admit that they could never give away a child on a permanent basis, no matter how many children they already had.

As one woman put it: "You can't give your child away. A mother is a mother, and a boy can never be as happy as he is with his own mother, and my sister can never be as good a mother to him as I am."

For this reason, very few infertile women and their husbands view fostering a sibling's child as a viable, long-term solution to their childlessness. However, in Egypt, fostering a sibling's child on either a formal or informal basis is the only viable alternative to biological parenthood for most poor urban infertile couples, because legalized adoption as it is practiced in the West is prohibited by Islamic law and is culturally unacceptable to most poor urban Egyptians.

In terms of Islam, the Islamic scriptures and family law make specific provisions for the care and treatment of orphans (Esposito 1982, 1991; Sonbol 1991). However, orphans cannot be officially "adopted," in that they cannot (1) inherit from adoptive parents, (2) receive the family name of the adoptive father if their own family name is known (or their family name is fabricated by the police, as is common practice for abandoned infants in contemporary Egypt), and (3) become fully acknowledged as the children of adoptive parents. (This does not preclude, however, permanent fostering arrangements, which will be described shortly.)

Interestingly, because of their lack of religious literacy, few poor urban Egyptians are aware that adoption is religiously prohibited, and many in fact believe that it constitutes a "good deed" in the eyes of God.[16] Of those who are aware of the religious prohibition against adoption, most explain it as "cheating"—as "changing God's religion"—to raise a child and give him a name, an inheritance, and a "blood" that are not really his own. The religiously inspired proverb "Those who raise other than their own children are building a house on other than their own land" is often cited to explain this sense of misappropriation.

However, even women who mistakenly believe in the religious permissibility of adoption view it, as well as any other form of permanent fostering of orphans, as a problematical and unacceptable institution. This is true even among infertile women, most of whom say that they and their husbands would refuse the idea of bringing an orphaned child into their own homes.[17] According to both infertile and fertile women, many of whom have watched the popular movies and television shows devoted to this theme, adoption of a child is a mistake on a number of grounds—even if, as some women realize, it is commonplace outside the Arab world. As apparent in women's own discourse on the subject, there are a multitude of powerful reasons militating against this practice.

First, there is the problem of illegitimacy. Adopted children are usually of unknown parentage and ancestry; that is, they are "strangers," who do not share the same "blood" as their adoptive parents.[18] Moreover, in most cases, they are probably illegitimate—making them an *ibn ḥarām*, or literally, a "son of sin." Because moral character is considered by most poor urban Egyptians to be transmitted hereditarily, or "through the blood," an illegitimate child can be assumed to be of "bad blood" and will probably grow up to become like its parents. Therefore, children who are "known," but are orphaned because of their parents' deaths, are considered by Egyptians to be better adoptive candidates.

As one woman explained: "If you bring a child from the orphanage, you don't know its origins. And no matter how good of an environment it grows up in, it still has its parents' blood. And if they're bad, it can go back to its origins [be bad, too]."

As another woman put it: "It's not *ḥarām* for the person who adopts the child, but the *child*, he himself is *ḥarām*, because he's the son of nobody. You don't know his parents. He's 'unofficial.' They call him '*ibn ḥarām*.' That child did nothing wrong in his life, but his parents, maybe he came 'in the wrong way,' so they gave him to an orphanage. It's different if his parents died. We will know of whom he is the son, and all his life he will be this person's child. He's 'known.'"

Second, there is the problem of parental intervention. According to poor urban Egyptians, if the biological parents of an abandoned child happen to be alive, they may eventually seek their child, causing trouble for the adoptive parents as well as for the child. Most poor urban Egyptians are convinced, perhaps based on their knowledge of familial fostering outcomes, that adopted children eventually return to their "real" parents, either by choice or because the biological parents have intervened.

Third, there is the problem of affinity. Namely, because an adopted child is not a blood relation and did not emerge from its adoptive mother's womb, most poor urban Egyptians believe that the "natural" feelings of affinity of the adoptive parents toward this child can never be as strong as they would be toward a biological child. As women explain, an adopted child is simply not as "precious" as a child of one's own, and this may cause some adoptive parents to mistreat, exploit, or neglect such a child, especially if a biological child is born after the adoption. Furthermore, if the child misbehaves or is aggressive toward his/her adoptive parents—which is apt to be the case with children who go wrong by virtue of the "bad blood" of their biological parents or who simply feel less loyalty to their adoptive parents by virtue of their "different blood" [19]—forgiving the child would be more difficult.

As one woman put it: "I couldn't get myself to love an adopted child enough, because one's own child is part of you, and you go through a lot to give it birth, so you necessarily take good care of it. Otherwise, it's like taking care of something that's not your own."

Fourth, there is the problem of erotic attraction. Namely, many poor urban women believe—and are supported by contemporary popular and Islamist discourse on the subject—that if a couple adopts a child and then happen to have a child of their own of the opposite sex, the children should not be raised together as siblings, because they are actually potential marriage partners. Such an arrangement is deemed abnormal and even sinful because of the potential for erotic attraction that seems semi-incestuous. Likewise, an adopted boy could theoretically marry his mother and an adopted girl her father. Dressing and undressing in front of such children as they grow older might provoke erotic feelings that might lead to sinful acts. Furthermore, if the child is given the family name of his adoptive father, he may grow up to marry his biological sister, who goes by a different name. Situations of this sort are frequently depicted on Egyptian television and in the movies.

Fifth, there is the problem of stigmatization of the child. Namely, because adoption is culturally unacceptable for the aforementioned reasons, an adopted child will be stigmatized by the adoptive parents' extended families, as well as community members. This will ultimately affect the child's psychological well-being. According to Egyptian women, other children will mock the adopted child, calling it "the one whose parents brought you from the orphanage." Not only will this permanently scar the child, but the child will suffer additionally from not knowing who its real parents are.

As one woman who had witnessed the mistreatment of an orphaned child explained: "One of my neighbors 'adopted' a girl. Whenever this girl passes by, people always make her feel she's adopted. 'This is the girl from the orphanage. They adopted her.' I was standing there one day, and they told me, and she was standing next to us. I'm sure she heard, and I felt very sorry for her. I'm sure this child will be psychologically affected. Where we live, all of us know each other. If we do something like this, all the people will talk."

Sixth, there is the problem of stigmatization of the adoptive mother. Namely, those who know about the adoption will gossip and will stigmatize the woman who is unable to give her husband children. They may tell her that she "stole" a child that does not belong to her or that she is raising a child for someone else who should really be doing the upbringing. Furthermore, most Egyptians assume that a husband would rather divorce his infertile wife than resort to this option, because his second wife is likely to provide him with offspring and proper heirs to his inheritance. Adopting is, in effect, tantamount to admitting that the wife (who is usually blamed for the reproductive failing) is hopelessly infertile, and it is considered wiser for a man to try his reproductive luck with another woman.

Finally, there is the problem of poverty. Namely, it is widely perceived by poor urban Egyptians that only the rich are allowed to adopt. The popular perception is that orphanages require adoptive parents to have money in the bank, land, and other financial assets with which to secure the future of the adopted child. Therefore, most poor Egyptians believe that they are prohibited from adopting.

As one woman summarized: "Adoption only occurs under very strict conditions. The mother has to work and have her own income, a house of her own, and she must promise to leave an inheritance [to the adopted child]. They must educate the child, and they have to come visit the parents in the house to see what it's like. So only rich people can adopt—those who have lots of money in the bank. But we're poor, so we're not even thinking about it."

For all of these reasons, obtaining a child from an orphanage is deemed either unacceptable or unrealistic by most poor infertile Egyptian couples. Nonetheless, in Egypt's major cities, state-run and charitable orphanages have existed since the late 1800s and continue to place orphaned children in the homes of infertile Egyptians of all classes. Such orphanages take in three major categories of admissions (Rugh 1984): (1) abandoned infants, assumed to be illegitimate; (2) foundling children up to age four, assumed to be abandoned by their impoverished parents; and (3) children brought by relatives (especially divorced or widowed parents), neighbors, or social agencies because of the critical inability to care for them. Although most of these children spend their lives in orphanages, some are allowed to be taken home by infertile couples as permanent foster charges. These include children who were lost or abandoned as infants or toddlers and therefore do not know their own names, and newborns (assumed to be illegitimate) who were abandoned at the doors of mosques, churches, police stations, hospitals, or even in the streets and were turned over to orphanages. Children who are old enough to know their names cannot be fostered, because the parents are presumed to be in search of them or, as is sometimes the case, may be in actual contact with them.[20]

Within their first year of life, most abandoned infants are fostered out to infertile Egyptian couples, usually those from the middle and upper classes. Although the fostering arrangement is almost identical to adoption as it is known in the West, there are some important differences. First, these foster children retain the name given to them by the police when they are found (Sonbol 1991). Essentially, when an abandoned child is found and turned over to the police, a police record is opened, and a name, parents' names, grandparents' names, place of birth, and time of birth are all fabricated by the officer filling out the report (Sonbol 1991). Giving the child such a "record," which is registered at the orphanage, is deemed important for birth and death statistics, for identifying the child, and for safeguarding the child in a society that regards illegitimate children as carrying the stigmata of their parents by way of moral contagion (Sonbol 1991).

When this child is "adopted," the new parents must accept becoming its guardian only, which is achieved through a court order. The child retains his or her name so that there will be no confusion over future heirs and so that the adopted child cannot lay claim to property or other rights from his or her adoptive parents (Sonbol 1991).

Accordingly, changing the name of the child to that of the adoptive father is a complicated matter that involves further fabrication. First, the permission of the Ministry of Social Affairs must be received; lack of permission is punishable by law (Sonbol 1991). If the approval is granted, the adoptive father must go to court and swear that the child is his biological child and that, by recognizing his paternity, he is legitimizing him. An adoptive mother cannot do this, because declaring an adopted child to be her biological child is tantamount to declaring oneself a "fallen woman" or prostitute (Sonbol 1991).

Although some couples do "adopt" their children through false claims of paternity, others simply change the child's name unofficially, a practice that is illegal. Furthermore, many abandoned children who are found are never taken to orphanages; instead, they are given over to and kept by infertile couples, who give the child the father's name and try to pass the child off as their own.

Abandoned infants found on porches, sidewalks, and apartment entryways are not uncommon in poor urban neighborhoods, and such children are usually directed by sympathetic neighbors to childless couples.[21] Although some couples may keep these children, others end up turning the infants over to the police, usually upon the advice of husbands' family members.

In addition, newborn infants are occasionally abandoned in the maternity wards of hospitals. For example, in the University of Alexandria's Shatby Hospital, the public maternity hospital, which serves mostly lower-class women, abandonment of newborn infants by their mothers is not uncommon, and, when it occurs, it is always the topic of speculation among patients and hospital staff. As with infants found in public places, these abandoned children are taken by the police from the hospital to the Muslim orphanage in Alexandria.

The Story of Hadaya, Zakaria, and Their "Adoption" of Imad

Given the need of infertile women to have children and given the need of abandoned children to have mothers and fathers, the following story, in which the needs of both an abandoned child and an infertile couple are met, seems an appropriate conclusion to this chapter. This story, in which I, the medical anthropologist, am one of the protagonists, serves to highlight the procedures, complexities, cultural biases, and outcomes involved in the fostering of orphaned infants in Egypt, as well as the ways in which family members influence this process. The story goes as follows:

Hadaya, a childless Nubian woman in her early fifties, had been "searching for children" for nine years following a postmiscarriage operation in a public hospital in Cairo. When she and her husband Zakaria moved to Alexandria so that he could take a job as a porter for a wealthy family, Hadaya decided to visit the University of Alexandria's Shatby Hospital for a postoperative problem that had developed "from down." When the physicians at Shatby Hospital examined Hadaya, they told her that she required surgery for a prolapsed vagina, the result of a previous hysterectomy. Unfortunately, the physicians in Cairo who had performed Hadaya's postmiscarriage operation nine years earlier had never bothered to inform her that they had "opened her belly" to remove both her dead fetus *and* her uterus and that, therefore, she would never be able to bear children. Although Hadaya's menstrual period had waned, she had continued to labor under the assumption that her uterus was still in her body and that she might still bear a child for her husband, Zakaria, who had only one grown daughter by a previous marriage.

When Hadaya received the bad news about her hysterectomy from the physicians at Shatby and then proceeded to confirm it with me, she was stunned and despairing. She told me that Zakaria, also Nubian and in his early sixties, was still hoping for a son and was being mocked by his relatives and the members of his Nubian community over his lack of male heirs. Given this situation, Hadaya feared that he would leave her for a younger fertile woman, especially if he heard the news of her absolute sterility.

Because of Hadaya's desperation and the friendship that had developed between us, I decided to attempt to help her. I asked her whether she might consider fostering an abandoned child, like the ones sometimes left behind by their mothers at Shatby Hospital. Hadaya told me she would be willing to consider this, so I learned the address of the Muslim orphanage from one of the nurse's aides at the hospital.

Although I was scheduled to leave Egypt in only one and a half months, I took my research assistant with me to the Alexandria orphanage. We were pleasantly surprised to find an attractive facility with an organized and courteous staff, including caretakers who obviously loved their infant charges. In a discussion with the orphanage director, we learned the basic requirements of "fostering" from this facility—namely, that the parents must be Egyptian nationals, Muslims, less than fifty-five years of age, who live in an apartment, have a physician's proof of their infertility, and are both willing to participate in the fostering process as a "couple." We explained to the orphanage director that the husband and wife in question were Nubian and wanted a "dark" child.[22] The director was gleeful, explaining to us that "black" children were more difficult to foster out by virtue of their "non-Egyptian" skin color and facial features. She also explained that the facility currently had a one-year-old black male and a four-month-old black female who would soon become "unfosterable" by virtue of their advanced ages and would be transferred to another more permanent orphanage facility. Given the precarious situation of both infants, she urged us to bring this Nubian couple to the orphanage immediately.

When I explained the situation to Hadaya, who was still hospitalized, she was skeptical, insisting that Zakaria would certainly refuse such a permanent fostering arrangement of an illegitimate child. However, I agreed, at her request, to speak to Zakaria and see whether I might be able to convince him.

When we met, I told Zakaria that I had happened to stop by the orphanage and had learned of the predicament of a black male infant, who was unfosterable because of his skin color. I told him how lovely the little boy was and that I thought he and Hadaya would make ideal parents for the child. With very little discussion, Zakaria said that he wanted to accompany me to the orphanage and "take a look" for himself. Within a week, we made our second pilgrimage to the orphanage, this time with Zakaria.

When Zakaria saw the little one-year-old boy named Imad—who was frankly cherubic and nearly ambulatory—he took him into his arms and said, "This is my son" (after cursing the "son of a bitch" who would have abandoned such an exquisite male child).

Although the subsequent bureaucratic details were painstaking and time-consuming—given that Hadaya and Zakaria were illiterate, were hard-pressed to find their marriage certificate, were above the maximum age of legal guardians, and were required to undergo an inspection of their basement apartment in the home of the wealthy Alexandrian—the orphanage director, the social worker involved in the case, and my research assistant and I facilitated the process as much as possible to ensure that the child would find its way into the home of this loving and charismatic Nubian couple.

However, Hadaya, who had once been thoroughly convinced that their relative poverty would prohibit them from fostering, continued to express her grave concerns that Imad would be stigmatized as an adopted orphan. In particular, she wanted her husband's family to believe that she had spent two months in the public maternity hospital because of a difficult childbirth. For, she was quite certain that, unless she and Zakaria were able to foster a child whom they could pass off as their own son, they would create a scandal within the Nubian community and would be ruthlessly mocked by members of Zakaria's *'a'ila*. Much to the dismay of Hadaya, Imad, the one-year-old boy who was on his way to becoming their permanent foster charge, was much larger than a newborn, had well-coordinated motor skills, and, when he smiled, sported his baby teeth.

Given Hadaya's apparent distress over the issue of Imad's greater-than-newborn size, I used my imagination and suggested to Hadaya and Zakaria that they might call Imad an "infant of gestational diabetes"—infants that are known to be larger than normal upon birth. Because diabetes is called *sukkar*, or "sugar," in Egyptian colloquial Arabic, I argued to Hadaya and Zakaria that the little boy should be called their "sugar baby"— a relatively gigantic son born following a difficult pregnancy, labor, and delivery at Shatby Hospital by the diminutive, but pot-bellied and purportedly diabetic Hadaya.

Although Hadaya was still skeptical, Zakaria found my own well-intended fabrication quite convincing and was soon rejoicing with his many relatives about the remarkable birth of his colossal son. Much to Hadaya's surprise, the members of Zakaria's *'a'ila* were more than willing to believe the story and felt nothing but happiness that God had chosen to compensate Zakaria for all the hardships he had suffered in his life.

Although I had hoped to witness and photograph the initial union of the happy new *usra* before my departure from Egypt, bureaucratic technicalities concerning the fostering agreement had not been ironed out by the time I left the field. However, my research assistant was able to follow through with the case and informed me, upon my return to America, that the foster family was united within a week of my departure. Reportedly, both "son" and "parents" were doing well and were ecstatically happy.

For me, facilitating this fostering arrangement was my greatest accomplishment in the field. For Imad, it was perhaps his only chance to grow up as the "son" of loving parents. For Hadaya and Zakaria, it was a once-unimaginable but joyous solution to their long-term childlessness. And for the members of Zakaria's *'a'ila*—who were willing to suspend their disbelief long enough to allow Imad into their hearts—it was a way to strengthen the *'a'ila* and to reabsorb Zakaria and Hadaya, stigmatized outcasts, into the womb of the family.

5. Endangered Neighbors

The evil eye can split the stone.
— An Egyptian proverb from the hadith

Maisa's Story

For twenty-eight-year-old infertile Maisa, it is women—and women alone —who make her life miserable. At home, Maisa is confronted daily by the verbal assaults of her spiteful mother-in-law, who torments her over her continuing childlessness. And, among neighborhood women, she is treated with suspicion and cautious avoidance, for these fertile women fear exposure of their children to Maisa's perceived uncontrollable envy.

Until the time of marriage, Maisa had never experienced such problems, and her life was frankly carefree. One of the younger children in a family of six siblings, Maisa was coddled and indulged, and she never wanted for material things, since her father was a moderately successful small businessman. When Maisa's interest in school waned in the third grade, she was allowed to stay at home, where her mother and older sisters taught her how to sew on the family sewing machine. By the time Maisa had reached adolescence, she had become an excellent seamstress and was even asked by neighbors to make pajamas and dresses for them. Furthermore, Maisa was considered by many to be one of the young neighborhood beauties, given her lovely eyes, voluptuous figure, and the care with which she dressed.

When Ragab, a young man from the neighborhood, came with his parents to ask for Maisa's hand in marriage, the arrangement seemed auspicious. Although Maisa did not know Ragab or his family well, she accepted him in her heart when she thought of him as a husband, and she was excited over the prospect of being a beautiful bride in the wedding dress she would make for herself. Although Ragab was thin and ordinary by any standard, he had a steady income as a self-employed carpenter and furniture maker, and his family home, where Maisa was to live after the wedding, was within visiting distance of her parents. Thus, Maisa entered into her marriage with high hopes—hopes that were eventually dashed not by Ragab, but by her continuing childlessness and the hurtful reaction of others to this condition.

Indeed, Maisa now knows that her infertility problem is severe: hopelessly blocked fallopian tubes resulting from the postoperative scarring following two pelvic surgeries, one for a fibroid tumor and one for ovarian cysts. Physicians at the University of Alexandria's Shatby Hospital, where Maisa has become a patient, have told her that her only hope of conceiving is through in vitro fertilization (IVF), which may cost thousands of Egyptian pounds. "All of my husband's income goes toward treatment, and lately I sold three bracelets for £3,000 [$1,200]. From where am I going to get the money to spend on IVF?" Maisa asks. "One year ago I sold these [bracelets] and now most of the money is gone on treatments—for doctors' prescriptions and transportation and ultrasounds."

Although Maisa has told Ragab that her tubes are blocked and that IVF represents her only hope, both of them have kept this information secret from Maisa's mother-in-law in an attempt to prevent further problems and the destabilization of their marriage. Frankly, for eight years now, Maisa has lived under the tyrannical reign of her mother-in-law, a woman who has chided Maisa over her childlessness since the sixth month of her marriage. "Sometimes she's good and sometimes she's bad," Maisa explains. "Sometimes when I come to Shatby, she asks me, 'What happened? Don't tire yourself and go so much. Wait and I'm sure God will give you some day.' On the other side, she hurts me with words. Maybe every day she says something to annoy me. Now I don't give her the chance; if she wants to sit and talk, I pretend I'm busy or I leave the room."

Although Ragab never takes the side of his mother, telling Maisa repeatedly, "Don't get upset. She doesn't mean it," Maisa knows that Ragab is under tremendous pressure from members of his 'a'ila, and especially his mother, to replace her with a fertile woman. Although she believes Ragab loves her, she fears for her marriage, which may be destroyed by the familial forces that she sees as pitted against her. Living in the same household with eighteen members of Ragab's extended family has only exacerbated her problems. Not only does Ragab's "buzzing" mother have direct access to him, but she is able to humiliate and stigmatize Maisa overtly—often in the presence of her husband and his relatives. Maisa describes several of these incidents.

From the beginning of marriage, I used to like to eat cheese a lot. All the time, my mother-in-law said, "Ah, she's pregnant." She made me feel and notice that each month I don't get pregnant. And, all the time, whenever she hears that someone is pregnant, she comes and tells me, then goes to that other person who is pregnant or has delivered a baby and says, "Maisa is very upset and losing weight because you were able to get pregnant and she can't." Whenever some of his relatives are around, "Oh, my poor son can't have a child," as if she's pitying him. My mother-in-law always says things. Whenever I'm sick and in bed, my mother-in-law tells me, "Ah, you must be pregnant," even when she knows I'm not. For example, one day, I was going to Kafr El-Dawwar with my mother-in-law to visit my sister-in-law and, when having lunch, there were pickled lemons. In front of the others, she said, "Put these pickled lemons in front of Maisa because you feel like having special foods when you're pregnant," and she knew I wasn't pregnant. She did it to hurt me. The ones surrounding us said, "Is that true? Honestly, you're pregnant?" I said "No." You can't know how I felt. I mean, I don't feel like a complete woman because I haven't had children. That's my feeling, and they *make* me feel that way. Maybe every day my mother-in-law says something. I hate the things that she does to me.

In addition to the everyday verbal abuse of her mother-in-law, Maisa's relations with her female neighbors are strained. Even though Maisa has a thriving home business as a seamstress—charging neighbor women £5 ($2) to make a dress from prepurchased fabric—women are cautious in their dealings with her, rarely bringing their children with them when they pick up their orders from Maisa's home. "People with children are scared that I give the evil eye to them," Maisa explains. "I noticed it. They don't take their kids away, but whenever they visit me, they don't bring their children, and all the time they tell me, 'He's sick, not in good health.' They say he's sick so they don't have to bring him so that I don't give him the evil eye. Most of them, they believe this, and I get upset, because why do they think such a thing about me? I love children, and I *never* think of giving them the evil eye."

Nonetheless, Maisa herself believes in the evil eye and its power to harm. "Yes, I *do* believe in the evil eye," she says, "because it's written in the Qur'an that the *Nabīy* [the Prophet Muhammad] had two sons,[1] and one day someone knocked on the door, so he hid the two children and instead of two children, he put a big stone and covered it as if the children were sleeping. After the person left, the *Nabīy* found the stone cut in two pieces. It was the evil eye."

Because such belief in the evil eye is widespread among her neighbors,

Maisa knows that she is suspect because of her infertility and her perceived uncontrollable envy of others' children. She explains:

> No one accused me of having it, but I feel this. For example, if a pregnant woman comes, they don't tell me until I see her belly is big and I know she's pregnant. They think because I don't have children I give the eye, because if you want something and can't get it, you *can* give [it]. There are two types [of people who give the evil eye]. Some people give it all the time. And if you're envying someone with something, you can give it, but it's not a permanent condition. Sometimes, even when I see a child, I do a small prayer so nothing happens to the child . . . so, if there is the evil eye, it won't happen. When I look at a child, it's not that I look in a bad way. It's because I love and miss children. But, if I saw a child and just by chance he got a fever, definitely they will say, "It's her eye."

The Stigmatization of Infertile Women

Among the urban Egyptian poor, the stigmatization of infertility begins at home and ends in the community, where infertile women such as Maisa are often feared as casting the evil eye—an envious glance so powerful that it can "split the stone" and make innocent children fall ill and even die. The fact that infertile women are actually feared by their neighbors (and, in some cases, by their husbands' female relatives as well) as endangering children attests to the magnitude of the stigma surrounding infertility and the power of this particular condition to shape infertile Egyptian women's daily lives.

In Egypt, the evil eye represents the reification of stigma—the making tangible of infertile women's marginality through the attribution of a force of evil that they are widely deemed to possess. In fact, everyday interactions with others in the community, and particularly fertile women and their children, may be a form of torment for infertile women; for they are forced to "manage" the social tension engendered by "mixed contacts" with "normals" (Goffman 1963), who may view their interactions with infertile women as patently harmful.

For poor urban infertile women, managing social tension involves, to a great extent, managing social information about themselves, a task that is made difficult in the intimate, often sex-segregated social environments of urban Egyptian communities. In these communities, the daily interactions of fertile and infertile neighbor women often replicate the social relations characteristic of infertile women and their husbands' female relatives vis-à-vis the production and management of stigma; namely, neighbor women tend to stigmatize the infertile women in their midst, while infertile women attempt to manage their stigmatization through a variety of resistant strategies. However, the key difference between female in-laws and neighbors is a tactical one: Whereas women in husbands' families usually employ direct measures against infertile women in order to purge the family of its social defect, neighbor women tend to utilize indirect measures designed mainly to protect themselves and their children against the evil thought to emanate from the eyes of infertile women. Although more subtle and evasive, these neighborly strategies are still the stuff of daily misery for infertile women like Maisa, who must prove their lack of malevolence and their love for neighborhood children.

Thus, among the urban Egyptian poor, the stigmatization of infertility becomes publicly manifested in the gynecocentric politics of everyday community life—politics involving a dialectic of hostility and tension among women, whose strategies include deception, avoidance, and information control. Such political struggles are the strategic turf of women rather than of men; for it is fertile women who, as the primary caretakers of their endangered children, must fight to protect their offspring from the infertile enemies in their midst, and it is infertile women who, as the victims of other women's fears, must attempt to resist their victimization through peaceful alliances or desperate retreats into further isolation.

Controlling Social Information

To understand the often tumultuous, hostile relationships between infertile women and their female neighbors, it is necessary first to examine the ways in which social information about infertile women is conveyed and controlled within urban Egyptian neighborhoods.

According to Goffman (1963), "social information" is best thought of as information about an individual's abiding characteristics—information that is reflexive, is conveyed by the individual through bodily expression in the immediate presence of others, and is thereby used by others to place individuals into socially recognized categories. This information can be of two types: that which is readily apparent to others, because of its visibility or because it is widely known; and that which is not readily apparent to others, because the individual is able to conceal it and has control over the circumstances under which it is conveyed. Thus, the spread of social information hinges upon issues of visibility and "known-aboutness"; those whose social information is literally embodied through, for example, various physical stigmata will be forced to cope with life situations differently from those whose social information remains "invisible" or hidden from the public view of potentially knowing others.

Social information may be stigmatizing, and, depending upon its visibility or known-aboutness, can serve to divide individuals into two categories: *discredited* persons, whose stigma is "known to us before we normals contact him, or to be quite evident when he presents himself before us" (Goffman 1963:41); and *discreditable* persons, whose stigma is "not immediately apparent, and is not known beforehand (or at least known by him to be known to the others)" (Goffman 1963:42). Accordingly, when individuals are discredited by virtue of the visibility or known-aboutness of the social information regarding their stigmata, then the major issue in their lives becomes one of "managing tension generated during social contacts" (Goffman 1963:42). On the other hand, when individuals are discreditable by virtue of the "hiddenness" of the social information regarding their stigmata, then the major issue in their lives becomes one of "managing information about [this] failing," including in some cases "passing" for normal (Goffman 1963:42).

In Egypt, infertile women share features of both discreditable and discredited personas. On the one hand, infertile women are discreditable by virtue of the fact that their reproductive tract problems are internal and "hidden" and hence not immediately apparent to others.[2] Thus, in interactions with strangers, infertile women must attempt to manage social information about their reproductive failing by avoiding the conversational topic of children. In Egypt, avoidance of this subject matter is extremely difficult, given that a person's marital status and reproductive history are often initial topics of conversation, especially among strangers. Nonetheless, by virtue of their discreditableness, infertile women do have some degree of control over how much information they convey about themselves to others, to whom they convey it, and the manner in which it is conveyed. As seen in the previous chapter, infertile women already employ such information management strategies in their interactions with in-laws, and these efforts are often aided and abetted by husbands and women's kin, who may even encourage dissimulation and prevarication for the sake of social harmony.

On the other hand, most poor urban infertile women are also "discredited" in that their failure to conceive is usually widely known within their home communities. In fact, in poor urban neighborhoods, keeping one's infertility a secret is virtually impossible, given that women's social networks are extensive and any social information about a woman's failure to conceive spreads rapidly.

In the poorer quarters of Egypt's cities, extensive biographical information about individuals is widely available to community members, given that urban neighborhoods are much like small towns, where the lives of residents are known to others. In Alexandria, poor urban neighborhoods often consist of several small city blocks of narrow, unpaved streets, each lined with two- to four-story cement-block apartment buildings, which are privately or governmentally owned. Within each of these buildings, large numbers of nuclear or extended families reside, usually in cramped rooms or small apartments. And, within each building and often between adjacent buildings, all occupants are known to each other, given that people's lives, and especially those of women, are often carried out primarily within this domestic arena. Moreover, in crowded urban apartment buildings, close physical proximity serves to blur the distinction between "public" and "private" as life spills out into public passageways (Nadim 1985), thereby increasing the potential for social surveillance and monitoring (El-Messiri 1978; Jowkar 1986; Rugh 1984).

This is especially true among women, whose lives are spent largely at home. As described in Chapter 2, women in poor urban neighborhoods often exist in the domestic realm, with marketing and visiting their major distractions. Forging friendships with other women in the neighborhood is a major form of recreation and a relief from boredom. For many poor urban women, their lives are deeply enmeshed in these relations of neighborliness, which may become "kin-like" when relatives live at a distance (Early 1993).

It is through such neighborliness in urban areas that gynecocentric networks of social support and influence are formed. However, some of this influence may be negative, in that women may use their social networks in ways that serve to oppress other women (Aswad 1978). Specifically, because much of poor urban Egyptian women's conversation revolves around the biographical details of each other's lives, such neighborly chatting—or what women call *kalām in-nās*, meaning literally "people's talk" or "gossip"—is the major vehicle for the dissemination of information about the socially or morally disapproved elements of women's lives, including their reproductive trials and tribulations. For infertile women, such spread of information, which is often beyond an individual's control,

Photograph 13. Neighbors baking bread. (Photograph by Mia Fuller)

serves to discredit them in their communities, making passing for normal impossible and forcing them to expend their energies in the management of social tension between themselves and other women.

Such spread of social information within the community has a number of characteristic implications for the lives of infertile women. First, social information *about* women is spread *by* women, given that these informal, neighborhood-based communication networks are usually composed exclusively of women. As women themselves note, "men don't gossip like women," and women's gossip, they add, may be vicious, in that it usually includes both informational exchange and critical (i.e., negative) social commentary. Thus, to reiterate a crucial point from the last chapter, women are often the staunchest supporters of traditions and social relations that constrain and limit each other's lives; in this case, they participate actively in their own oppression by criticizing women who do not meet agreed-upon standards of "normal womanhood" through motherhood.

Second, these women's communication networks may extend well beyond the community and back to the natal villages of infertile women whose families are of rural origin. In Alexandria and Egypt's other major cities, many poor urban neighborhoods are composed largely of rural migrants, and, in some neighborhoods, migrants may hail from the same village or rural vicinity (Nadim 1985). Thus, social information about infertile women in the urban migrant neighborhood may spread "back home" through the village ties kept by neighbors. Infertile women may find that information about their failure to conceive is widely known in both urban and rural locales, leaving them literally with no place to hide their reproductive failing. In fact, infertile women often report visits to their natal villages in which social information about their infertility has preceded them; in other words, they literally arrive back home stigmatized, experiencing little in the way of pleasant interaction.

Third, because of the intragender-based nature of neighborhood communication networks, infertile women bear the burden of the "discreditedness" for their failure to produce children; their husbands, even when they are the source of the infertility, are rarely stigmatized by community members. Women themselves attribute this gendered difference to two major factors: women's closer association than men with the quotidian aspects of pregnancy, childbearing, and child-rearing; and the gender-based separation of spheres of activity for men and women.

With respect to the former factor, the bearing and nurturance of children is the major role of poor urban women; thus, hindrances to this role, including the problems of infertility, are perceived to be *their* problem and *not* those of their husbands—no matter who is to "blame." With respect to the latter factor, men, generally speaking, carry out their lives outside of the domestic realm and hence are free from the intense social scrutiny of neighbors. Although men may gather informally in the late afternoons and evenings at neighborhood cafes to drink tea and coffee, smoke waterpipes, play backgammon, or watch soccer and other sporting events on television, they lack the community-based information networks of women. Thus, when men gather, the passage of social information *about each other* is not their major concern and, when it is, it is usually not related to men's reproductive histories and problems. The result is that infertile husbands, even when "known about," tend not to suffer social stigmatization within the community in the same way as their wives. In fact, as previously discussed, they may not suffer stigmatization at all, because of the protective efforts of their wives to conceal male infertility problems.

Fourth, because of the extent to which social information about female community members is widely disseminated in urban neighborhoods, most poor urban Egyptian women know of or are personally acquainted with one or more women who are infertile. In many cases, they possess rather detailed information about their infertile neighbors' specific complaints, both reproductive and marital—indexing the strength of neighborhood communication networks as effective vehicles for the dissemination of social information.

For infertile women themselves, knowing other neighbors who are also infertile can make them feel less alone and can provide them with therapeutic companions in their reproductive quests (Inhorn 1994). And, among fertile women, intimate knowledge of neighbors' reproductive complaints can make some more sensitive to infertile women's plight, generating both pity and compassion. However, among fertile women, compassionate responses are not the rule. As we shall see, familiarity more often than not breeds contempt, in that increased knowledge seems to exacerbate some women's negative appraisal of infertile women as inherently dangerous by virtue of their destructive envy.

"Normal" Women's Views of the Infertile

Both fertile and infertile Egyptian women agree that the overall view of infertile women, at least among the urban poor, is "not a good one," because of the widespread conviction that only motherhood makes a married woman normal and complete. Because infertile women are widely perceived as incomplete, they are, at best, the subjects of pity, and, at worst, the objects of fear among those who believe that envious individuals cast the evil eye. Thus, in addition to their worries about their reproductive health, their marriages, and their relations with kin, poor urban infertile women must contend with the sometimes thinly veiled pity and contempt of neighbors, as well as the knowledge that they are the frequent subjects of *kalām in-nās*, or "people's talk."

Indeed, this largely negative appraisal is clearly reflected in fertile women's discourse on what they perceive to be the predominant views of infertile women—namely, pity, fear, and disdain.

As one woman explained: "They pity her, of course, and they talk behind her back. 'She didn't have children. Her husband will leave her.' People here don't do anything except talk about other people, their bad fortunes, their lives."

Another woman remarked: "Some people pity her. Some talk behind her back. Some are happy she's suffering. Some people think the infertile woman can give the [evil] eye. Some say, 'She's no use. There's no good to come out of her.' You can never know what's in their consciences."

And, as another woman put it: "People don't necessarily believe she gives the evil eye, but they say bad things about her like, 'She didn't get pregnant. God didn't give her a child.' Mostly behind her back, but sometimes in front of her. They view her as incomplete; they actually think something is a little wrong with her. They view her as a weird person."

INFERTILE WOMEN AS PITIABLE

As revealed in this discourse, fertile women with living children often consider infertile women to be pitiable for being deprived of the experience of motherhood and for missing children in their lives. Of all of the neighborly attitudes toward infertile women, pity is the most benign and is usually manifested among fertile women who are "wise normals" (Goffman 1963) —those who choose to play the role of sympathetic others to their infertile neighbors. Fertile women who manifest a kind of sympathetic pity toward their infertile neighbors tend to be of three types, including: (1) those who themselves experienced brief periods of postmarital infertility and thus are more empathic toward the plight of infertile women based on their own close calls with reproductive failure; (2) those who have close relatives (for example, a sister, a cousin, or an aunt) who are infertile and whose stigma they are involved in managing as members of the infertile woman's *'a'ila*; and (3) those whose religious convictions convince them that infertility is "from God" and hence beyond any individual woman's control.

With regard to the first group, many poor urban Egyptian women experience delays in conception at one time or another in their lives, delays that are sometimes construed as periods of "infertility."[3] For example, it is not at all unusual for young Egyptian brides, some of whom are barely postpubescent, to experience delayed conception during the first postmarital year. Similarly, delays in conception are common following the weaning of a child or discontinuance of a birth control method among women who have already proven their fertility. When such conceptive delays occur, many poor urban Egyptian women panic, thinking that they may never become pregnant, and many of these women seek therapy, either ethnomedical or biomedical or both, for what they perceive to be their infertility problem. Sometimes therapy succeeds, and sometimes therapy is not even required, because most of these women are not truly infertile and will become pregnant spontaneously without treatment.

Yet, the fact that infertility worries are so common—even among women who are quite fertile—makes some of these women much more sympathetic toward women who seem to be permanently barred from motherhood. Many poor urban women who have come close to infertility consider themselves lucky to have proven their fertility; for they, too, believe that they would have faced the kinds of problems with their husbands, in-laws, and neighbors that they see among their infertile acquaintances.

With regard to the second group, some fertile women are much more sympathetic toward infertile women because of their own close relationships with infertile relatives, including siblings, first cousins, and aunts and uncles.[4] Knowing an infertile relative, and particularly an infertile sister, tends to have the same effect as having experienced delayed conception personally—namely, promotion of feelings of pity and sympathy for other women, including neighbors, who cannot conceive.

Finally, some women are much more sympathetic toward infertile women because of their firm belief that God bestows infertility on some women for a reason—a reason that cannot be questioned and that places infertility and its solution beyond human agency. With the growing Islamic revival in Egypt, such religiously inspired beliefs about infertility seem to be increasing among the urban poor, with beneficial effects on the ways in which some "religious" women treat their infertile neighbors. Yet, even women who are not particularly religiously devout may share the conviction that infertile women are not to blame for their problem, since it is a condition created by God for a reason.

Such wise normals, or fertile women who sympathize with the infertile, tend to express their concern in a number of ways: (1) in expressions of hope and support for their infertile neighbors; (2) in prayers for a solution to infertile neighbors' problems; (3) through advice on and encouragement of infertile neighbors' therapeutic quests, including in some cases provision of the names of "good" physicians and traditional healers or accompaniment of the infertile woman to and from therapeutic destinations; and (4) friendship rather than avoidance, including in some cases the employment of the infertile woman as a kind of surrogate mother to one's own children.

This last expression of sympathy—of giving one's children to an infertile babysitter—is particularly important because of its dual meaning. On the one hand, fertile women claim to loan infertile women their children out of feelings of sorrow for the infertile woman's plight and to allow the woman to experience that which she is missing. On the other hand, as will

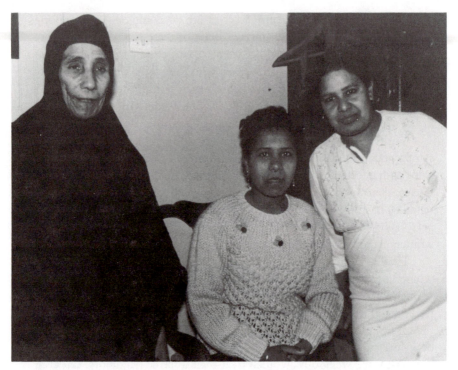

Photograph 14. Neighbor women. (Photograph by Marcia Inhorn)

be described shortly, giving an infertile woman one's own children (usually for a brief period of time) is thought by some fertile women to be the most effective means of preventing or reducing an infertile woman's envy and, hence, her likelihood of casting the evil eye on one's offspring.

For their own part, infertile women tend to question the motives of sympathetic others when they give their children to them or express words of encouragement and support. As they note, most fertile women can never be trusted to express the same sentiments "behind the infertile woman's back," although undoubtedly some fertile women are genuine in their expressions of sympathy and concern. Yet, as infertile women also recognize, even expressions of sympathy and support cannot mask the pity that accompanies these words and actions—a sentiment that most infertile women despise, because it reminds them that they are, in fact, pitiable in the eyes of "normals."

As one infertile woman lamented: "All of them [my neighbors], they pity me, and of course, I don't like that, because I don't like their pity. All the time, they tell me, 'Search for doctors, and I hope that one day you get a child.' It happens a lot. What else do they have to do here than talk about other people?"

INFERTILE WOMEN AS EVIL EYE GIVERS

Yet, to reiterate a crucial point, pity is the most benevolent of the sentiments commonly expressed by fertile women toward their infertile neighbors. A much more common response is fear mixed with loathing of the infertile woman as a despicable and dangerous being—one to be dealt with through her social ostracism in the community.

Community ostracism of infertile women typically takes two forms. On the one hand, it replicates rather closely the kind of stigmatization of infertile women by their in-laws—namely, direct attempts to disparage and distance these women through malicious comments, criticism, and "dirty looks." Although not all infertile women experience such overtly hostile behavior on the part of their neighbors, a significant proportion encounter run-ins with neighbors who have openly insulted them over their childlessness.[5] As with in-laws, malicious neighbors often remind infertile women about their inability to become pregnant or question their femininity, either by calling them males or mocking their infecundity.

As one infertile woman who had been "hurt by the words" of hostile neighbors recounted: "You can never know how some Egyptian women are going to make you feel if you're not having children and she's carrying a child. Because they talk to you about children and say to you, 'Oh, how good you are! You can sleep at night because you have no children crying.' They do this to make you feel less than them."

Another infertile woman lamented: "Some neighbors who married at the same time as I did and who have children used to hurt me with words. 'Aren't you going to have children? This is it? You're finished?' Now, I keep away from people, because any word hurts, even if they don't mean it."

Another infertile woman gave this account: "My neighbors have annoyed me a lot. One of them said, 'God won't give you children.' Another one, we had a fight, and I told her, 'You are not to judge [me] because you swear a lot and blaspheme our religion.' So my neighbor told me, 'Oh, yes, and you're the one who God doesn't want to give children. Don't talk about religion!' And another old woman in our building has a granddaughter, and I was saying, 'Oh, she's ugly' [to protect her from the evil eye], and the friend of this woman said, 'You try to get something as good as her shit!' Egyptians are bad in this way. When we fight or have a problem, they use [my childlessness] to hurt me."

Such verbal tactics serve to reinforce the social distance that many fertile women desire to put between themselves and the infertile women in their midst. In fact, the second main form of social ostracism comprises actual physical avoidance of infertile women, which is considered necessary by many fertile women to ensure the safety of themselves and their children from *ḥasad*, or deleterious envy.

To understand the community reaction to infertile women, it is imperative to understand how poor urban Egyptians' attitudes toward the infertile are shaped by their pervasive belief in the evil eye—considered to be the major negative sequela of envy. In fact, among the urban Egyptian poor, the term *ḥasad* glosses as both "evil eye" and "envy," a connection that has been explained as follows: "In . . . Egypt and the Middle East, people believe that envy (*ḥasad*), working through the agency of the glance (*nazar*), has efficient action and can destroy or harm the objects or people against which it is directed. The word *ḥasad* is used both as a noun (envy, or the evil eye), and as a verb (to envy, to cast the evil eye): The act of envying and its action are taken to be synonymous" (Ghosh 1983:211).

As noted in this passage, belief in the power of the envious glance to cause harm is widespread not only in Egypt but throughout the Middle East, a region considered to be one of the "core areas" where evil eye beliefs are found (Maloney 1976a). Yet, evil eye beliefs are not restricted to the Middle East; they appear to be widely distributed throughout the Mediterranean region, northern Europe, the northern half of Africa, South Asia, parts of Central America, and among immigrant groups in North America (Dundes 1992; Maloney 1976a). Given this wide distribution, it is not surprising that evil eye beliefs lack a specific association with any particular world religion, including Islam. For example, although the evil eye is mentioned in the Islamic scriptures, the belief in evil eye predates Islam, appearing in both the Bible and in Sumerian texts as early as five thousand years ago (Dundes 1992). Furthermore, although Egyptians may refer to Islam to justify their evil eye beliefs, Muslims in other parts of the world, such as Southeast Asia, appear not to abide by such beliefs (Maloney 1976a).

Moreover, it is important to note that beliefs about the causes and consequences of the evil eye, as well as counteractive measures, appear to vary considerably cross-culturally (see, for example, Dundes 1992 and Maloney 1976b). For example, within the Middle Eastern region alone,

the evil eye may or may not be thought capable of causing illness or striking inanimate objects, and it may or may not be associated primarily with
socially marginal individuals (Maloney 1976b). Whereas in Iran, it is "unusual" people—or "persons who for some reason or other do not fully
belong to the closely knit community, either because they are strangers or
because they have some physical defect or abnormality, not necessarily of
the eye or sight" (Spooner 1976:78)—who are suspected of being vehicles
of the evil eye, in rural Egypt, anyone is thought capable of casting the evil
eye, with those living in closest proximity (i.e., envious neighbors) being
prime suspects (Ghosh 1983:213).

Yet, amid the cultural diversity, there are certain recurrent features of
evil eye belief and practice that are of tremendous importance to this discussion. First of all, in a wide variety of cultural settings, children—and
particularly more highly valued male children—are believed to be one of
the main targets of the evil eye, with their sickness, injury, and even death
constituting possible outcomes (Dundes 1992; Maloney 1976b). Thus, in
many settings, belief in the evil eye serves as a primary explanatory model
for infant and child morbidity and mortality (e.g., Harfouche 1992). Indeed, around the world where evil eye beliefs are found, mothers fear the
power of others' envy to provoke the ill health of their children, and they
take precautionary measures to guard their children against the evil eye
whenever possible.

Second, given these beliefs concerning child health, it is not surprising that women—and particularly reproductively troubled women
incapable of fulfilling their motherhood expectations and desires—are
deemed particularly likely to cast the evil eye on children, who comprise the
coveted object of these maternal expectations and desires (Maloney 1976b).
Spooner explains women's particular susceptibility to evil eye suspicions
as follows: "Since their social role is more strictly defined than men's, and
they are at a physical and social disadvantage to start with, any unusual
behaviour, or any trait that prevents them from fulfilling their women's
function, may make them suspect: e.g., *barrenness*, brashness, unexplained
visits, etc." (Spooner 1976:80, emphasis added).

This presumed link between the envy of barren women and poor child
health outcomes certainly holds true for urban Egypt. It is widely believed
by poor urban Egyptians that anyone who is envious can cast the evil eye,
including men and fertile women,[6] and that infertile women vary in their
potential to cast the evil eye because some are more jealous and hateful than
others. But most poor urban Egyptians nonetheless contend that infertile

women are more likely to cast the evil eye on others' children for the simple reason that women "deprived" of children cannot help but to envy them. Furthermore, some poor urban Egyptians consider infertile women to be dangerous to fertile women themselves, especially those who are pregnant or who have demonstrated their reproductive success repeatedly. The danger of infertile women to fertile women and their children, furthermore, is often confirmed in popular discourse by "real-life" accounts involving unfortunate incidents of illness, injury, or death thought to be proof of an infertile woman's envious glance.

As one fertile woman who believes in the evil eye explained: "Infertile women can envy someone else's children and hurt them. It's common and it happens. If a woman who doesn't have children carries a baby and envies him, this baby will be hurt. Of course, it's not all infertile women. Some are very kind and would take care of others' children. And it doesn't matter if you have children or not; you can still give the evil eye. *Anyone* can give the evil eye. If you're eyes are 'full' [you have everything you want], you will not envy. But, because infertile women are deprived of children, they're more likely to envy."

Another woman put it this way: "All over Egypt they believe in the evil eye. Of course, anyone can give the evil eye, but some people say, 'In the name of God' or 'God praise the prophet' and so this prevents you if you're envious. And some people just give the evil eye continuously. This is why no one talks to a woman without children or why they stay away from her—lest she give the evil eye to their children. If she sees a child and says 'It's beautiful' and carries it and something happens to it, they blame her. So women [with children] are usually very careful."

In addition, women who believe in the evil eye and infertile women's tendency to cast it on children justify their convictions by noting that the evil eye is "mentioned in the Qur'an and the hadith." In reality, the evil eye lacks specific reference in the Qur'an (Spooner 1976), although the following Qur'anic passage (chapter 113), and especially its last line, is often invoked in support of evil eye beliefs in Islamic countries:

> In the Name of God, the Merciful, the Compassionate,
> Say: "I take refuge with the Lord of the Daybreak,
> from the evil of what he has created,
> from the evil of darkness when it gathers,
> from the evil of women who blow on knots,
> from the evil of an envier when he envies."

References to the evil eye in the hadith, however, are more specific. In fact, the oft-cited Egyptian proverb "The evil eye can split the stone" derives from a story in the hadith in which the Prophet Muhammad warns his daughter Fatima to protect her infant sons from the evil eye by hiding them and "replacing" them with a large stone wrapped in a swaddling cloth. When women come to admire the infants and notice their apparent large size, the stone that has replaced them is split in two by the power of the evil eye of an envious admirer.

Yet, even though many poor urban Egyptian women are able to cite such religious support for the evil eye concept, some continue to be skeptical about the existence of the evil eye—or at least infertile women's presumed heightened role in casting it. As they reason, a woman cannot envy that which she has never experienced; put more metaphorically, a person who has never tasted shrimp and who therefore does not know what she is missing can never envy a shrimp eater. By this logic, then, if the evil eye exists, *fertile* women with children are more likely to cast the evil eye on other women's children, perhaps out of jealousy over their comparative beauty or accomplishments.

However, such "skeptics" constitute a definite minority.[7] By and large, poor urban Egyptian women—and especially those with potentially endangered children—believe in the evil eye and continue to take precautions in their interactions with infertile neighbors.

As one such "believer" explained: "Of course, people are afraid [of infertile women]. I myself fear to give my kids to an infertile woman. She could give them the evil eye because she wants them very much. It's like a kind of food that is too expensive for her—like shrimp. When she sees it, she *has* to give it the evil eye."

As suggested by this speaker, fertile women fear exposing their children to infertile neighbors and may, in fact, go to great lengths to avoid infertile women and/or hide their children from them. Among fertile women, such avoidance strategies are deemed the most effective preventive mechanism. In some cases, the avoidance is obvious; for example, some women literally pull their children off the street to hide them from an infertile passerby. In other cases, the avoidance is more subtle; for example, some women pretend that the absence of their children from an infertile woman's sight is accidental when, in fact, these mothers have taken great pains to hide their children and then to lie to the infertile woman about the children's whereabouts.

Lying about one's children is deemed by many mothers to be another effective strategy to ward off an infertile woman's envy. Typically, these lies involve a de-emphasis of a child's positive attributes so as to make him or her seem less appealing—and therefore less enviable—to the infertile woman. Thus, infertile women are often told that a child is ill when, in fact, the child is healthy, or that a child is stupid when, in fact, the child is clever. In addition, some women with many children—a common phenomenon among the urban poor—lie about their family sizes, reducing the number of children so as to make the infertile woman less envious.

Yet, as noted earlier, some fertile women contend that avoidance of infertile women and accompanying dishonest cover-ups are the wrong approach, serving only to intensify an infertile woman's jealousy and, therefore, her potential to cause harm. Instead, these women employ a diametrically opposed strategy: namely, placing their children in an infertile woman's care, so as to diminish her feelings of deprivation, jealousy, and covetousness and, hence, her likelihood of casting the evil eye. Although this strategy meets with mixed responses from infertile women, who suspect that they are being "used" as babysitters because of their neighbors' underlying fear, it is nonetheless a strategy that is advocated by significant numbers of fertile women.

As one such woman explained: "I know of a woman without children and she keeps the neighbors' children all of the time. Even if she *can* give the evil eye, this prevents her because you make her feel less envious. Unlike if you hide your children from her, this would make her feel bad. Then God will make something happen to your child and you will blame it on her. But usually a woman without children is more affectionate, so she would take very good care of your child."

In addition to these specific strategies, fertile women also employ a number of generic measures to prevent infertile women from casting the evil eye on their children or to counteract the evil eye when it has already been cast. These include burning incense in a household in which an infertile woman (or any individual suspected of giving the evil eye) has just visited. In addition, many women wear as jewelry or attach to their children's clothing various evil-eye-preventive charms, including coins, blue beads, and figures of eyes or an outstretched palm (which is meant to represent the hand of Fatima, the Prophet Muhammad's daughter). Amulets, consisting of small parcels of paper upon which a *shaikh* has written verses from the Qur'an, are also popular (see also Inhorn 1994).

Infertile Women's Responses to Community Ostracism

For their part, infertile women often realize that they are viewed as abnormal and even dangerous by women in their communities—even if they themselves disbelieve in their own power to cause harm to other people's children.[8] Furthermore, infertile women are often able to articulate the ways in which this fear and loathing has led to the various strategies of protection and avoidance described above. Although virtually all infertile women report feeling offended and hurt by such attitudes and actions, their responses to neighbors' behavior may take two quite distinct forms. Namely, some infertile women choose to manage the tension generated during social contacts with fertile women by being overly solicitous of them and their children and by attempting to assimilate, or "pass" into the fertile world. Others choose to avoid such "mixed contacts" altogether in overt statements of resistance against the stigmatizing fertile community. In other words, infertile Egyptian women may choose two contrasting stigma management styles: assimilation or resistance.

Although assimilation is the less common strategy, some infertile women do their best to fit in—to "pass for normal"—in their communities by befriending fertile women with children, normalizing their relationships with them, and thereby overcoming fertile neighbors' apprehensions about evil eye risks. Infertile women of this assimilative persuasion are more likely to view their neighbors as potential friends rather than as enemies and to work at establishing intimate relationships with them, often by entrusting their neighbors with confidences about themselves and their infertility problems. In other words, these women attempt to increase their chances of social acceptance in the community by working to create a protective circle of wise normals. Often, however, they must work diligently at gaining community acceptance through self-conscious efforts at managing the uneasiness—the "pathology of interaction" (Goffman 1963)—present in their interactions with normals. But, if they succeed, they may be rewarded with kindness and may be able to report that "my neighbors love me."

Furthermore, women in this group are quick to profess their great love for children and to shower their neighbors' children with affection. These expressions of tenderness, along with an enthusiastic willingness to care for neighbors' children, are mechanisms by which infertile women prove their innocence regarding the evil eye and allow community mothers to feel at ease with them. Such infertile women are often proud that neighbors' children love them and spend more time with them than with their own mothers. Furthermore, by serving as successful caretakers of children, these women are able to convince their neighbors that their eyes were "full" (i.e., not evil).

Infertile women of this persuasion also tend to participate wholeheartedly in the many Egyptian rituals involving women and children (e.g., wedding festivities, birth ceremonies, circumcisions, baptisms). Furthermore, they are not reluctant to admire children—although those among them who believe in the evil eye tend to say one of the formulaic religious phrases containing the name of God or the Prophet Muhammad or both as a preventive measure against their own envy.[9]

Thus, some infertile women are determined to gain acceptance in their communities—thereby overcoming to some degree their social stigmatization—by ingratiating themselves among their "normal" neighbors. When their efforts to ease social tension are successful, they are often rewarded through acceptance and are allowed to pass for normal in the fertile community. Although their neighbors often continue to pity them, these infertile women are willing to accept this sentiment in order to experience relatively normal lives within their urban communities.

However, most infertile women choose a markedly different stigma management strategy, characterized by self-isolation from the community of "normal" women and resistance to its tyranny. Infertile women of this persuasion tend to view their fertile neighbors not as friends but as enemies, who can only hurt them if they attempt to gain social acceptance. In many cases, this mistrust of "normals" is based on painful experiences with neighbors, who may have asked too many questions and then failed to keep social information confidential, insulted them, avoided them, or accused them of giving the evil eye to their children. Such experiences, which are often compounded by stigmatization within the husband's extended family, make these infertile women extremely reluctant to mingle with "normals." As a result, they choose to resist unnecessary interaction— both as a matter of pride and as an active defensive strategy. Many of these women report—sometimes defiantly—that "I have no relationships with my neighbors."

Furthermore, just as fertile women fear infertile women as evil eye givers, infertile women in this group fear this fear—and avoid the accompanying avoidance. As they see it, if they mix with women and children and then some tragedy occurs involving one of these children, they will be blamed for the misfortune, and this is a risk that most of these women are simply unwilling to take. Thus, they tend to shy away from children as much as possible—and even avoid looking at children as they pass by—so as to achieve impunity in their communities. For these women, the various child-intensive ritual activities of their neighbors are particularly problematic, and they tend to avoid them at all costs, even when they are specifically invited to participate. In other words, infertile women of this persuasion become "situation-conscious" (Goffman 1963), or obligated to "protect" normals in various ways, in part by voluntarily withholding themselves from situations guaranteed to generate social tension.

One infertile woman put it this way: "If an infertile woman must be around a child, she says 'In the name of God' because she fears that if something happens to that child, she will be blamed. Because we women who have no children are sensitive in this respect, we don't go to [the homes of] women who have children. *We feel.*"

In summary, then, most poor urban infertile women attempt to manage their stigmatization in their communities by avoiding their potential stigmatizers and resisting their attempts to dehumanize them. This defensive strategy often means that relationships with neighbors are minimal or absent—a highly aberrant situation for women in poor, crowded, and communicatively interactive urban Egyptian neighborhoods.

Yet, these infertile women prefer lives of isolation, alienation, and even quiet desperation in their cramped apartments to lives of public exposure, social scrutiny, and potentially painful ostracism. Such ostracism bespeaks the power of infertility to shape Egyptian women's everyday lives. As we shall see in the final chapter, this ostracism also indexes the power of children—so desired by *all* Egyptians but *especially* by the infertile—to serve as the crucial agents of adult normalization.

6. Child Desire

Marry and multiply for I will make a display of you on the Day of Judgment.

— A saying of the Prophet Muhammad

Salma's Story

"The most important thing in my life is children. There is nothing else as important. There is nothing else. It is children. I don't want anything else at all."

These are the words of Salma, a poor Alexandrian woman whose ardent desires for a child have been thwarted by an infertility problem whose resolution may never come. Born into a large rural family consisting of four sons and two daughters, Salma always thought that someday she, too, would bear many children for her husband. But, so far, Salma's dream has not been realized, and she fears her husband may leave her for want of children in their lives.

Like so many of the other women whose stories have been told in the preceding chapters, Salma's troubles began in childhood, when her farmer father dropped dead one day, leaving a pregnant wife and five children, including the still suckling Salma. Salma's father's brothers wanted to take the children to raise them, just as they took Salma's father's land to raise his crops. But Salma's mother, Ratiba, could not bear parting with her children nor the children with her, so she fled with her young brood to Cairo, where she found a one-room apartment and a job in a soap factory. For several years, Ratiba worked in both the factory and as a seamstress in her home in order to put food on the table for her young children, and wealthier neighbors who knew of Ratiba's plight donated clothing and money for her children during the holiday feasts. Although Ratiba's behavior and her devotion to her children were beyond reproach, Ratiba's husband's brothers continued to disapprove of this arrangement and spoke badly of Ratiba for having resisted their demands. When the children were sent back to their natal village for brief visits, their uncles often attempted to coerce them into staying, telling them that their mother was a "bad woman." As Salma recalls, "Sometimes they wanted us to stay there, but we never accepted. We wanted our mother. I mean, we used to love her a lot. We didn't want to stay with anybody because we loved her so. She was affectionate and sweet, and she used to pray and she knew God very well."

Eventually, Ratiba consented to marrying her *ibn 'amm*, a paternal first cousin, who had been married four times previously but had been unable to produce his own offspring. Because he loved children so much, he proposed to his widowed cousin, vowing to raise her six children as his own. Indeed, he proved to be a loving and responsible stepfather, working as hard as Salma's own mother to "feed us and raise us so that nobody would lead us astray," according to Salma. However, because both Salma's mother and stepfather were "from the *fallāḥīn*," they did not believe in the importance of education. Neither Salma nor her five siblings were allowed by their parents to go to school, although many of the children in their lower-income Cairo neighborhood attended school until the sixth grade. For Salma, who was considerably younger than her only sister and consequently spent most of her days at home with no playmates, being able to go to school was a dream—one so important to her that she took her small savings to buy a notebook and a pencil, imagining that she was studying and writing like the pupils in the elementary school nearby. But, according to her parents' wishes, Salma never saw the inside of a classroom. As a result, she grew up illiterate, unable to sign even her own name. Salma laments:

> I don't know how to read and write Arabic. I wished I would have been educated, like any educated woman, because knowledge is nice. You can know everything in science. It was not my fate to be educated. My parents were poor, and we were many. And, when we were still in the village, my father wanted many children to work on the land. Because he used to say, "We are *fallāḥīn* to cultivate and harvest; *this* is our education." Because working on the land—cultivating and harvesting—provides the food and drink of the educated. It is not important to be educated. That's what he told us.

Although Salma never received any formal education, she was schooled in domesticity. Her mother and older sister taught Salma how to cook, which she enjoyed, and how to clean the house. They also prepared her for a proper life of female modesty and seclusion. Salma explains:

I was always at home—locked up. I never went out to play in the street. I was always, my childhood, I spent at home. And my friends used to come and stay with me a little while at home and then they would tell me, "Come play outside." And I told them, "No, my mother would beat me." She always told us, "Never go outside. Never play with boys. Never speak to a boy. It is a shame to speak to a boy, because you are a girl." So I grew up fearing boys . . . I was *very* scared. I was always staying at home. Up until now, I'm staying at home. I don't like going outside.

One day after Salma's older sister was married and her older brothers were in their teens, Salma's mother came home from work, ate lunch with her children, gave them some pocket money, went to sleep, and died. Because Salma's stepfather had also died two years earlier, the children were split up and sent to their relatives to be raised. Salma ended up at her paternal aunt's, whose husband owned a small cafe in Cairo. Occasionally, Salma would cook at the cafe, although her older brothers disapproved of her working, even in a family business. But it was through work that Salma came to know Sadiq, an employee at the cafe who was to become her future husband.

In his late thirties at the time, Sadiq was nearly twenty years Salma's senior, and because of his tendency to get into fights, he had never stayed at one job for very long. But because Salma and her family found Sadiq to be basically good-natured and kind, they consented to the engagement, which lasted for three months. Sadiq had never saved enough money for a proper bridewealth or an apartment of his own, but, with help from Salma's family, he bought Salma an attractive *shabka*, consisting of a chain, a ring, and two wedding bands, one for him and one for her. Salma's family threw a small engagement party just for relatives in Cairo, and three months later, Sadiq's family in Alexandria hosted a small wedding party. Although Sadiq and Salma planned to move to Alexandria, the wedding night itself was spent in Cairo, in order for Salma's family members to "see her blood" (i.e., the bloodied defloration handkerchief).

Because Sadiq was unable to afford a separate apartment, he brought his new bride back to live in the small, one-room, government apartment rented by his elderly father, who planned to live with his son and daughter-in-law. Fortunately for the newlyweds, Sadiq's father, who was paralyzed and remained outstretched on a small sofa, was also stone deaf. But he was not blind, and thus the young couple were forced to sleep behind an opaque curtain that Sadiq fashioned over the canopy bed. As Salma explains:

It was against my will that he was staying with me. I couldn't wear my night-gowns in front of him. I was shy, because he was an old man. When he slept, I ran and bathed and prayed in this room and dressed normally. . . . He stayed here a long time [eight years] until he died a year and a half ago. When he died, he died here on my shoulder. He slept on my shoulder and he died. It was from God. I loved him a lot. He was old and he used to bother me, but I loved him. Why? Because my husband always told me, "It's *ḥarām* [sinful] not to take care of him. He is miserable, and he loves you. So don't upset him. Take care of him." So I took care of him all the time until he died. Do you be-lieve he used to fill the house for me when he was alive? He filled all my free time; I saved it for him. Now the room is empty. I imagine that the room is empty, and I imagine that it's a sea where I can't find anyone. Really! He was an old man, but I loved him. He filled all my time—bathing him, combing his hair, changing his clothes. So I had no time left at all.

In effect, Salma's aged father-in-law was like her only child, for she and Sadiq had never been able to have children of their own. Because Sadiq made it clear to Salma within weeks of their marriage that he ardently de-sired a child by his beautiful, dimple-cheeked wife, Salma began "searching for children" within six months of their wedding. Salma laments:

I went to doctors, and each one said something different. They never said the same thing. One said, "There is nothing wrong." The other said, "You need an operation." The other said, "Take this medication." And I used to repeat it for six or seven months and when I found no use, I went to another doctor. And everything was expensive. Medications are expensive. And from here to there, I spent all my money. I sold all my gold. There's no use. I thought when I went to doctors, I thought they had a solution for my problem. But they didn't say correctly, not one correct word. They don't say exactly what's wrong with you. Nothing. All they do is write a treatment and that's it. And I swallow the treatment and bring another, but they don't say if I have or don't have [a prob-lem], or if I'll get children or not. They don't say any of this. They're all alike.

Eventually, Salma found a physician who would make a tentative diag-nosis. She told him about all of her treatments, and without examining her, he said, "Since you did all this and no pregnancy, you took all these treatments and no pregnancy, then your tubes must be blocked." Although Salma was extremely upset, barely holding back her tears, she agreed with the doctor to undergo a diagnostic laparoscopy at the University of Alex-andria's Shatby Hospital. The laparoscopy showed that both of Salma's fallopian tubes were indeed blocked and that she needed an operation to open them. When Salma returned home, she was extremely upset, and she told Sadiq, "That's it. I'm not going to any more doctors. If you want to get remarried, get married, but divorce me. I don't want a partner [co-wife]." She adds, "My psychological state was very bad. I was quite fed up, and I felt like one who would like to throw oneself into the sea. By God!"

Although Sadiq, too, was extremely demoralized by this bad news, he felt sorry for Salma and believed that she might be cured if she could only undergo tubal surgery. But, because he had no money to pay for such an operation, Sadiq took out a small ad in the newspaper, seeking any physician who would undertake Salma's operation for free. He also sent the letter with a copy of the diagnostic laparoscopy report to the dean of the faculty of medicine. Although the advertisement received no response, the dean of the medical school did reply to Sadiq and referred Salma back to Shatby Hospital to be treated as a charity case.

Since that day, Salma has been a regular patient at Shatby Hospital, where she has undergone an extensive series of ultrasounds. She is not certain whether she will eventually undergo surgery, artificial insemination, or in vitro fertilization, since the doctors there have told her nothing about her case. However, she was heartened to know that the doctor found "three eggs" on a recent ultrasound, which he told her was a good sign (even though Salma was shocked to learn that women produce eggs like a chicken!).

If Salma is unable to become pregnant following treatment at Shatby, she fears that Sadiq will remarry for children. She knows that he desperately wants children, even without saying so. And sometimes he is open about it, telling her, "If you don't have a child, I'll go get married." At first, this statement would send Salma into a frenzy, and she would sleep at a relative's house for several days until Sadiq or one of his family members would come to retrieve her. But on one such occasion, an elderly female relative of Sadiq's began encouraging him to remarry. When Salma learned of this from his immediate family members, she decided not to leave the house ever again.

Frankly, Salma believes that the only reasons Sadiq has not yet replaced her with another woman are his deep love and sympathy for her, his appreciation of the kind way she cared for his father, and his still heartfelt hope that Salma may be cured of her blocked tubes and bear him a child in the near future. "Yes, he loves me, and I love him, but there must be a child to have love," Salma says. "It's a must. And also, love is more when there is a child. Love is more than when you don't have children. You find affection in the house a lot, and the voice of children is nice."

Salma has numerous other reasons for wanting and needing children. For one, since the death of her father-in-law, she is extremely lonely, spending most of her days and nights by herself in the small, one-room apartment. In order to support Salma's infertility therapy, Sadiq, a ship mechanic, travels on the Mediterranean three out of every four weeks, leaving Salma under the protection of their large German shepherd named "Rambo." For Salma, who does not work and who mingles little with her neighbors, the isolation and loneliness are nearly unbearable. She laments:

> My feelings are that I wish to have a baby to talk to and he talks to me and to entertain each other and to fill this emptiness, because I have a lot of free time and I don't work. I am staying at home. The one who has children, they fill all of her time, not like the one who doesn't have children. I'm free all of the time. I sleep alone. I wish that there was someone beside me. I don't have a mother or a father, not even a sister beside me. Whenever I sleep and I'm so lonely in bed, I feel sorry for myself. [She started crying.] I *wish* I had a daughter to be my mother, my sister, my friend. I wish to have a child, I mean, to fill my life.

In addition, Salma believes that only by having children can a couple create a "family." "The family is basically the children," she explains. "I mean, what basically makes the family is the child, not just a mother and a father only. No, there must be a child, even to have a mother and a father. In Egypt and in *all* countries, there must be a family—a father and a mother and a child. No two people would be living together like this. This is the problem that I have."

Indeed, Salma believes that all infertile couples have problems and that only by having children are these problems resolved. "Here, they look for children more than they look for money, those who don't have [children]. And those who have [children], they exert themselves to be able to raise their children and educate them and this. Because they love children very much—very much. It's not important to have money, but it's important to have children. *This* is the decoration of life on earth. There are people who live happily without children, but very rarely. Maybe they are one percent. But one hundred percent want children."

Perhaps most important, Salma wants to feel the love of motherhood, which she believes is a natural instinct requiring fulfillment. She says:

> If I had children, I would love my children more than anyone else. I would love my child more than his father and more than my siblings, too. When you have a child, you will love it more than both because of motherhood. Because

your heart saw this child before your eye did. I mean, one's heart has seen the child before one's eye has seen it. See how much love there is then? Nine months you're waiting for it; you want to see if it's a boy or a girl, beautiful or ugly. Isn't that right? And after you deliver it, you find yourself wishing to see it older—a man. And if it's a girl, you want to see her a bride. You would enjoy her. If I had a child, I don't want anything else. Just one baby, and I don't want anything from this whole world. Greedy, no! I can't get one nor two. So when it's one, that's enough. I'm satisfied.

Like so many infertile women, Salma has contemplated fostering a child from an orphanage or from within her family, but has decided that this would be bad for the child, even if she and Sadiq proved to be good foster parents. She explains:

For one to adopt a child, it won't work. I mean, in our neighborhood, this is considered to be a *baladi* [low-income and "traditional"] area, it doesn't work here, because it will be known. When he grows up, they will tell him that "You are from the orphanage," and they will cause him to have a psychological complex. So I don't want this for the preservation of the child's psychology, because when he becomes a young man he will get hurt. And if I take from my siblings, from my nieces or nephews, when I raise it and it grows up, it will know its mother and father and go to them. Then I would have raised it for nothing. And if I get it from the orphanage, they will tell it. This makes it unfair. I am destroying him, not bringing him up. . . . It's as if someone has built a big, big building and all in one second a bomb falls on it and razes it. He would be finished this way. And I don't want to do this.

Thus, for Salma, all of her hopes for a child rest in God, who, after all, is the one who "makes everything." As Salma concludes, "I mean, it's God, who if he wants to give children to someone he gives them girls or if he wants to give them boys he gives them boys, and those whom he doesn't want to give, he doesn't give."

As of now, God's choice for Salma remains unclear. But she prays to him each and every day that he will see fit—sometime very soon—to make her a mother.

Infertility, Population Growth, and Egyptian Pronatalism

As apparent in their stories, poor infertile Egyptian women such as Salma, Maisa, Nafisa, Aida, and Fayza face a devastating problem, for they typically carry the triple burden of blame and negative evaluation for the failure to conceive, the social consequences contingent upon that blame, and the responsibility of overcoming the reproductive failing through an often un-fruitful therapeutic quest. Furthermore, many infertile Egyptian women face triple stigmatization: for being women in a patriarchal society that legitimizes male power, authority, and ideological superiority on multiple levels; for being poor women in a society that is markedly class stratified; and for being infertile women in a society that places motherhood above all other female role expectations and identities.

Moreover, as seen in the preceding chapters, infertility itself sets in motion a political drama—political in that it involves the use and abuse of social power and influence in the most intimate domains of everyday life, and a drama in that it involves the staging and management of in-fertility "crises" by contesting parties vying for control over marital and reproductive outcomes. Indeed, to use a masculinist metaphor, the social crisis of infertility in Egypt involves a multipartied "gender war," in which the "battle" is not necessarily between the sexes. Rather, in wittingly or unwittingly upholding a deeply entrenched patriarchal system, Egyptian husbands are sometimes pitted against their wives, wives are often pitted against husbands' female relatives, husbands' female relatives are at times pitted against wives' female relatives, and fertile women are typically pitted against infertile female neighbors. Placed in the center of such social re-lational struggles, infertile women find themselves coping with marital duress, including the ever present threat of polygynous remarriage or pro-nouncements of divorce on the part of their husbands; cruel harassment by husbands' extended family members, who remind them of their failure to provide their husbands and husbands' families with offspring; and overt and covert ostracism within the community by neighbors who fear infertile women as a source of danger. Engaged in tumult not of their own making, many infertile women such as Salma attempt to bring peace to their mar-riages, to their familial and community relations, and to their own lives by embarking upon therapeutic quests, or "searches for children," as they themselves call these quests, which are consuming of their limited finan-cial, physical, and emotional resources (Inhorn 1994). For many of these women, as well as for those intimates who attempt to assume power and authority over their lives, motherhood is viewed as the only acceptable life option—one that becomes an engulfing pursuit for those who are unable to achieve it.

But some crucial questions, only partially foregrounded in the preceding chapters, remain. First, why is having children so very important to Egyptians, and to poor urban Egyptians in particular? And why are infertile women such as Salma and the others whose voices have been heard throughout this book seen as "missing" motherhood and children in their lives? To answer these questions is, to a large extent, to answer the key question that continues to baffle population policymakers: namely, why do Egyptians continue to "overpopulate" their country, despite decades of active effort by the Egyptian and other interested governments (primarily that of the United States) to enforce population control and family planning measures? To a great extent, in Egypt, the forces fueling the stigmatization of infertility and those fueling population growth are one and the same, because both are intimately tied to the overarching issue of Egyptian pronatalism, or the intense ideological emphasis in Egypt on the desirability of having children.

Surprisingly perhaps, in the now voluminous literature on Egyptian population issues, Egyptian pronatalism—or the *why* of wanting children rather than the fact of having children—has received relatively scant attention. Instead, there has been an obsessive and rather narrow demographic focus among scholars and population policymakers on Egyptian population growth, as well as the best means of reducing that growth. This limited focus on the population growth/reduction equation is problematic on a number of grounds.

First, ever since the early 1960s, when Egypt became the first Middle Eastern Muslim country to initiate a state-sponsored, U.S.-backed, population-control program (Stycos et al. 1988), the population discussion in Egypt has preceded almost entirely from the questionable assumption that Egypt has a population "problem," which largely accounts for its stalled economic development. The primary trope around which such discussion continues to revolve is one of "geography versus demography": namely, that a rapidly growing population, which has more than doubled since 1947, is outstripping Egypt's habitable (and usable) land, an area constituting only 4 percent of the country's total, mostly arid land mass. As noted by political scientist Tim Mitchell (1991:18), the popularity of this image of "space and numbers" is summed up in one World Bank report as follows: "These two themes—the relatively fixed amount of usable land and the rapid growth of the population—will be seen as leitmotivs in the discussion of Egypt's economic problems."

However, as argued by Mitchell (1991) in his penetrating critique of the Western "development" of Egypt, there is no prima facie evidence

Photograph 15. Children in a poor urban neighborhood. (Photograph by Mia Fuller)

for the assumption that Egypt's population is somehow too large for its cultivable area. Rather, using development industry sources themselves, Mitchell precisely documents how Egypt's massive dependence on grain imports since 1974 owes not to its excessive population growth, but rather to a Western-development-industry-supported shift to heavy meat consumption among Egypt's urban middle and upper classes. Not only does Egypt now grow more food for animals than for humans, but since 1974 it has imported ever-increasing amounts of grain, including American feed grains, to support a growing livestock industry. In short, if "overpopulation" is Egypt's problem, one must question whether the "over" prefix refers to animals or human beings. Mitchell, for one, concludes: "The image of a vast, overbreeding population packed within a limited agricultural area is therefore quite misleading. Egypt's food problem is the result not of too many people occupying too little land, but of the power of a certain part of that population, supported by the prevailing domestic and international regime, to shift the country's resources from staple foods to more expensive items of consumption" (Mitchell 1991: 22).

Second, because the largely Western-generated discourse on Egypt's purported overpopulation problem has penetrated all levels of population scholarship and policymaking, reducing population growth has become the raison d'être of the population establishment (much of it Western) in the country. This has meant that population growth has been closely monitored, demographically surveyed, statistically calculated, projected well into the future millennium, and hotly debated as a worrisome political, economic, and even religious issue. Since the 1960s, population scholars have kept careful track of population growth rates of all kinds, as well as those other rates, such as birth, death, life expectancy, infant mortality, total fertility, and contraceptive usage, that enter into the population growth calculus. Thus, detailed, up-to-date, demographic statistics are available on Egypt's population size (estimated at 58.3 million as of mid-1993); its annual growth rate (2.3 percent as of 1993); its population doubling time at the current rate of growth (30 years); its population size projected to the year 2010 (82.5 million); and its population size projected to the year 2025 (104.6 million) (Population Reference Bureau 1993). Furthermore, it is known that Egypt's total fertility rate, or the number of children a woman can be expected to bear at the current rate, is 4.2 (as of 1993), and that less than half (44 percent) of married Egyptian women use "modern" contraception.

Along with these measures, a burgeoning literature on what might be called the normative and behavioral aspects of Egyptian population growth and reduction has developed. This literature includes numerous studies of attitudes toward and usage of contraception among Egyptian women (e.g., DeClerque et al. 1986; Fox 1988; Gadalla, Nosseir, and Gillespie 1980); surveys of desired family size among Egyptian households (e.g., Cochrane, Khan, and Osheba 1990; Gadalla 1978; Gadalla, McCarthy, and Campbell 1985; Stokes, Schutjer, and Poindexter 1983); and analyses of changing Egyptian population reduction policies, including their successes and failures (e.g., Gadalla and Rizk 1988; Stycos et al. 1988).

But this almost exclusive focus on population growth/reduction has meant that other important issues are missing from Egyptian population discourse. Most important here, Egyptian infertility—also a population and certainly a family planning issue (Inhorn 1994)—has been either ignored or trivialized as insignificant in light of the purported problem of Egyptians' apparent "hyperfertility." To wit, whereas every conceivable measure of Egyptian fertility and population growth has been calculated, accurate statistics on rates of infertility in the country are unavailable (Inhorn 1994). Externally generated estimates of Egypt's primary infertility rate have put the figure at about 8 percent of all married couples (Farley and Belsey 1988). However, Egyptian infertility investigators suspect that this figure is an underestimate, judging from the relatively high levels of infertility, especially from infection-scarred fallopian tubes, among Egyptian women in various clinical-epidemiological studies (Abdullah, Zarzoor, and Ali 1982; Serour, El Ghar, and Mansour 1991), as well as the exceptionally high rates of infertility among Egypt's southern neighbors (including Sudan), countries that comprise the so-called infertility belt of sub-Saharan Central Africa (Inhorn 1994).

Furthermore, in accepting the notion that Egyptians are "hyperfertile" and in need of reproductive regulation, population scholars and policymakers in Egypt have largely disregarded infertility as a significant social problem—one engendering the kinds of human suffering described in the chapters of this book and elsewhere (Inhorn 1994). Additionally, they have overlooked all that the study of infertility can reveal about fertility trends and reproductive desires. Namely, fertility and infertility exist in a dialectical relationship of contrast, such that understanding one leads to a much greater understanding of the other (Inhorn 1994). Infertility, in particular, provides a convenient lens through which fertility-related beliefs and behaviors can be explored. These include, among other things, ideas about conception and how it is prevented both intentionally and unintentionally; understandings of, attitudes toward, and practices of contraception; and beliefs about the importance of motherhood, fatherhood, and children themselves.

Indeed, it is from the study of infertility that issues of pronatalism, or child desire, are perhaps best understood. Namely, those who are missing children and who therefore have had much cause to reflect on their object of desire are often in the best position to articulate why children are so very important on a number of levels, ranging from the personal to the political. Yet, no studies in Egypt have ever attempted to survey infertile men and women about such matters. Nor have *fertile* Egyptians' beliefs about the importance of children been adequately assessed. Saad Gadalla's 1978 book, *Is There Hope? Fertility and Family Planning in a Rural Egyptian Community*, goes the farthest of any study to explore why (very fertile) Egyptians in one rural community desire children. In this book, Gadalla and his co-investigators rely in part on in-depth interviews conducted with a representative sample of both Egyptian husbands and wives "to reveal the prevailing reproductive norms and to gain insight into their influence on family size and fertility behavior" (Gadalla 1977:325). However, the book is fundamentally a demographic treatise, and hence it relies heavily on a large-scale "Knowledge, Attitudes, and Practice" (KAP) survey to get at rural Egyptians' reproductive motivations and desires. Gadalla acknowledges the limitations of this type of large-scale survey investigation, stating that "cultural norms about reproduction are not synonymous with, or cannot be measured by, a mere expression of desires or ideals in response to oversimplified questions" (Gadalla 1978:4). He argues instead that "it is also essential for an adequate understanding of these reproductive prescriptions to explain the social, economic, and psychological forces which support their existence, the situations under which they operate, and the cultural rewards and punishments which urge people to conform" (Gadalla 1977:325).

In effect, Gadalla asks Egyptian population investigators to move beyond facile demographic methodologies and explanations to get at the psychological, sociocultural, and (political-)economic forces that underpin people's reproductive desires and behaviors. Yet, nearly two decades later, little sophisticated, nuanced work on the complex human motivations for having children has been carried out in Egypt, including among anthropologists interested in human reproduction or women's lives.

When pronatalism is indexed (usually in passing) in the Egyptian population literature, two simplistic arguments for why Egyptians want children are generally forwarded. One falls under the demographic-economistic rubric of "wealth flows." The other has to do with Islam and what Carla Makhlouf Obermeyer (1992) has called the "fateful triangle" model attributing a pernicious association among Islam, women, and demographic outcomes.

With regard to the former, much demographic analysis of why people around the world want children focuses on the direction of wealth flows between generations (Caldwell 1982). From this perspective, having children is viewed as a rational, economic decision by parents, who weigh the cost of having children against future economic returns. Although having children may be initially costly, these same children will eventually contribute economically to the household and, in many societies, can be expected to provide economic security for parents in their old age.

In the case of Egypt, the wealth flows model is typically invoked as the primary "explanation" for Egyptian pronatalism. Namely, it is argued that Egyptian parents desire children, usually many of them, as labor power—first, to help them in agricultural production and, second, to take care of them in their old age, given that Egypt lacks both institutionalized social security and elder care. Although this appears to be a reasonable explanation of Egyptian pronatalism, especially in rural areas, it is clearly insufficient. In urban centers such as Cairo and Alexandria, where nearly half the Egyptian population now resides, the vast majority of households are landless, and household heads, often working in menial factory or informal-sector jobs, must support their dependent children until late adolescence or even marriage. In urban households at least, children are often viewed by parents as economic liabilities rather than as assets, and having a small family, ideally two or three children at the most, is considered by many urbanites to be the only sensible option. Although parents hope that their children will support them in old age, many parents now lament the fact that their adult children, and especially their sons, can no longer be counted on to "repay" them in this way. Thus, at least in urban areas, the wealth flows model—in which the flow of wealth from parents to children and vice versa is supposedly rationally determined by parents as working in their favor—is not particularly persuasive as a primary explanatory model for pronatalism.

The second most popular and more "cultural" explanation of pronatalism in Egypt (as well as the rest of the Middle East) focuses on the role of Islam in promoting child desire, and especially strikingly high fertility among women. In this "fateful triangle" model, it is argued that Islam, as a particularly patriarchal and pronatalist religion, supports conditions conducive to high fertility in Egypt and other parts of the Middle East by subordinating women in the realms of education, employment, and legal rights. Thus, by virtue of their low status and restricted access to other means of fulfillment, women want motherhood and many children by default. Furthermore, given Islam's purportedly unique "fatalism," it is argued that Egyptians, as well as other Middle Eastern Muslims, believe that the decision to have children is ultimately beyond their control; hence, they ignorantly accept "God's will" by having additional children year after year.

However, as both Obermeyer (1992) and Gadalla (1978) argue, relying on Islam as a sufficient model to "explain" Middle Eastern pronatalism and demographic outcomes is clearly inadequate. First, it is possible to disprove demographically that adherence to Islam's pronatalist religious doctrine leads to equally high fertility levels throughout the Middle Eastern region, or even within a single Middle Eastern country such as

Egypt (where, for example, urban and rural fertility levels vary quite significantly). Second, the "fateful triangle" model ignores the great diversity of Islam, including within the Middle East, as well as the significant diversity in Middle Eastern women's status. Third, this model is inattentive to the contradiction between norms, including religious ones, and people's behavior, as well as to the ambiguities inherent within the normative structure of any society (Obermeyer 1992). Perhaps most important, however, this "fateful triangle" model falls back on Orientalist stereotypes about Islam as a religion that is uniquely patriarchal, militantly pronatalist, and absolutely determinative of the daily lives of followers, particularly women.

As already suggested in Chapter 1 of this book, Islam may play an important role in Egyptian women's lives, but it is certainly not the only determinant, nor is it somehow uniquely patriarchal in its religious doctrine. Islam *does* valorize motherhood and children, as we shall see in this chapter, but it *does not* offer rigid prescriptions to women on how many children they must bear or what kind of mothers they must be. Only with the recent advent of politicized Islam in Egypt have women been told to abandon contraception and return to exclusive mothering. Indeed, the Islamist call for a return to higher fertility levels has caught Egyptian women in a bind. Namely, Egyptian women have been exhorted by the Egyptian state over the past three decades to limit their fertility. They—and not men—have been the "targets" of population control and family planning programs, programs that have worked diligently to convince them of the religious permissibility of birth control. Yet, it can be argued that population control and family planning programs directed almost exclusively at Egyptian women have served to undermine their motherhood roles, while paying little if any attention to the reality of Egyptian women's daily lives, their felt needs for motherhood, or their desires for children. It is this undermining of motherhood that Islamists in Egypt have caught wind of and have placed squarely on their political agenda. By revalorizing motherhood and continuous childbearing, Islamists claim to be giving women their rightful due as the very foundation of the Muslim family, which the Egyptian state is accused of sabotaging.

However, neither Islamists in Egypt nor the Egyptian state nor population policymakers for that matter can claim particular knowledge of or sensitivity to what Egyptian women want for themselves. Because the state, Islamists, and population policymakers proceed from their own political agendas, they attempt to convince women of the advisability of their programs, often without considering women's own knowledge and opinions. Hence, such programs as state-sponsored population control in Egypt, which "target" women, have literally operated in the dark with regard to the *real* knowledge, attitudes, and practices of their female constituencies. Given this inattention to women's lives and desires (let alone the almost complete neglect of men in population discourse), it should come as no surprise that Egypt's population control efforts have been judged to be weak and ineffective in several international assessments (Stycos et al. 1988). In other words, until the desires for children are understood among "target" populations of Egyptian women *and* men, programs that attempt to change Egyptians' fertility behavior are unlikely to be successful.

Virtually all Egyptian women—urban or rural, rich or poor, educated or illiterate—want children, for reasons that have remained obscure until now. Women such as Salma speak of their ardent desires for children, desires that they see almost all Egyptian women, and most Egyptian men, as sharing. Furthermore, Egyptian women see themselves and their fellow citizens as much more pronatalist than people in other countries.

As one woman put it: "Here in Egypt, we Orientals like to be surrounded by children. Here, even educated people have four or five, because we *love* kids. From what I see, children are not that important in other places and the percentage of children is less than in Egypt. We love children more and like to have more children than any other country."

This desire among Egyptians for children—and the attendant disappointments and difficulties posed by infertility—must be viewed from three interrelated levels of analysis: the individual psychosocial, the social structural, and the political-economic. From the perspective of individuals, the psychological motivations to conceive and then parent children to adulthood require exploration in order to understand why infertility is associated with personal failure and existential crisis. From the perspective of the social group, the benefits of bringing children into society and the effects that children have on social relations must be analyzed in order to understand why infertility is such a grave social onus, one that poses a threat to social reproduction. Finally, the benefits to Egypt's predominantly Muslim body politic of having children are extremely important in any contemporary analysis of pronatalism, because of the ways in which Islamism serves as a countervailing force to Egyptian state efforts to reduce population growth. An exploration of pronatalism and the consequent stigmatization of infertility from these three levels of analysis—particularly as they apply to the urban Egyptian poor—is the goal of this concluding chapter.

Child Desire from a Psychosocial Perspective

To understand why infertile Egyptian women are stigmatized for "missing motherhood" in their lives, it is crucial to understand what children mean to individual members, both male and female, of Egyptian society. To understand this is to understand in large part what it means to be an adult—and, on an even more basic level, a person—in Egypt.

As emphasized by Rugh in *Family in Contemporary Egypt* (1984), the Western, Enlightenment-inspired ideal of "individualism" is virtually lacking in Egypt, where "doing one's own thing" is not only devalued but actively discouraged. Individual actions are usually taken in consideration of how these actions will affect other members of the group—the most important social group being the family. Families in contemporary Egypt can be viewed as patriarchal connective systems (Joseph 1993; 1994), in which individual members are deeply enmeshed in familial relational matrices that serve to shape individuals' deepest senses of self.

However, even though the relationship between individual and familial identity is extremely important in Egypt, it would be a mistake to assume that individual Egyptians' egos merge entirely with those of other family members. Egyptian men and women, like men and women everywhere, have personal hopes and dreams and desires—that is, personal ego-gratification needs—that are quite separate from those of other individuals. What part the desire for children plays on this level of individual psychodynamic fulfillment—and how the inability to produce children affects individuals' self-definition—is extremely important and is the first issue to be analyzed here.

Personal desires for children among poor urban Egyptian adults, both men and women, comprise three major categories, which, for heuristic purposes, can be called: (1) *normalcy desires*, or the equation of normal adult personhood with marriage and parenting; (2) *immortality desires*, or the conviction that personal perpetuity can be achieved through children, who serve as extensions of self; and (3) *quality of life desires*, or the existential equation of happiness and life-meaning with having children.

NORMALCY DESIRES

In terms of normalcy desires, it is important first to reiterate that marriage is a near-universal phenomenon for adult Egyptians, with virtually every physically and financially able person achieving married status at some point in life. The universality of marriage is no accident. The Islam-inspired inculcation of the desirability of marriage among individual members of Egyptian society is so effective that adult personhood is currently defined in Egypt by the achievement of the dual, inextricably linked statuses of being married and being a parent. The equation of the married parent status with adulthood is demonstrated in numerous ways: for example, by the fact that a grown woman is called a *bint*, or girl, unless she marries and thereby becomes a *sitt*, or woman; the fact that every effort is made by families to normalize their adult children by marrying them off; the fact that young men devote extraordinary efforts to accruing bridewealth payments in order to marry; and the fact that, once married, conception desires on the part of the husband and wife and their families are immediate and are the source of significant problems if unfulfilled due to infertility. In fact, in Egypt, full adulthood for both men and women cannot be truly achieved until parenthood is achieved. Norms of being in Egypt dictate the rite of passage to parenthood, and those whose reproductive passage is literally and figuratively "blocked" by infertility are barred from becoming normal adults, according to widely accepted normative standards. Put another way, in Egypt, being married is not enough; being a normal adult also requires having children.

Becoming a normal adult through the achievement of married-parent status is a cultural imperative that most Egyptians do not question. So deeply engrained is the ideology of married parenthood that Egyptian men and women only face the degree of its cultural embeddedness when, by virtue of their own reproductive pathology, they are made socially pathological in their inability to achieve reproductive normalcy. When this happens, infertile individuals—as well as all of those around them—acknowledge the threat of permanent social marginality and ostracism. This threat, which, among women, includes evil eye suspicions, is one of the most terrifying prospects ever to face individuals in a society emphasizing group conformity. The terror of permanent marginality receives expression in the oft-cited comparisons made by infertile individuals between "infertile self" and "fertile others." Standing outside the "fertile crowd" is an unenviable position—one that Egyptian men and women do not wish upon themselves. For, to stand outside the crowd is to feel and to be acknowledged as "less than" others—and not only less than, but "not quite as human as" and even "dangerous" to others. In other words, having children is part and parcel of the overall desire to achieve normal adult *personhood* in a society that defines personhood in this way. Naturally, then, becoming a "complete" person by becoming a parent is a major motivation for having children and is one of the most basic reasons for the severe stigmatization of those who fail to pass reproductive muster. As the demographer John Weeks notes in his discussion of Muslim pronatalism in Egypt and elsewhere:

> Underlying all of these reasons [to have children] is perhaps the most important motivation of all—the desire for social approval. When a community believes that parenthood is important, it rewards parents with its most precious commodity—the approval of others. Equally important is the threat of rejection if we fail to meet society's expectations. To ensure that a sufficient number of children is born, virtually every human group has institutionalized pronatalist pressures—pressures to marry and procreate—which tend to be pervasive, subtle, and usually taken for granted, so much so that the decision to bear children is often misconstrued as "voluntary." Nothing could be further from reality. We are socialized from birth to learn the rules of childbearing and believe that they are right, and this is reinforced by everyday life that puts us in contact with the norm-enforcement process, since other people have a keen interest in how we behave. (Weeks 1988:18)

In Egypt, this pressure to achieve parenthood goes beyond issues of achieving community acceptance as a normal adult individual. Additionally, it involves the achievement of normal sexual and gender identity. Having children stands as proof of that which makes men men and women women. For women, bearing children represents the most important confirmation of a woman's femaleness—of having reproductive parts and processes that allow her to gestate a fetus and give birth to this child. Women who, by virtue of their infertility, are unable to become pregnant are often called "males" to signify their questionable sexual identity. Furthermore, only by becoming a mother can a woman prove her gender identity *as a woman*. In Egypt, motherhood is seen as "completing" a woman, for only through motherhood can a woman express her natural maternal instinct. Thus, women who are "deprived" of their own children are seen as "incomplete," as "less than" other women, for they are unable to experience those maternal feelings that make other women whole and normal.

For men, these sexual and gender identity issues are equally, if not more, important. As with women, proof of a man's sexual identity, or maleness, hinges upon the demonstration of his ability to impregnate his

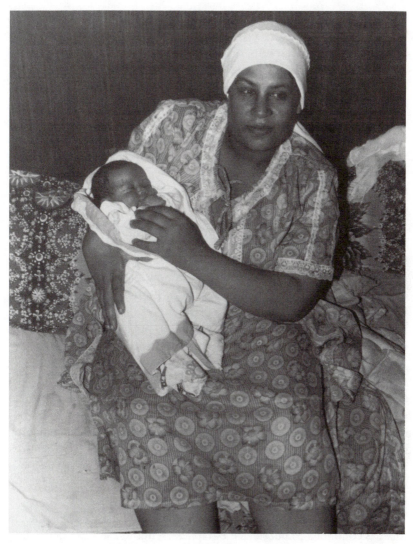

Photograph 16. A mother and her newborn child. (Photograph by Marcia Inhorn)

wife. Men whose wives remain barren are suspected of being impotent—of being "no good for women"—by virtue of unmanly sexual organs that fail to function properly. But the ability to impregnate bespeaks more than male virility. As described in Chapter 1, at the core of Egypt's patriarchal value system is the widespread belief among the Egyptian masses in monogenesis, or male procreativity. Men—not women—are thought to be the procreative partners, producing fetuses through the process of spermatogenesis. If men's sperm, or "worms," "carry the kids," as Egyptians are apt to put it, then women's wombs are viewed as mere receptacles, or vessels, for men's omnipotent substantive input. This belief in the virile, life-giving force of men is absolutely crucial in understanding Egyptian *men's* pronatalist tendencies. Indeed, it is a large part of the reason why Egyptian men, consciously or unconsciously, want children, whom they see as being "part of them," "belonging to them"; why they obtain ego gratification from producing many children, and especially sons; why they sometimes discourage or even prevent their wives from using birth control and in other ways pressure their wives to bear children for them (Inhorn 1996); and why they may willingly cast off wives who are not up to the task of childbearing and who thereby thwart the demonstration of their most essential, superior power. That is, if men prove their masculine procreativity through reproductive feats of multiple impregnations—thus eliminating any doubt of their power to bring life into this world—then infertility (male or female) looms as a dangerous challenge to this exclusive, masculine domain of procreativity, which Egyptian men throughout the centuries have ideologically appropriated for themselves (Inhorn 1994).

Because of this powerful patriarchal ideology, which is still alive and well among the Egyptian masses, Egyptian women face extreme pressure to facilitate the masculine procreative act by nurturing—in utero and beyond—the children that men bring into this world. This is perhaps one of the key reasons why motherhood alone receives undisputed ideological and practical elevation in Egypt and why alternative roles and identities for the vast majority of Egyptian women, particularly those of the lower classes who subscribe to this monogenetic belief system, are extremely limited.

This lack of female role proliferation in Egypt is a phenomenon that has continued to puzzle demographers, feminist theorists, and others interested in improving women's status in the country. All of them have pointed to the continuing lack of participation of most Egyptian women in the educational system, in nonagricultural economic activities outside the home, and in politics and other forms of social activism. As noted by Audrey Chapman Smock and Nadia Haggag Youssef in a review of the status of Egyptian women in the late 1970s:

> It has been shown that the position of the Egyptian woman is not exactly a favorable one. Cultural strictures requiring the seclusion of women continue

to limit a woman's role options primarily to being a wife and mother. Adult Egyptian women have very low rates of participation in school attendance, employment, and political activism. Even when compared with the figures for other Arab states, the percentage of adult Egyptian females who are literate and the female proportion of the total nonagricultural, economically active population are not encouraging. (Smock and Youssef 1977:73)

Essays such as these invariably attribute asymmetrical gender role distribution in Egypt to "sociocultural factors," such as the role of Islam in oppressing women. They also point to the failure of the Egyptian state in committing its resources and energies to the improvement of women's status and the achievement of gender equality in all realms of Egyptian social life. However, to some extent, these analyses of Egyptian women's role restrictions miss the mark. Although it is easy to assign responsibility for women's role restrictions to patriarchal institutions such as religion or the state, it is necessary to examine patriarchal values themselves and the ontological assumptions underlying them. As argued here, belief in male procreation is at the ideological core of patriarchy in Egypt, serving to promote gendered social relations that subvert women into the unidimensional role of mothers to men's children. If women are deemed nurturers of men's "child productions," then all other roles are deemed less important or even unimportant when compared to this one. In short, this deeply engrained belief in male procreation is perhaps the core operative ideology underlying the "cult of motherhood" in patriarchal Egypt.

IMMORTALITY DESIRES

However, proving personal, sexual, and gender identities in the aforementioned ways is not the only reason why Egyptian men and women desire children on an individual level. Child desire is also inextricably linked to fears of death and resultant felt needs to achieve personal immortality.

In terms of immortality desires, it is probably true that fear of death is a human universal. In societies such as Egypt, where mortality rates are relatively high and few individuals live until a ripe old age,[1] death is everywhere, threatening to strike with little warning. Because deaths of one's family members, neighbors, and friends are so common, one's own mortality is a heightened anxiety. Although the vast majority of Egyptians are religious, believing that the circumstances and timing of death are part of God's predetermined plan for every individual, they nonetheless fear the finality of death and the possibility that death will obliterate memories of their lives.

This fear of permanent obliteration is extremely pronounced among Egyptians—perhaps not more so than among individuals in any other society, but pronounced nonetheless. Both Egyptian men and women, but especially men, speak often of their desires to create lasting "memories" of themselves during life and after death. Children are seen as the ultimate memory of an individual's having "left a trace" on this earth. The oft-cited expression "The one with children is not dead" bespeaks the concerns of both men and women in Egypt to achieve a kind of personal perpetuity after death. Just as parents receive the teknonymous titles "Father and Mother of So-and-So"—*needing* these teknonyms in order to be normally addressed by others—children are typically referred to as the "Son and Daughter of So-and-So," especially after their parents die. Thus, for both men and women, having children gives an individual a proper name in life and guarantees that "your name won't die with you" after death. Both male and female children, furthermore, carry their father's family surname to future generations in a society that values patrilineal continuity. For men at least, having children to immortalize their names is a personal motivation that cannot be underestimated.

Thus, for most poor urban Egyptians—whose other options for immortality through, say, good deeds, tangible contributions to society, or professional accomplishments are quite limited—children are their primary ego-extensions, literally extending their parents' names and memories into future generations. As Egyptians are fond of saying, "With children, you feel you *are* something, you're living *for* something, you *brought* something in this world."

In this light, then, it becomes apparent that infertility threatens not only notions of normal personhood, but desires for personal immortality as well. In short, infertility and immortality are diametrically opposed phenomena; if infertility exists, personal immortality cannot be achieved. Therefore, fear of infertility and the stigma that surrounds infertility in Egypt are closely linked to fears of death and the possibility that infertility will thwart opportunities for immortality.

QUALITY OF LIFE DESIRES

Although Egyptian men and women desire children for reasons that may be seen as egocentric, to view personal desires for children as selfish would be a mistake, given that most Egyptians both say and behave as if they generally enjoy children and love their own. To the best of their financial, physical, and emotional abilities, most Egyptian parents care for their chil-

dren and attempt to provide for their needs, on both a material and affective level. Affection and concern for children are the general rules among
Egyptian parents, and those individuals, primarily fathers, who are known
to be tyrannical, abusive, or uncommitted to their offspring are seen as
highly aberrant human beings. Typically, Egyptians boast of their great
"love for children," and, more often than not, they display this love rather
profusely.

Indeed, children are highly valued in and of themselves for they are
considered to bring great joy, happiness, cheer, and sweetness to their parents' lives and to a home. Egyptians are fond of equating the importance
and delight of children with the importance and delight derived from the
human senses—calling children the "taste," "sound," "light," and "smell"
of life.

Given the enjoyment thought to derive from children, many Egyptians are adamant that a "life without children" cannot be happy under any
circumstances. Children are thought to bring quality of life to a household—and, by extension, to the marital partners in that household. Thus,
by contrast, childlessness can only be seen as a miserable condition, leading to lives that are, to quote Egyptians, "empty," "bored," "meaningless,"
or "like boiled food without salt and pepper to give it taste."

In fact, to say that Egyptians live *for* and *through* their children is
not overstating the case. Most Egyptian adults (at least among the lower
classes) do not marry for the love they feel or expect to feel for their
spouses; hence, the quality of life they expect to derive from marriage
alone is limited. Rather, quality of life is expected to emerge from the joy
of "bringing children" into the household. In reality, children may provide
a couple with their greatest continuing sources of love, happiness, and affection—even when the husband and wife have learned to love each other,
but especially when they have not.

For men, coming home after a hard day's work to find their children
eager to see them is considered one of the greatest joys in life—one that
gives a man's work "meaning," as he knows he is toiling "for something."
As men are fond of saying when they reflect on their familial commit-
ments, "God is above, and my children are down here."

For women, whose lives of culturally enforced domesticity revolve
around the household, children *are* their careers. It is children who provide
a woman with her major role in life, and it is they who keep her company when her husband is away at work and who fill the otherwise empty
hours in days with few distractions. Reflecting on their domestic seclusion,

women who do not work are fond of saying, "A husband is only for the night, but your children are with you all day."

Moreover, as children grow older, often leaving the household upon marriage, Egyptian parents continue to equate the quality of their own lives with the pride, joy, and satisfaction they derive from having parented their children to adulthood. Grown children are seen as individuals' greatest "accomplishments in life," especially when they provide their parents with "something to brag about to others." Many parents also look to their grown children as their primary friends and companions, with daughters becoming "like sisters" to their mothers and sons "like brothers" to their fathers.

It is apparent, furthermore, that deriving quality of life from one's children is even more pronounced in recent times, which, for most poor urban Egyptians, are marked by extreme economic stresses, fragmentation of extended families and kin-based social networks, resultant social isolation from traditional forms of economic and emotional support, and widespread anomie and alienation. To wit, the economic pressures that have led to massive rural-to-urban migration within Egypt and migration of Egyptian men to countries outside of Egypt have also led to dramatic changes in the structure of the Egyptian family, especially in urban areas. Large extended families, typical of rural areas, have undergone a metamorphosis in the cities. Extended families have splintered into nuclear families, in large part because of housing shortages and the lack of spacious, extended-family-sized apartments. Over the past four decades, the nuclearization of the urban Egyptian family has been pronounced and has reached a stage of normalcy. Whereas postmarital patrilocal residence was once viewed as imperative, neolocal residence is now viewed as ideal—as long as reasonable proximity to relatives can still be maintained. However, as housing has become less and less available over the years, families have spread farther afield, so that easy visiting distance can no longer be guaranteed.

As described in the preceding chapters, the isolation of young urban husbands and wives from their extended kin groups has had both positive and negative effects. On the one hand, separation from families has dramatically altered the marital relationship for many men and women, who have come to rely upon each other for support of all types. For women in particular, the freedom from direct social controls imposed by in-laws has been a liberating experience for some and has led to increased feelings of independence and autonomy. On the other hand, men and women who lack the resources and support of their extended families and who are geographically and socially distant from them may face extreme isolation, loneliness, and despair. This is especially true when living quarters are dark, dank, and cramped; when marital strain is present for any reason; when economic pressures are severe, meaning that basic subsistence needs cannot be met; or when men feel compelled to migrate away from their families in order to relieve these suboptimal conditions.

Feelings of alienation are even more pronounced when husbands and wives are unable to have children. For poor urban infertile women stranded in one-room apartments, surrounded by neighbors who are estranged from them, isolated from their kinswomen, and entirely reliant on their often disgruntled husbands for economic and emotional support, the lack of children for whom to care presents itself as an awful void—a vacuum so enormous that many infertile women spend the bulk of their lives in deepening states of depression and despair. For their husbands, whose relatively short lives are often spent as "beasts of burden" in backbreaking forms of manual labor for which they receive little remuneration, the lack of children to support makes lives of hard work seem meaningless and futile, and this frustration is often taken out by them on their already desperately depressed wives.

Thus, infertility only serves to exacerbate the anomie of contemporary urban living in Egypt and the alienated feelings of the urban proletariat, who face economic duress and social isolation from traditional forms of support. Because children are thought of as bringing joy to life, many Egyptians, and perhaps the disenfranchised urban poor in particular, desire children as symbolic capital—their reward and compensation for all that is lacking in their lives of hardship and despair. Although realities are often much different, children are at least viewed by many poor urban Egyptians as "something to live for," as the primary form of hope and relief from lives of quiet desperation. This existential fear of living a life of despair—like the fears of personal deviance and mortality described above—is one of the major factors underlying the desire for children in Egypt and the stigmatization that inevitably accompanies the inability to produce such joyous offspring.

Child Desire from a Social Structural Perspective

But Egyptian men and women are not alone in their desires for children and in their consequent fears of infertility. Children are extremely important for reasons that can only be construed as social, and infertility can be seen to pose a threat to group structures—from the level of the nuclear family to that of Egyptian society at large. In other words, social reproduction is at stake when individual members of society are unable to reproduce biologically.

In addition to the personal ego needs fulfilled by having children, having children is perceived by Egyptians as socially instrumental on a number of important levels. From a social structural perspective, the replacement value of children to society is but one factor underlying child desire. Rather, the socially based reasons for having children can be seen to comprise three major categories, which, for heuristic purposes, can be called: (1) *social security desires*, or the conviction that children are necessary in a number of ways to secure their parents' and families' survival; (2) *social power desires*, or the belief that children serve as a valuable power resource in the realm of patriarchal social relations; and (3) *social perpetuity desires*, or the perceived need to continue group structures into future generations.

SOCIAL SECURITY DESIRES

Although the wealth flows model of child desire described earlier in this chapter is, in and of itself, an insufficient explanation of Egyptian pronatalism, the frequency of this model's invocation as an explanatory paradigm in the Egyptian population literature bespeaks the importance of children as "wealth" for Egyptian parents and their families. Children are, in fact, perceived as a form of investment in the future; for their costs to parents, especially when they are young, may be offset by their multiple future returns, especially as they grow into adulthood and can help to secure the existence of aging parents and other family members.

In fact, old-age security is often cited by scholars as one of the primary reasons why Egyptians want children (Ammar 1966; Gadalla 1978; Morsy 1980a; Rugh 1984). As rightfully noted, Islam encourages adult children to care for their aging parents, since parents comprise the first category of "needy persons" to whom voluntary financial charity is due (Omran 1992; Schleifer 1986; UNICEF 1985). Given the general lack of government programs for health insurance and retirement benefits in Egypt, many elderly parents do, in fact, constitute "needy" persons, who rely entirely on their children for financial support in old age. This is perhaps especially true among the urban poor, who usually lack property and are unable to save their meager earnings over their lifetimes.

Thus, among the urban Egyptian poor, old-age security issues are a major concern for most parents, who hope that their adult children will not only finance their final days on earth but also supply a roof over their heads. Traditionally, when both aging parents are still alive, they live alone or with any unmarried offspring. However, if one parent dies, the survivor typically moves into the residence of an adult child, which, in times past, was generally the eldest son. Today, however, parents bemoan the fact that their adult sons, having chosen to live in their own apartments, "forget" them far too easily in favor of their wives and children, and thus can no longer be relied on for old-age support of any kind. More and more commonly in urban areas, adult daughters and their husbands are assuming the duties of guardianship of elders, moving aged mothers and fathers into their own small apartments when these parents become widowed or in need of care. Because nursing homes are a rarity in Egypt and are patronized primarily by the well-to-do, housing and health care for aged parents, even when they are quite ill, continue to be the responsibility of adult children, who typically nurse their parents in their own homes until they die.

Arriving at "old age"—which is much younger than by Western standards—without a means of financial support, housing, or nursing care is obviously a terrifying prospect, especially for poor urban Egyptian women, who usually rely throughout their lifetimes on others for their economic survival. Having children, therefore, is considered the best way (although no longer a guarantee) of securing a reasonable future in old age—security that is definitely threatened by infertility. In fact, as they approach middle age with little hope of achieving parenthood, infertile couples often lament their future fate, with its real possibility of destitution, homelessness, and miserable death in anonymity. For they can only point to the popular saying "The daughter is good for rottenness [when one is old and sick and rotting], and the son is good for the coffin [when one dies and needs a son to attend to the funeral arrangements]."

However, children provide other kinds of social security as well. For one, they may contribute to the economic sustenance of the family through their unremunerated labor power or through independent income generation. In rural areas in particular, children are desired as family workers, who may provide an invaluable source of unpaid labor to both their farmer fathers and to their hardworking mothers, whose domestic chores are significant and time-consuming (Ammar 1966; Gadalla 1978; Lane and Meleis 1991; Morsy 1980a). Sons in particular are desired to be the "back" of their fathers—men whose heavy agricultural labor is, indeed, backbreaking and debilitating over time. Landowning peasants without their own children to assist them in farmwork and to engage in subsistence-level household food production may face significant economic disadvantage—and even problems of survival—if they are forced to hire agricultural workers from within or outside the extended family.

Among the urban poor, the situation tends to be somewhat different. Although poor families who run their own formal- or informal-sector businesses rely on their children as a source of labor (and as heirs to the family business when parents die), children are less likely in urban areas to be engaged as family workers, since their fathers tend to be the paid employees of others. In fact, today, poor urban parents lament the rising costs of having children, who are likely to be economically dependent upon their fathers until late adolescence, when sons begin to find jobs and daughters marry. Nonetheless, teenaged and adult children, especially when they are still single, can often be counted upon to contribute economically to the family. When sons enter the work force in Egypt or abroad, either before or after they complete their mandatory military service, they are generally expected to contribute all or part of their wages to the family coffers—even if all of this money is put aside as savings for their future marriages. In the case of daughters, who are much less likely to seek outside employment unless their families are truly destitute (in which case they are likely to work as maids), mothers may rely on them for their unremunerated domestic service, especially when there are younger children in the household to be cared for. Some daughters, such as Maisa, whose story was told in the last chapter, contribute financially to their families through informal-sector labor, particularly sewing done at home. Furthermore, growing numbers of poor parents, especially those transitioning into or out of the lower-middle class (MacLeod 1991), have come to realize the economic benefits to the family of allowing their daughters, especially educated ones, to work in "respectable" jobs outside the home. Indeed, the growing legions of women factory, service-industry, and government workers in Egypt are comprised mainly of young, single women, who continue to live at home and who are likely to contribute all or part of their wages to the household (thereby offsetting some of the costs to their parents when they eventually marry) (Ibrahim 1985a; MacLeod 1991).

Children who can generate income are especially important to women who are widowed or divorced. Although some widows are entitled to government or private pensions upon their husbands' deaths, a divorced mother has only her adult children "behind her" when her husband leaves, for it is they, and not her ex-husband (who is not required by Muslim family law to pay extended alimony), who will normally be her source of economic support. Similarly, young women who are divorced by their husbands but have no father to return to are expected to be taken care of by their adult brothers, care that may include housing them and their young children until they are able to remarry. In fact, one of the reasons why having only one child—or even two for that matter—is seen as unrealistic by poor urban Egyptians is that children, and especially daughters, may desperately need their sibling when life problems arise after their parents die. Just as infertile couples are seen as being "alone in the world" without children, only children are widely viewed as "orphans" upon the death of their parents—even if the only child has married and created a family of his or her own.

When all is said and done then, issues of social security are extremely important in understanding desires for children among the urban Egyptian poor. Although the needs for children are changing in Egypt as more and more people move from rural to urban areas, children are still viewed as instrumental to survival in both rural and urban settings, given that the Egyptian government cannot be relied on to provide for the economic welfare of its needy citizens. If children are imperative to familial economic survival, especially of parents in their old age, then the inability to produce children certainly represents a grave economic threat. Indeed, infertility can be seen as an economic tragedy for those who succumb to it—not only because such individuals face a lifetime of impoverishing treatments, but because they are forced to contemplate a bleak future of being old, alone, and without children to support them.

SOCIAL POWER DESIRES

But children provide another form of security, especially for women in Egyptian society. Namely, children are viewed as a form of "power" in the realm of social relations, particularly when struggles arise between contesting parties. For poor urban women, children *are* their major source of power, for it is children who usually serve as crucial leverage in contestations between wives, their husbands, and their in-laws.

Although the power of children to lubricate social relations—and the paradoxical power of infertility to interfere with or even destroy those relations—has been highlighted throughout this book, it is worth reiterating here that the power of children to normalize social relations is a *major* factor underlying child desire in Egypt. This is particularly true for women, whose pronatalist tendencies are certainly linked to their relative lack of alternative social roles and power resources within an overtly and covertly patriarchal social system. The patriarchal circumscription of women's lives on multiple fronts (e.g., in education, employment, religious participation, politics) serves to fuel women's own pronatalist attitudes and behaviors. Living under patriarchy, it is Egyptian women—rather than men—who come to see having children as their primary means of social advantage in their everyday lives and interactions. Thus, patriarchy and the expectations for women engendered by a deeply engrained patriarchal value system are issues that must be addressed in any discussion of Egyptian pronatalism, as well as in the discussion of the threat that infertility poses to the social reproduction of patriarchal relations themselves.

The relationship between patriarchy and women's pronatalism is most evident in the arena of gender politics, or the inter- and intragender relational strategies of Egyptian men and women. Namely, patriarchy is most directly manifested in the ways in which men and women interact hetero- and homosocially. In Egypt, the ability of men to wield their social power over women is clear in patterns of behavior that are upheld (at least theoretically) by men and generally tolerated, if not enjoyed, by women.

Women most fear men's social power in the realm of marriage. Within marriage, men are viewed by women as "in control" on multiple levels—control that many women deem to be patently unfair, but timeless and irreversible. For one, men control the financial purse strings, for it is they, and not their wives, who generate the family's income. Women who desire work as a means of alleviating economic hardship are usually forbidden by their husbands from seeking employment, for women's work exposes men as poor providers. Thus, when husbands' wages are inadequate to support their families, wives and children must suffer in silence or face the wrath of frustrated "breadwinners."

Husbands, furthermore, often limit their wives' physical mobility, in an attempt to prevent their wives' "exposure" to the potential lust of other men. Thus, among the urban poor, husbands are free to participate actively in the nondomestic, "outside" world of work, recreation (mostly at cafés), and communal religious participation. But their wives may be forced, sometimes under direct orders, to spend their lives "inside" their homes and home communities. When women do participate in nondomestic activities, they must be modest and circumspect in their behavior, and are generally expected to guard their own and their husband's honor by avoiding interactions with unfamiliar men.

In addition, husbands tend to make behavioral demands on wives that the latter are expected to accept without question. These may include, among other things, continuous domestic service to husbands in terms of food preparation, laundry, and so forth; expectations of co-residence with and domestic service to husbands' kin; restrictions on the degree of social interaction with women's own kin and neighbors; and male control over the amount and tenor of conjugal emotional, communicative, and sexual involvement.

Most important, men are seen by women as being in substantial—if not absolute—control of marital outcomes. Whether a marriage continues, is transformed by polygyny, or ends in divorce are all decisions that men tend to make alone, usually with little if any input from their wives. Women are multiply restricted in seeking changes in their marital status—not only because negotiating with husbands to improve a marriage may be difficult if not impossible, but because women are legally and culturally limited in seeking divorce to end a bad marriage. Therefore, women see themselves as subject to the whims of men, who, when "bad," can make their marriages miserable and then leave their wives with little warning.

Among women, having children is seen as a way of building some security into this otherwise precarious situation. Although reality often proves otherwise, it is at least widely maintained by poor urban Egyptian women that children "tie a husband to his wife"—literally preventing polygyny or divorce. Children are seen as creating love between a husband and wife, thereby helping to overcome the feelings of estrangement that often accompany spouses as they enter into arranged marriages. Having children is seen as helping husbands and wives to "feel a connection" to one another and to cement feelings of marital commitment that might otherwise fail to emerge. In addition, it is children themselves who are seen as the major preventive against divorce. For, as Egyptian women observe, husbands and wives who are not comfortable with one another and who therefore lack commitment as spouses often stay together in a marriage "just for the sake of the children."

Because of the marital security children are believed (at least by women) to engender, having children is deemed necessary to ensure a successful marriage. Among Egyptians, marriage is for family-building, with children being an essential part of any definition of the "family." Within their own families of procreation, men and women want to feel "powerful": men as "heads" of the *usrāt* they have created, and women as "queens" of the household. Thus, marriages that are childless are deemed structurally aberrant, given the absence of culturally defined notions of the "couple" or of "nuclear families" constituted of a husband and wife alone. Not only is the inability to achieve structural parity with other married "family-builders" considered ominous, conjugally speaking, but marriages that are devoid of children are also deemed devoid of the happiness and improved quality of life that children are seen as providing. Thus, infertility is considered a grave social onus to a marriage, which, lacking the "tying power" of children, is expected by most Egyptians to fail.

The fact that many infertile couples remain together for a lifetime—and that their marriages are more successful than many fertile marriages encumbered by children—is a reality of which few poor urban Egyptians, including the infertile themselves, are apprised. Nonetheless, this marital success is evidence of changing marital praxis among the urban poor, with movement toward a more "companionate" form of marriage thought typical only of the middle and upper classes. That this change in marital praxis has yet to be accompanied by changes on the level of marital ideology is reflected in women's beliefs in the tying power of children and their strong desires to have children for this very reason.

However, even though children are less powerful in "tying" a husband than many Egyptian women realize, children may constitute a powerful resource in women's negotiations with other interested parties. This is especially true of in-laws, whose relationships with daughters-in-law tend to be strained, but especially when children are not forthcoming from the marriages of their sons. Although the desire to please in-laws cannot be considered a primary factor underlying the desire for children among either Egyptian men or women, Egyptian women are nonetheless aware that their children are their major claim to power and status within their husbands' families. Assuring such elevated status is particularly important for daughters-in-law in patrilocally extended households. There, their children may "protect" them from some of the more flagrant forms of control and expectations of service perpetrated by mothers-in-law and other senior women over junior women in the household. As seen in Chapter 4, infertile daughters-in-law who lack the protective power of children may be subject to overt abuses and social stigmatization by senior women, even when these women live in separate residences. Generally speaking, it is senior women in husbands' families who, by "buying into" a patriarchal system under which they, too, have been oppressed, serve to reproduce patriarchal relations that are detrimental to the lives of other women, and especially the infertile.

SOCIAL PERPETUITY DESIRES

Such senior women "buy into" patriarchy in part through their overzealous interest in the reproductive lives of male family members. To wit, it is women who typically encourage their male family members to "marry and multiply" and who make miserable the lives of men's wives when they fail to facilitate familial reproductive agendas. Although the gendered aspects of this social pressure are detailed at length in Chapter 4, it is important to reiterate here *why* women perpetuate these patriarchal relations. Namely, women remain members of their own patrilineages, while their children belong to the patrilineages of their husbands. Thus, women's concerns over patrilineal continuity—and their own chances of finding future support within the patrilineage—must be directed at sons and brothers and, by extension, the reproductive partners of these men.

Women's reproductive zealotry and their negative reaction to infertile female in-laws has much to do with desires for social perpetuity—or the need for patrilineal extended families, as corporate entities, to continue into the future. Given the corporate nature of Egyptian society in general and family life in particular (Rugh 1984), social perpetuity is an extremely compelling group concern, and it is played out most obviously in the efforts of husbands' patrilineal extended-family members to ensure that children—and especially male children—are born, so as to "carry the family name" to future generations.

Just as individuals in Egypt desire children to preserve their individual memories, patrilineal extended families in Egypt desire the reproductive success of constituent family members in order to insure the strength and social memory of the *'a'ila* itself. Even though urban Egypt lacks the kind of corporately functioning, patronymic descent groups found in other areas of the Middle East (Eickelman 1989), patrilineal *'a'ilāt* characterized by multiple generations of large families are considered by most poor Egyptians to be powerful, in that the name of the *'a'ila* will have "a big tail."

Sons, and especially eldest sons, are inculcated with the message that they *must* produce children for the sake of the family's perpetuity, and the inculcation of this message among Egyptian men is often very effective. But carrying the family name to future generations is but one aspect of social perpetuity that concerns poor urban Egyptian men. On a more concrete level, Egyptian men are often extremely cognizant of patrimony issues, or the ways in which family enterprises, land, housing, and other properties will be bestowed upon future generations. Having children and especially male heirs to the family patrimony is one of the major reasons why Egyptian men desire children. Even poor men, who may leave behind little in the way of inheritance, view their children as the only preventive against the dispersion of their patrimony to "strangers." This is of special concern to men involved in the building of family businesses, who want to insure by producing male heirs that their "exhaustion has been worthwhile."

Given the desires of both men and women to insure family futures, it comes as no surprise that infertility is viewed as deeply threatening to the social reproduction of larger family structures. When individual members of the family are unable to reproduce, the future of the family itself is at stake, with members fearing (usually unreasonably given Egypt's relatively high birth rate) that "the family will die out." Since individuals are generally loath to blame their own family members for reproductive failure, it is the "strangers" who marry into the family who are deemed, often without sufficient evidence, to be the unreproductive partners. Given Egypt's patrilineally based family structure, it is unfortunate daughters-in-law who therefore carry the burden of the failure to conceive and are tormented by their in-laws for ruining the family's reproductive fortunes.

Child Desire from a Political-Economic Perspective

Issues of social perpetuity also receive expression in Egyptians' desires to "help and continue their country" through the production of future generations of children. Indeed, child desire in Egypt has nationalistic dimensions, in that Egyptians have become increasingly concerned about the future of their Muslim nation vis-à-vis the politically and economically powerful Christian West.

Without a doubt, this concern about the reproduction of Egypt as a Muslim society has been fueled by the growing Islamic movement in the country. With the notable rise of Islamism in Egypt over the past two decades, many Islamist theologians in the country have become engaged in what might be called a "demographic war" against the Christian world, including the minority Christian population in Egypt. Specifically, they have stated their frank opposition to Egypt's family planning movement, associating it with a Western (and particularly a U.S.) conspiracy to limit the size of the Egyptian and, ultimately, the worldwide Muslim population in relation to the world's Christian population (Lane and Rubinstein 1991; Omran 1992; Omran and Roudi 1993). The question of numbers has been a key issue in this debate, because Islamists who adopt this stance argue that the larger the number of Muslims and the higher their rate of growth, the greater their power and the closer they are to pleasing God and the Prophet Muhammad as his messenger (Omran 1992). They proclaim, furthermore, that a Muslim "multitude" is ordained by Islam and that failure to achieve it is a deviation from the "right path" of the religion. Family planning, therefore, having originated in the Christian West, represents a clear conspiracy to reduce the absolute number of Muslims and to diminish their relative power, according to Islamists who deliver this message (and who disregard the fact that contraceptive use is much more prevalent in Western countries than in the rest of the world) (Omran 1992).

Thus, today in Egypt, the visible resurgence of Islamic codes of dress and behavior is inextricably linked to a new movement of pronatalism sweeping the country, and especially in politically disenfranchised, poor urban areas. Despite exerted efforts by the Egyptian government, government-supported Muslim clerics, and Egyptian Muslim family planning advocates to convince Egyptians of the stated need for, permissibility of, and even "invention" of family planning in Islam (Omran 1992), Islamist groups are encouraging Egyptians to follow another path: one of uninhibited reproduction through the discontinuance of birth control, resultant large family sizes, and the exclusive devotion of women's energies toward the care and religiously guided upbringings of their large Muslim broods.

The strategies by which contemporary Islamists, be they groups or individuals, attempt to inculcate these messages among Egyptians are varied and frankly require further investigation.[2] Nevertheless, it appears that Islamist elements within Egyptian society have targeted their efforts in large part toward religiously illiterate, poor urban Egyptian men and women through a number of inherently political strategies.

Local Islamist clerics and popular televised Islamist theologians have been particularly effective in spreading the Muslim pronatalist message to the poor. Some have publicly attacked the practice of family planning by Egyptian Muslim couples, as well as the establishment of family planning services in the country (Omran 1992). While Muslim theologians throughout the centuries have traditionally interpreted the Islamic scriptures as permissive in allowing family planning (primarily for the purposes of birth spacing and to prevent health hazards to mother and child) (Musallam 1983; Omran 1992; Omran and Roudi 1993), these "new" Islamist clerics who oppose family planning point to the Qur'an in support of their opposition. Namely, they cite multiple pronatalist passages in the Qur'an pertaining to the beauty of motherhood and of children, the begetting of whom constitutes the purpose of marriage. Furthermore, they argue that family planning contradicts the will of God and doubts his ability to provide for the *rizq*, or sustenance, of each and every child, even those born into poor families.[3] Additionally, they contend that the use of family planning will bring with it promiscuity, moral decline, secularization, and all the evils that it has purportedly caused in Western countries. And, on a "policy" level, some of these theologians argue that the so-called "population problem" does not apply to the Islamic world, which has enough resources to sustain several times its present population (Omran 1992).

Ultimately, Islamists of this ilk have attempted to convince Egyptian Muslims—in many cases successfully—that the use of family planning is disloyal to the religion, given that God through the Prophet Muhammad urged Muslims to "marry and multiply." The effectiveness of this last message is particularly apparent in oft-cited comments made by Egyptian Muslims—and counterstatements made by Egyptian Christians—expressing fears about the reproductive proliferation of the "other group" and the consequent need to multiply the numbers of one's own kind. Thus, the increasing Islamization of Egyptian society is manifested in part in informal but apparently effective campaigns to *increase rather than decrease* the absolute numbers of Egyptian Muslims. The spread of this message and its implementation among poor urban Egyptians certainly contradicts governmental efforts to curb population growth in the country. Ultimately, the demographic consequences of this ideological debate have yet to be seen.

Thus, to summarize, contemporary interpretations of Islam by increasingly powerful Islamist elements in Egyptian society are serving to reinforce rather dramatically culturally grounded pronatalist tendencies. But the question that remains to be answered here is: What are the effects of these increasingly pronatalist sentiments on the Egyptian infertile?

As described in Chapter 2, many infertile Egyptian women take great solace from their religion and may use religious arguments as a kind of "defense" to justify their infertility as decreed by God, who is ultimately "testing" their patience and faith in his power. Thus, religious conviction is one of the major coping strategies for infertile women and for their husbands as well, who, by "knowing God," may be much more patient regarding remarriage. Islam, then, serves as a most potent ameliorating force, mitigating the stigmatization of infertility in a setting in which this affliction is viewed as quite threatening for all of the reasons already described.

However, although Islamic doctrine about the inevitability of and reasons for infertility among some Muslims is inherently destigmatizing, contemporary interpretations of Islamic doctrine threaten to increase the stigmatization of women who are unable to comply with the "multiplication of offspring" tenets prescribed by Islamist groups in contemporary Egyptian society. Egyptian women themselves worry openly about the fate of infertile women in an increasingly Islamic, child-desiring nation. As they state, "If everyone is having more kids, infertile women will have many more problems."

Thus, Islam itself can be seen as having countervailing effects on the infertile Egyptian women whose lives and struggles have been portrayed in this book. On the one hand, Islam provides their major source of strength and self-help. On the other hand, its pronatalist tendencies are today being manipulated in a way that, unfortunately, widens the gap between fertile women with many children and infertile women, who can only imagine the beauty of the children "missing" from their lives.

Notes

Chapter 1: Infertility and Patriarchy

1. For definitions of patriarchy by theorists of the Middle East, see Hatem (1987a), Moghadam (1993), Nelson (1991), and Sharabi (1988).

2. It is important to differentiate three analytically distinct referents for the term "reproduction": (1) social reproduction, or the overall reproduction of a particular social formation, including the perpetuation of groups in society; (2) reproduction of the labor force itself; and (3) human or biological reproduction (Moore 1988; Yanagisako and Collier 1987). In this book, I will attempt to show how the failure of biological reproduction threatens both social reproduction and the reproduction of labor, since all three forms of reproduction are connected.

3. For recent scholarship on Egyptian feminism, see Badran (1988; 1993; 1994; 1995); Baron (1994); Hatem (1984; 1993); Marsot (1978); Moghadam (1993); and Philipp (1978).

4. In the colloquial parlance of the urban Egyptian poor, the uterus is called the *bait il-wilid*, or literally "the house of the child," while achieving orgasm is referred to as "bringing." For a further discussion of beliefs about and terminology for reproductive parts and processes among the urban Egyptian poor, see Inhorn (1994).

5. Not all radical critiques of Islam and patriarchy come from Western feminists. Fatna A. Sabbah, a Muslim Middle Eastern feminist scholar, has published perhaps the most critical assessment of the view of women under Islamic patriarchy, entitled *Woman in the Muslim Unconscious* (1984). Because her critique was potentially offensive to Muslims, she chose to write the book under a pseudonym.

6. The literature on Egyptian women and work is beginning to proliferate. For recent examples, see Abu Nasr, Khoury, and Azzam (1985); Hammam (1979); Ibrahim (1985a, 1985b); Lane and Meleis (1991); MacLeod (1991); Mohsen (1985); Morsy (1990); Rugh (1984, 1985); Sullivan (1981); and Toth (1991).

7. See, for example, Bill (1972), who has distinguished between seven different traditional classes in the Middle East.

8. In this book, I prefer to use the term "urban poor" rather than "working class" to designate the class position of my informants. "Working class" implies participation in the nondomestic labor market, which is true of informants' husbands but not of informants themselves. Because most of my informants did not work outside the home, never had, and did not anticipate future employment, to call them "working class" would be misleading and would suggest that a woman's class position is determined by her husband's occupation. Furthermore, the term

"working class" includes both the poor and the lower-middle class. In this study, most of the women and their husbands were poor.

9. In the literature on Egyptian women, for example, the following subjects, in addition to honor and shame, have been privileged: veiling, women and work (see note 6 above), feminism (see note 3 above), family life and personal status laws, fertility, spirit possession, female circumcision, and, recently, Islamism. To take but one example, the literature devoted exclusively to veiling includes El Guindi (1981), Hoodfar (1991), MacLeod (1991), Williams (1980), and Zuhur (1992), and many other books and articles include discussions of or passing references to veiling.

Chapter 2: Missing Motherhood

1. All informants' names used in this book are pseudonyms.

2. See my earlier book, *Quest for Conception: Gender, Infertility, and Egyptian Medical Traditions* (Inhorn 1994), for a complete account of these beliefs about infertility etiology among poor urban Egyptian women.

3. By definition, a female becomes a woman, or *sitt*, only when she has been deflowered on her wedding night. Thus, an elderly spinster who has never married continues to be referred to as a "girl," or *bint*. On the contrary, a barely pubescent girl who is married off at the age of twelve or thirteen will be referred to as a *sitt* from that point on, even when she appears more "girlish" than "womanly."

4. The verb *khallafa* means, literally, "to leave [someone] behind," "to have offspring," or "to have descendants" (Cowan 1976). Infertile women are usually referred to through negation of the verb *khallafa* as ones who did not have offspring.

5. The "housewife," a recent historical creation within the middle-class West, is now being created throughout the Third World as a result of development policies and the capitalist mode of production, which define women's productivity in relation to money (Bennholdt-Thomsen 1988; Moore 1988; Sacks 1989). According to the Ministry of Information report *Egyptian Women*, the majority of Egyptian women are "housewives" (Egyptian Ministry of Information 1985).

6. The notion of one male breadwinner with a "family wage" to support his wife and children in a feminized domestic realm is a middle-class ideology that developed in eighteenth- to nineteenth-century Europe and differed from the reality of the vast majority of the poor population (Connell 1990; Moore 1988). Nonetheless, feminist historians have shown how working-class people historically removed their women and children from the work force in an attempt to approximate a bourgeois life-style (Tong 1989).

7. Although the Egyptian state is officially committed to women's work, its position is paradoxical, according to Hatem (1986a). In the late 1970s under the pressure of increasing Islamism, the state encouraged women to return home to care for their families. This paradoxical position has been seen in Egyptian labor laws regarding women, which are constantly breached (Smock and Youssef 1977), and in the fact that factories offer benefits to women but usually not childcare (Ibrahim 1985a).

8. Statistics on Egyptian women's economic activity and labor force partici-pation vary, depending upon the source. The figures presented here are among the highest estimates, with other sources reporting lower figures.

9. Many authors have noted how a shift from a subsistence to a monetized economy restricts women's economic independence, as women come to rely in-creasingly on their husbands for cash. With the advent of capitalism, the economic partnership between husbands and wives is dissolved, and women are left at home as a marginalized, secondary work force (Gendzier 1981; Young 1981).

10. A number of scholars studying women and work in Egypt note that women work only out of economic necessity. Because it is considered more ac-ceptable for women to work while they are still single or if they are divorced, most married women who work would quit if economic circumstances in the household were better. See, for example, Hammam (1979); Ibrahim (1985a, 1985b); Khattab and el-Daeiff (1984); MacLeod (1991); Morsy (1990); Rugh (1984; 1985); and Yous-sef (1978).

11. The acceptance of the patriarchal "man the provider" norm and the threat-ening nature of women's work to the maintenance of this norm have been noted by numerous scholars working in the Muslim Middle East. See, for example, Boddy (1989); Bowen (1993); El Saadawi (1980); Hoodfar (1988); Kandiyoti (1991); Mer-nissi (1985); Moghadam (1993; 1994); Nelson (1976); Omran (1992); Rugh (1982; 1984; 1985); and UNICEF (1985).

12. Cases publicized in the Egyptian media about prostitution by middle-class working women support traditional fears about working women's corrupt-ibility (Mohsen 1985).

13. The stigma of women's work in the Arab countries in general has been noted by Azzam, Abu Nasr, and Lorfing (1985). As scholars of Egypt have noted, work may bring women money and even power, but rarely prestige and status (MacLeod 1991; Rugh 1985). As MacLeod puts it, work is an "ambiguous gain" for women.

14. The cultural conservatism of southern Egyptians, or Ṣaʿīdīs, is reflected in a popular discourse of Ṣaʿīdī jokes among northern Egyptians. These numer-ous jokes poke fun at the ignorance and backward mentality of rural southern folk. Even among Ṣaʿīdī women, a popular expression points to the "locked" brains of their Ṣaʿīdī menfolk.

15. Rugh (1985) traces the slowly changing attitudes toward women's work in Egypt to: (1) rising inflation and the need for two incomes; (2) rising expecta-tions about basic needs, especially regarding children's education; and (3) middle-class women's example. As she sees it, the need for money is gradually overcoming cultural resistance to women's work among the lower classes.

16. Even though public attitudes toward employment may be slowly chang-ing in Egypt, traditional sex roles and responsibilities are not. Therefore, women who work remain saddled with domestic responsibilities and childcare (MacLeod 1991; Mohsen 1985; Rugh 1984).

17. Informal work conducted from inside the home is often "approved" by men. As Rugh (1985) describes, women's work is judged by five criteria: (1) how protected (in terms of the opportunities for moral indiscretion) the work area is;

(2) how publicly it displays a family's need; (3) how much status is connected with the work; (4) how much income is earned; and (5) how much it interferes with a woman's other responsibilities. Given these criteria, part- or full-time work at home, such as sewing, is viewed as unproblematic and may bring a woman some status if she is able to generate income from her work and becomes known for its high quality.

18. As reflected in the photographs in this book, many poor urban Egyptian women suffer from mild to severe obesity. This is perhaps especially true of infertile women, who tend to eat out of boredom and who may have more food available to them, given that they have fewer mouths to feed in the household. Obesity itself may lead to infertility, primarily through negative effects on a woman's ovulation. Not surprisingly, so-called "ovulatory-factor infertility" is one of the two major etiological types of infertility in Egypt, along with tubal-factor infertility (Inhorn 1994).

19. Although infertile Egyptian women rarely express their emotions in public forums, they are often quite willing to emote among intimates, as was also discovered by Abu-Lughod (1986) in her study of Egyptian Bedouin women. Because of my own assurances of confidentiality and the private settings in which I conducted my interviews with infertile women, I was privileged to be the recipient of women's emotional discourse and to witness their emotional turmoil. See Inhorn (1994) for further details.

20. Before I conducted my anthropological study of infertility in Shatby Hospital, two master's degree candidates, one in nursing (Yassin 1985) and one in public health (Abou-Zeid 1987), conducted psychologically oriented studies of the "personality traits" of infertile Egyptian women also presenting to Shatby Hospital. Both of these studies employed purportedly objective "personality tests" (i.e., standardized psychometric questionnaires developed in the West) in an attempt to assess such personality dimensions as "neuroticism," "introversion," "anxiety," "phobia," "obsession," "psychosomatic complaints," "depression," and "hysteria." Infertile women were found in both studies to manifest such psychological disturbances significantly more often than their husbands and more often than fertile women also tested. Yet, neither study addressed the question of the validity of the Western-based psychometric instruments applied in this cross-cultural setting, and neither attempted to assess the psychological problems found among study participants, such as "depression," from a clinical diagnostic standpoint. In addition, because both studies focused rather narrowly on intrapsychic phenomena, they did not address the psycho*social* nature of infertility and the various social stressors that may affect an infertile woman's personality profile. Clearly, sensitive psychological research on the problem of infertility among Egyptian women is still needed.

21. Few poor urban Egyptian women know the exact translation of this and other relevant Qur'anic verses, although some of them have an approximate idea. The vast majority of women profess—and often apologize for—their lack of knowledge of the Qur'an and their religion in general, although they consider themselves to be religious.

22. Although Egypt has proclaimed an official "Mother's Day" on March 21 of each year (Egyptian Ministry of Information 1985), al-Shaarawi argues that

Egypt does not need this festival, because, as an Islamic society, Egypt celebrates Mother's Day "every moment of the year" (Stowasser 1987:281).

23. Poor urban Egyptian women are particularly amused by the Islamist dress code for women, which, in its more extreme variants, involves almost complete coverage of a woman's body except for her eyes. Poor urban women, who find such garb to be excessive, like to joke how these *Sunnī*, or Islamist, women wear the latest fashions under their Islamic cloaks, which they like to show off to each other at festive gatherings such as weddings.

Chapter 3: Conjugal Connectivity

1. Schistosomiasis is a parasitic blood fluke infection that affects the majority of rural Egyptians at some point in their lifetimes. It is acquired through contact with the infected water of Egypt's rural canal system. If not treated, the chronic infection leads to, among other things, enlargement of the spleen, leading to splenectomies, or surgical removals of the spleen, among many Egyptian villagers.

2. Individuals who are tyrannical in their behavior are often called "pharaohs," in reference to the way in which Egypt's ancient pharaohs were thought to have ruled the country.

3. As noted in Chapter 1, the 1979 amendments to Egypt's personal status laws dictate that a first wife must be notified that her husband has taken a second wife, so that she may decide whether to file for divorce.

4. Men and women who are not considered attractive by Egyptian standards are nevertheless "married off" in most cases with the help of their families, who attempt to find suitors for them. However, adults with mental or physical disabilities often remain unmarried for life.

5. Van Spijk, Fahmy, and Zimmerman (1982), Mohsen (1985), and Rugh (1984) also argue that appearance is the single most important factor in initial attraction of a man to a woman, even among Egypt's middle class. Indeed, Sabbah (1984) argues that the other attributes of a woman, such as her intelligence or personality, are not important criteria, because the very definition of female beauty, of the "ideal woman" in Islam, involves silence, obedience, and immobility.

6. It is rumored that many a young woman who has lost her virginity before marriage has been "saved" by a midwife, who, using her hand, can produce blood from the girl's vagina, which no longer has an intact hymen. Nevertheless, it is certainly accurate to state that most Egyptian women, and especially those from the lower classes, are virgins on their wedding nights.

7. Although the vast majority of Egyptian Muslims are Sunni, the use of the term *Sunnī* in Egypt implies that a person is a "religious" (i.e., fundamentalist) Muslim. Nowadays, *Sunnī* men tend to display their Muslim identity through the growth of an untrimmed beard. Many of these men also have prominent "prayer spots," which are actually calluses, on their foreheads.

8. It appears that the incestuous, "cousin-as-sibling" problem is overcome in two ways: (1) older male cousins take younger female cousins as brides, thereby

ensuring a "generational distance" between the husband and wife; and (2) male and female cousins who have been raised in different geographical locales marry, thereby ensuring a "geographical distance" between the husband and wife.

9. Although official statistics on infertility in Egypt are lacking, the percentage of couples who have never conceived is estimated to be at least 8 percent, and, as reported by urban gynecologists, infertile women may constitute up to one-third of their patients (Inhorn 1994).

10. According to Omran and Roudi (1993), polygyny in the Middle East is notorious not because of its frequency, which is only 3 to 4 percent in the region as a whole, but rather because of its possibility. Women, and especially infertile women, live in fear of this possibility (Atiya 1982; Baron 1991).

11. The terror of divorce, the plight of divorcées, and women's reluctance to seek divorce have all been noted by other scholars working in Egypt. See, for example, Baron (1991); El Saadawi (1980); Mohsen (1985); and Rugh (1984).

12. Bourdieu (1977) has noted the asymmetry between men's and women's abilities to marry and remarry in the Middle East. Whereas "the man is always a man" in his ability to marry—and hence "deviant" men are often able to find wives—"deviant" women, such as divorcées and the infertile, may face considerable difficulties when it comes to marriage.

13. In this study, male infertility was present in four of these cases, but three of the husbands had never been informed by a single physician that they, too, were partly responsible for their wives' failure to conceive.

14. See Inhorn (1996) for a more detailed discussion of some of the marital problems and pressures faced by poor urban women with children. See also Rugh (1984).

15. Barakat (1985) describes recent changes in Middle Eastern marriage practices, including a decrease in both arranged and endogamous marriages, an increase in expected bridewealth payments, a decrease in the age gap between spouses, and a decrease in rates of polygyny. However, he (along with Rugh [1984]) points to the continuing high rate of divorce, especially early on in marriage, when children have not yet been conceived. What is meant by "high," however, is a matter of interpretation. For example, the divorce rate in Egypt, occurring in approximately one quarter of all marriages, is still half that of the United States (Fluehr-Lobban 1990).

Chapter 4: Relatives' Responses

1. Generally speaking, a marriage is not consummated until the evening following the official wedding celebration. When a marriage contract is written in advance of the wedding—even months or years earlier—most poor urban Egyptian couples do not cohabit and do not engage in sexual relations.

2. In the *Hans Wehr* Arabic-English dictionary (Cowan 1976), *usra* is defined as "family; dynasty; clan, kinsfolk, relatives," whereas *'a'ila* is defined as "family, household." The conceptual distinction between *usra* as nuclear family and *'a'ila* as extended family is a recent one in Egypt. For example, Rugh in her 1984 ethnography on *Family in Contemporary Egypt* does not mention the term *usra*, although

she defines *bait*, which means literally "house," as "the smallest family unit specified by Egyptian terminology" (1984:55). According to Rugh, the term *'a'ila* can be used to refer to either a nuclear family or an extended group of kin. However, since the publication of Rugh's book, the terms of reference for "family" have obviously changed, as reflected in the *usra* versus *'a'ila* dichotomy now widely adopted in urban settings.

3. In this study, about 40 percent of infertile couples did not experience marital interference from members of the husband's or wife's *'a'ila*. About one-third of infertile women actually reported good relations with their in-laws, including their female in-laws, who were sometimes supportive and even protective of them. However, about 60 percent of infertile couples experienced some form of familial interference in their marriages, the vast majority from members of the husband's *'a'ila*. In two-thirds of these cases, overt interference was experienced by the wife vis-à-vis her husband's relatives.

4. Men's efforts to disband infertile unions tend to be carried out "behind the scenes" and are characteristically enacted "man to man." The fact that women tend to deal directly with other women and men with other men is, to some degree, a reflection of persistent gender divisions in Egyptian society, particularly in the realm of daily activities. In this study, only six infertile women, including Aida, whose story was described in Chapter 3, reported having been overtly harassed by male members of their husbands' *'a'ilāt*.

5. On an affective level, relationships between parents and their daughters are often closer than those between parents and their sons, given that daughters tend to foster emotionally intimate relationships with their mothers (and sometimes their fathers) well into their adult years. Nonetheless, because of deeply engrained societal preferences for sons, especially among men, sons often retain privileged positions within the family structure, even when on an emotional level they are not as "close" to their parents as their sisters.

6. The reportedly strong mother-son relationship, which has contributed to the weakening of the marital bond throughout the Middle East (Mernissi 1985), has been described as eroticized, even incestuous (Hatem 1986c). Supposedly, the son serves as a substitute for a woman whose relationship with her own husband is attenuated. Accordingly, a mother's emotional dependence upon her son becomes marked, while his reaction to his overly needy mother becomes ambivalent. Although such an interpretation of the mother-son relationship may be appropriate for some parts of the Middle East or for earlier periods of Egyptian history, I concur with Early (1993), who argues that the mother-son relationship has been overemphasized in discourse on the Egyptian family, is undergoing dramatic change, and does not necessarily bear a resemblance to this classic description. As we shall see, most mothers' closest ties are to their daughters, for a myriad of reasons to be described later in this chapter.

7. Of the twelve marriages in this study between infertile women and eldest/only sons, only three marriages could be described as "stable." The rest were experiencing difficulties, and in three of these cases replacement of the infertile wife by her husband was imminent.

8. Supposedly "accidental" burning deaths are not uncommon among Egyp-

tian women, especially in rural areas where kerosene is used to light lamps and stoves. A significant proportion of these deaths are probably suicides.

9. Although mothers and sisters are usually infertile women's closest confidantes, this may not always be the case. Because of patrilocally based residence patterns, infertile women may live at some distance from their own family members, making it difficult to visit mothers and sisters regularly or to entertain them in their own homes. Without regular contact, the sharing of personal information may be difficult, and many women report that they do not want to "worry" or "upset" their mothers and sisters whom they cannot see on a regular basis. In such cases, women may find alternative confidantes, primarily friends but occasionally other members of their own or their husbands' families. In some cases where no "sympathetic others" are to be found, infertile women "keep their secrets to themselves," divulging their innermost feelings and concerns to no one else, including their husbands. In this study, several women reported that they were able to tell their stories and discuss their problems for the first time only as a result of this research. In each case, such disclosure was deemed cathartic by the women themselves.

10. Gadalla (1978), Hatem (1986c; 1987b), and Rugh (1984) have reported Egyptian women's preference for, intense identification with, and extreme closeness to their daughters, despite their need for sons in a patriarchal society where sons are valorized. However, the vast majority of literature on Egypt and on other parts of the Middle East describes the valorization of sons and women's reliance on sons under a patriarchal system without describing women's actual preferences for their daughters.

11. The Egyptian Ministry of the Interior reported that of the 775 cases of homicide in 1988, 49 of them were to "wipe out shame," a euphemism for honor killing (Lane and Daponte 1994). Honor killing may occur when a family has been "shamed" by the premarital or extramarital relations (even if they are only rumored) of a female member of the family. Typically, the girl/woman who has committed the illicit act, and especially if she has become pregnant as a result, is killed by her father, brother, uncle, or male cousin. If the man who has dishonored her is known, he may be killed by her relatives, also. Although honor killings are relatively rare, they still occur today in culturally conservative areas of Egypt, including Ṣaʿid and the rural Nile Delta. When they occur, they are reported, often sensationally, by the news media. Thus, most poor urban Egyptian women have heard heinous stories about honor killings, which probably serve to dissuade them from pre- and extramarital sex, as well as other forms of immoderate behavior.

12. Although it is uncommon, members of wives' ʿaʾilāt may occasionally exert pressure on an infertile couple to "get treated or get divorced." Most of these cases involve male infertility and pressure on the wife by her mother or other female relatives to divorce her infertile husband. Wives' family members may feel that an infertile husband is "depriving" his wife of children and that she should therefore be allowed to experience motherhood through marriage to another man.

13. In this study, for example, 9 percent of infertile couples had been or were currently involved in fostering the children of relatives.

14. Occasionally, other siblings—including women's brothers and the siblings of husbands—as well as friends of either spouse may offer their children for

fostering. In this study, two infertile couples were raising a child given to them by the wife's brother, while two others were raising children provided by a friend of the wife or husband. Interestingly, despite the often hostile relationships between infertile women and their husbands' sisters, five infertile couples in this study had been offered a foster child by a sister of the husband; three couples accepted and two rejected the offer.

15. Of the nine infertile couples in this study who had experienced familial fostering, six eventually returned their foster charges, usually per their siblings' requests.

16. In this study, of the ninety-one infertile women questioned, 58 percent believed that Islam allows adoption, and 20 percent of these women deemed it a "good deed." Similarly, 64 percent of the fifty-five fertile women questioned believed in adoption's religious permissibility. Only 34 percent of the infertile women and 20 percent of the fertile women questioned were aware of the Islamic prohibition on adoption, and the rest (8 percent of the infertile and 16 percent of the fertile) were unsure of the religious opinion on this practice.

17. In this study, thirty-seven of fifty-seven infertile women (65 percent) with an opinion on the subject refused the idea of adoption on a personal level. Furthermore, twenty-eight of thirty-nine (72 percent) said their husbands would never accept the idea. Only eleven women said that both they and their husbands would accept the idea of parenting an orphaned child; in a few of these cases, couples had actually inquired at Alexandrian orphanages about this possibility.

18. The importance of *nasab*, or relationship by blood, to both family life and inheritance practices is underscored by Islam (Sonbol 1991). Because of the emphasis on "blood" in family relationships, the issue of paternity is a very important one in Islam, with several hadith emphasizing blood relationship as the only basis for paternity (Mernissi 1985; Sonbol 1991).

19. The widespread Egyptian belief that "blood makes fonder" feelings is the basis for the questioning of the loyalty of adopted children to their adoptive (and non-"blood"-related) parents.

20. Orphanages often act as a source of social relief for poor families (Rugh 1984; Sonbol 1991). Parents who are widowed or divorced and are either unable to care for their children or are disallowed from doing so by their new spouses may place their children in orphanages but continue to visit them on a regular basis.

21. In this study, four infertile women and one fertile one reported that they, their husbands, or family friends had found an abandoned infant left on a porch or sidewalk. Three of the infertile women who had wanted to keep these abandoned infants had pleaded with their husbands to do so. But their husbands, usually upon the advice of family members, had decided that the children should be taken to the police station, from which they were then transferred to orphanages.

22. Nubians, who comprise a separate ethnic group in Egypt, tend to have darker skin than the average non-Nubian Egyptian.

Chapter 5: Endangered Neighbors

1. Actually, these were the Prophet's grandsons, Hussein and Hassan, the children of his daughter Fatima.

2. It could be argued, however, that infertile women are discredited by their visible lack of pregnancy. On the other hand, many fertile women also spend significant periods of their lives in a nonpregnant state. Thus, it would seem that infertile women do not demonstrate the physical stigmata of most discredited persons.

3. In this study, twenty-five of the ninety fertile women (28 percent) considered themselves to have been infertile at one time, usually during the first year of marriage.

4. In this study, twenty-nine of fifty-two fertile women questioned (56 percent) had an infertile relative, either in their own family, in their husband's family, or in both.

5. In this study, 17 percent of the infertile women had experienced verbal disparagement by their neighbors.

6. As with other traditional belief systems in Egypt (see Inhorn 1994), there is significant heterogeneity of belief about the evil eye and who is most likely to cast it. For example, some Egyptians argue that both men and women can cast the evil eye, while others argue that the envy that causes the evil eye to be cast "is not usually in the nature of men." Still others argue that men can envy "material things," but not children. Furthermore, some Egyptians argue that certain individuals are born with the evil eye and, hence, are permanently malignant to others. According to a number of women in this study, such individuals possess eyes that are "round" in shape.

7. In this study, thirty-eight of fifty-two fertile women (73 percent) questioned said that they, like most Egyptians, believe in the evil eye and infertile women's propensity to cast it on children. Although ten women were skeptical about the existence of the evil eye, they acknowledged that the belief is widespread and that infertile women are often suspected of harboring envious feelings toward children.

8. Not surprisingly, infertile women are less likely than women with children to believe in the evil eye, and especially their own power to cast it. In this study, for example, only twenty-four of ninety infertile women questioned (27 percent) believed in the evil eye, as opposed to 73 percent of fertile women.

9. Evil eye believers contend that these formulaic religious phrases, if uttered at the moment of envious arousal, will prevent the evil eye from being cast.

Chapter 6: Child Desire

1. Egypt's death rate is $\frac{31}{1,000}$ (as of 1993). Life expectancy at birth is age 60—59 for males and 62 for females (Population Reference Bureau 1993).

2. For example, in this study, Islamist medical practitioners were observed to urge poor, religiously illiterate female patients to discontinue the use of birth con-

trol, telling them that birth control was *ḥarām*, or sinful in the religion. Such messages tended to create cognitive dissonance among patients, who had already absorbed government messages about the religious permissibility of family planning.

3. Many poor women rely on the concept of *rizq* to justify why they experience unplanned pregnancies and why they decide not to terminate them through illegal abortions. As they explain, no matter how many children a couple begets, God helps parents to find a way to clothe and feed them. As one Islamist woman put it, "Disregarding the Egyptian economy, God says that there isn't a creature on earth whose *rizq* is not on God. Even if you're poor with lots of kids, God will give your children their own *rizq*."

Glossary of Arabic Terms

'a'ila (pl.: *'a'ilāt*): extended family.

aṣīl(a): of noble origins, good upbringing; well mannered.

aṣl: upbringing.

bait il-wilid: lit. "house of the child," as in womb, uterus.

baladī: traditional, native, folk, indigenous.

bint: girl; virgin.

bint 'amm: father's brother's daughter (i.e., patrilineal parallel cousin).

dammu khafīf: lit. "light-blooded," as in a pleasant, amiable person.

dammu ta'īl: lit. "heavy-blooded," as in a bad-tempered, unpleasant person.

dāya: traditional midwife.

dhakar: male.

dukhla: lit. "entrance," as in the wedding night (penetration).

fallāḥīn: peasants, farmers.

faraḥ: wedding party.

ghalāba: a woman who is subdued, conquered, vanquished, or defeated.

ḥālti il-nafsīya: state of mind, mood.

ḥarām: sin; forbidden (usually referring to Islam).

ḥasad: envy, the evil eye.

ḥubb: love.

ibn 'amm: father's brother's son (i.e., patrilineal parallel cousin).

ibn ḥarām: lit. "son of sin," as in a bastard, illegitimate child.

'idda: legally prescribed waiting period according to Islamic law during which a woman may not remarry after being divorced or widowed.

'ifrīt: mischievous spirit.

kalām in-nās: lit. "people's talk," as in gossip.

karāma: dignity, pride, self-esteem.

katb il-kitāb: the official writing of the Islamic marriage contract.

khair: goodness, wealth.

khallafa: to have followers, offspring, or descendants; to leave someone behind.

khuṭūba: engagement.

kunya: teknonym, consisting of "mother" or "father" followed by the name of the eldest son (or daughter if a son is absent).

mahr: bridewealth.

maksūrit il-gināḥ: lit. "broken-winged," as in a woman who is oppressed and in need of support.

mu'akkhar: lump-sum divorce settlement to be paid by a man to his ex-wife.

mu'min: faithful.

nabīy: prophet, as in the Prophet Muhammad.

nafs: human being, self, personal identity, soul, psyche, spirit, mind.

nafsīya: psychology; frame of mind.

nasab: relationship by blood.

nifsi: intense personal desire or wish, as in "I wish" or "I crave."

rizq: sustenance; means of subsistence.

Ṣaʿid: Upper Egypt.

Ṣaʿīdī: Upper Egyptian.

shabka: gift of bridal gold from the groom.

shadīd: severe.

shaikh: Muslim religious leader or cleric.

sharaf (a.k.a. *ʿirḍ*): honor.

sharīʿa: Islamic legal code.

sitt: woman; nonvirgin.

sitt il-bait (pl.: *sittāt il-bait*): housewife.

sukkar: lit. "sugar," as in diabetes.

Sunna: the way of the Prophet Muhammad.

Sunnī: religiously devout; also, the major branch of Islam.

ṣūwaf: vaginal suppositories.

ṭalāq: divorce.

ṭalāq al-bidʿa: divorce of innovation, that is, when a husband pronounces three divorce oaths at the same time, thus immediately and irrevocably dissolving the marital union.

ṭanīn: lit. "buzzing," as in social pressure through private conversation.

Umm Il-Ghāli: lit. "Mother of the Precious One"; a teknonym for an infertile woman.

Umm Il-Ghāyyib: lit. "Mother of the Missing One"; a teknonym for an infertile woman.

Umm Il-ʿIwaḍ: lit. "Mother of the Compensation"; a teknonym for an infertile woman.

usra (pl.: *usrāt*): nuclear family.

References

Abdel Kader, Soha
- 1987 "A Survey of Trends in Social Sciences Research on Women in the Arab Region, 1960–1980." In *Social Science Research and Women in the Arab World*, ed. UNESCO, 139–75. London: Frances Pinter.

Abdullah, S. A., A. Zarzoor, and M. Y. Ali
- 1982 "Epidemiological Study of Infertility in Some Villages of Assiut Governorate." *Assiut Medical Journal* 6:266–74.

Abou-Zeid, Azza A.
- 1987 "Personality Traits of the Infertile Couple." Master's thesis. High Institute of Public Health, Alexandria University, Alexandria, Egypt.

Abu-Lughod, Lila
- 1986 *Veiled Sentiments: Honor and Poetry in a Bedouin Society*. Berkeley: University of California Press.
- 1989 "Zones of Theory in the Anthropology of the Arab World." *Annual Review of Anthropology* 18:267–306.
- 1990 "The Romance of Resistance: Tracing Transformations of Power Through Bedouin Women." *American Ethnologist* 17:41–55.
- 1993 *Writing Women's Worlds: Bedouin Stories*. Berkeley: University of California Press.

Abu Nasr, Julinda, Nabil F. Khoury, and Henry T. Azzam
- 1985 "Introduction." In *Women, Employment and Development in the Arab World*. Berlin: Mouton.

Acker, Joan
- 1986 "A Review Essay." *Feminist Issues* 6:87–92.

Ahmed, Leila
- 1989 "Arab Culture and Writing Women's Bodies." *Feminist Issues* 9:41–55.
- 1992 *Women and Gender in Islam: Historical Roots of a Modern Debate*. New Haven, CT: Yale University Press.

Althusser, Louis
- 1971 *Lenin and Philosophy*. New York: Monthly Review Press.

Ammar, Hamed
- 1966 *Growing Up in an Egyptian Village*. New York: Octagon.

Ardener, Edwin
- 1975 "The Problem Revisited." In *Perceiving Women*, ed. Shirley Ardener, 19–27. London: Dent.

Aswad, Barbara C.
- 1978 "Women, Class, and Power: Examples from the Hatay, Turkey." In *Women*

in the Muslim World, ed. Lois Beck and Nikki Keddie, 473–81. Cambridge, MA: Harvard University Press.

Atiya, Nayra
1982   Khul-Khaal: *Five Egyptian Women Tell Their Stories*. Syracuse, NY: Syracuse University Press.

Azzam, Henry, Julinda Abu Nasr, and I. Lorfing
1985   "An Overview of Arab Women in Population, Employment, and Economic Development." In *Women, Employment and Development in the Arab World*, ed. Julinda Abu Nasr, Nabil F. Khoury, and Henry T. Azzam, 5–37. Berlin: Mouton.

Badran, Margot
1988   "Dual Liberation: Feminism and Nationalism in Egypt, 1870s–1925." *Feminist Issues* 8:15–34.

1993   "Independent Women: More Than a Century of Feminism in Egypt." In *Arab Women: Old Boundaries, New Frontiers*, ed. Judith E. Tucker, 129–48. Bloomington: Indiana University Press.

1994   "Gender Activism: Feminists and Islamists in Egypt." In *Identity Politics and Women: Cultural Reassertions and Feminisms in International Perspective*, ed. Valentine M. Moghadam, 202–27. Boulder, CO: Westview Press.

1995   *Feminists, Islam, and Nation: Gender and the Making of Modern Egypt*. Princeton, NJ: Princeton University Press.

Barakat, Halim
1985   "The Arab Family and the Challenge of Social Transformation." In *Women and the Family in the Middle East: New Voices of Change*, ed. Elizabeth Warnock Fernea, 27–48. Austin: University of Texas Press.

Baron, Beth
1991   "The Making and Breaking of Marital Bonds in Modern Egypt." In *Women in Middle Eastern History: Shifting Boundaries in Sex and Gender*, ed. Nikki R. Keddie and Beth Baron, 275–91. New Haven, CT: Yale University Press.

1994   *The Women's Awakening in Egypt: Culture, Society, and the Press*. New Haven, CT: Yale University Press.

Barrett, Michele
1988   *Women's Oppression Today: The Marxist-Feminist Encounter*. London: Verso.

Bennholdt-Thomsen, Veronika
1988   "Why Do Housewives Continue to Be Created in the Third World, Too?" In *Women: The Last Colony*, ed. Maria Mies, Veronika Bennholdt-Thomsen, and Claudia von Werlhof, 159–67. London: Zed.

Bill, James A.
1972   "Class Analysis and the Dialectics of Modernization in the Middle East." *International Journal of Middle East Studies* 3:417–34.

Boddy, Janice
1989   *Wombs and Alien Spirits: Women, Men, and the Zar Cult in Northern Sudan*. Madison: University of Wisconsin Press.

Bouhdiba, Abdelwahab
   1985   *Sexuality in Islam*. London: Routledge & Kegan Paul.
Bourdieu, Pierre
   1977   *Outline of a Theory of Practice*. Translated by Richard Nice. New York: Cambridge University Press.
Bowen, Donna Lee
   1993   "Pragmatic Morality: Islam and Family Planning in Morocco." In *Everyday Life in the Muslim Middle East*, ed. Donna Lee Bowen and Evelyn A. Early, 91–101. Bloomington: Indiana University Press.
Bowen, Donna Lee, and Evelyn A. Early
   1993   "Introduction." In *Everyday Life in the Muslim Middle East*, ed. Donna Lee Bowen and Evelyn A. Early, 1–16. Bloomington: Indiana University Press.
Brink, Judy H.
   1987   "Changing Extended Family Relationships in an Egyptian Village." *Urban Anthropology* 16:133–49.
Brydon, Lynne, and Sylvia Chant
   1989   "Introduction: Women in the Third World: An Overview." In *Women in the Third World: Gender Issues in Rural and Urban Areas*. Hants, England: Edward Elgar.
Caldwell, James C.
   1978   "A Theory of Fertility: From High Plateau to Destabilization." *Population and Development Review* 4:553–77.
   1982   *A Theory of Fertility Decline*. London: Academic Press.
Cochrane, Susan Hill, M. Ali Khan, and Ibrahim Khodair T. Osheba
   1990   "Education, Income, and Desired Fertility in Egypt: A Revised Perspective." *Economic Development and Cultural Change* 38:313–39.
Connell, R. W.
   1990   "The State, Gender, and Sexual Politics: Theory and Appraisal." *Theory and Society* 19:507–44.
Coulson, Noel, and Doreen Hinchcliffe
   1978   "Women and Law Reform in Contemporary Islam." In *Women in the Muslim World*, ed. Lois Beck and Nikki Keddie, 37–51. Cambridge, MA: Harvard University Press.
Cowan, J. Milton, ed.
   1976   *The Hans Wehr Dictionary of Modern Written Arabic*, 3d ed. Ithaca, NY: Spoken Languages Services.
Crapanzano, Vincent
   1973   *The Hamadsha: A Study in Moroccan Ethnopsychiatry*. Berkeley: University of California Press.
de Certeau, Michel
   1984   *The Practice of Everyday Life*. Berkeley: University of California Press.
DeClerque, Julia, Amy Ong Tsui, Mohammed Futuah Abul-Ata, and Delia Barcelona
   1986   "Rumor, Misinformation and Oral Contraceptive Use in Egypt." *Social Science & Medicine* 23:83–92.

Delaney, Carol
    1991   *The Seed and the Soil: Gender and Cosmology in Turkish Village Society*. Berkeley: University of California Press.
di Leonardo, Micaela
    1991   "Introduction: Gender, Culture, and Political Economy—Feminist Anthropology in Historical Perspective." In *Gender at the Crossroads of Knowledge: Feminist Anthropology in the Postmodern Era*, ed. Micaela di Leonardo, 1–48. Berkeley: University of California Press.
Dundes, Alan, ed.
    1992   *The Evil Eye: A Casebook*. Madison: University of Wisconsin Press.
Dwyer, Daisy Hilse
    1978a   "Ideologies of Sexual Inequality and Strategies for Change in Male-Female Relations." *American Ethnologist* 5:227–40.
    1978b   *Images and Self-Images: Male and Female in Morocco*. New York: Columbia University Press.
Early, Evelyn A.
    1982   "The Logic of Well Being: Therapeutic Narratives in Cairo, Egypt." *Social Science and Medicine* 16:1491–97.
    1985   "Catharsis and Creation in Informal Narratives of Baladi Women of Cairo." *Anthropological Quarterly* 58:172–81.
    1993   "Fertility and Fate: Medical Practices Among *Baladi* Women of Cairo." In *Everyday Life in the Muslim Middle East*, ed. Donna Lee Bowen and Evelyn A. Early, 102–8. Bloomington: Indiana University Press.
Egyptian Ministry of Information
    1985   *Egyptian Women*. Cairo: Egyptian Ministry of Information.
Ehrenreich, Barbara, and Deirdre English
    1978   *For Her Own Good: 150 Years of the Experts' Advice to Women*. New York: Anchor.
Eickelman, Dale F.
    1989   *The Middle East: An Anthropological Approach*. 2d ed. Englewood Cliffs, NJ: Prentice-Hall.
El Guindi, Fadwa
    1981   "Veiling Infitah with Muslim Ethic: Egypt's Contemporary Islamic Movement." *Social Problems* 28:465–85.
El-Messiri, Sawsun
    1978   *Ibn Al-Balad: A Concept of Egyptian Identity*. Leiden: E. J. Brill.
El Saadawi, Nawal
    1980   *The Hidden Face of Eve: Women in the Arab World*. Boston: Beacon Press.
Esposito, John L.
    1982   *Women in Muslim Family Law*. Syracuse, NY: Syracuse University Press.
    1991   *Islam: The Straight Path*. New York: Oxford University Press.
Farley, T. M. M., and E. M. Belsey
    1988   *The Prevalence and Aetiology of Infertility*. Paper presented at the International Union for the Scientific Study of the Population, African Population Conference, Dakar, Senegal, November 1988.

Fernea, Elizabeth Warnock, and Basima Qattan Bezirgan
  1985   "'A'ishah bint Abi Bakr: Wife of the Prophet Muhammad." In *Middle Eastern Muslim Women Speak*, ed. Elizabeth Warnock Fernea and Basima Qattan Bezirgan, 27–36. Austin: University of Texas Press.

Fluehr-Lobban, Carolyn
  1990   *Modern Egypt and Its Heritage*. Pittsburgh: Carnegie Museum of Natural History.

Foucault, Michel
  1977   *Discipline and Punish: The Birth of the Prison*. Translated by Alan Sheridan. New York: Vintage.
  1978   *The History of Sexuality*. Vol. 1, *An Introduction*. New York: Random House.

Fox, Karen F. A.
  1988   "Social Marketing of Oral Rehydration Therapy and Contraceptives in Egypt." *Studies in Family Planning* 19:95–108.

Friedl, Erika
  1989   *Women of Deh Koh: Lives in an Iranian Village*. New York: Penguin.

Gadalla, Saad
  1977   "The Influence of Reproductive Norms on Family Size and Fertility Behavior in Rural Egypt." In *Arab Society in Transition*, ed. Saad Eddin Ibrahim and Nicholas S. Hopkins, 323–42. Cairo: American University in Cairo Press.
  1978   *Is There Hope? Fertility and Family Planning in a Rural Egyptian Community*. Cairo: American University in Cairo Press.

Gadalla, Saad, James McCarthy, and Oona Campbell
  1985   "How the Number of Living Sons Influences Contraceptive Use in Menoufia Governorate, Egypt." *Studies in Family Planning* 16:164–69.

Gadalla, Saad, Nazek Nosseir, and Duff G. Gillespie
  1980   "Household Distribution of Contraceptives in Rural Egypt." *Studies in Family Planning* 11:105–13.

Gadalla, Saad, and Hanna Rizk
  1988   *Population Policy and Family Planning Communications Strategies in the Arab States Region*. Vol. 2 of *State of the Art in the Arab World*. UNESCO.

Gendzier, Irene L.
  1981   Foreword to *The Hidden Face of Eve: Women in the Arab World*, by Nawal El Saadawi, vii–xix. Boston: Beacon Press.

Ghosh, Amitav
  1983   "The Relations of Envy in an Egyptian Village." *Ethnology* 22:211–23.

Gilmore, David D.
  1987   "Introduction: The Shame of Dishonor." In *Honor and Shame in the Unity of the Mediterranean*, ed. David D. Gilmore, 2–21. Washington, DC: American Anthropological Association Special Publication 22.

Ginsburg, Faye, and Rayna Rapp
  1991   "The Politics of Reproduction." *Annual Review of Anthropology* 20:311–43.

Goffman, Erving
    1963   *Stigma: Notes on the Management of Spoiled Identity*. Englewood Cliffs, NJ:
            Prentice-Hall.
Good, Mary-Jo DelVecchio
    1980   "Of Blood and Babies: The Relationship of Popular Islamic Physiology
            to Fertility." *Social Science & Medicine* 14B:147–56.
Gramsci, Antonio
    1971   *Selections from the Prison Notebooks*. London: Lawrence and Wishart.
Greenwood, Bernard
    1981   "III(a) Perceiving Systems: Cold or Spirits? Choice and Ambiguity in
            Morocco's Pluralistic Medical System." *Social Science & Medicine* 15B:
            219–35.
Haddad, Yvonne Yazbeck
    1980   "Traditional Affirmations Concerning the Role of Women as Found in
            Contemporary Arab Islamic Literature." In *Women in Contemporary Mus-
            lim Societies*, ed. Jane I. Smith, 61–86. Lewisburg, PA: Bucknell University
            Press.
Hammam, Mona
    1979   "Egypt's Working Women: Textile Workers of Chubra el-Kheima."
            MERIP Reports 9(9):3–7.
Harding, Sandra
    1986   *The Science Question in Feminism*. Ithaca, NY: Cornell University Press.
Harfouche, Jamal Karam
    1992   "The Evil Eye and Infant Health in Lebanon." In *The Evil Eye: A Case-
            book*, ed. Alan Dundes, 86–106. Madison: University of Wisconsin Press.
Hatem, Mervat
    1984   "Women's Rights, Development and Feminist Politics in Egypt." Paper
            presented at the National Women's Studies Conference, New Brunswick,
            NJ, June 24–27.
    1986a   "The Enduring Alliance of Nationalism and Patriarchy in Muslim Per-
            sonal Status Laws: The Case of Modern Egypt." *Feminist Issues* 6:19–43.
    1986b   "The Politics of Sexuality and Gender in Segregated Patriarchal Sys-
            tems: The Case of Eighteenth- and Nineteenth-Century Egypt." *Feminist
            Studies* 12:251–74.
    1986c   "Underdevelopment, Mothering and Gender Within the Egyptian
            Family." *Arab Studies Quarterly* 8:45–61.
    1987a   "Class and Patriarchy as Competing Paradigms for the Study of Middle
            Eastern Women." *Comparative Studies in Society and History* 29:811–18.
    1987b   "Toward the Study of the Psychodynamics of Mothering and Gender in
            Egyptian Families." *International Journal of Middle East Studies* 19:287–
            306.
    1993   "Toward the Development of Post-Islamist and Post-Nationalist Femi-
            nist Discourses in the Middle East." In *Arab Women: Old Boundaries, New
            Frontiers*, ed. Judith E. Tucker, 29–48. Bloomington: Indiana University
            Press.

Helie-Lucas, Marie-Aimee
    1994   "The Preferential Symbol for Islamic Identity: Women in Muslim Personal Laws." In *Identity Politics and Women: Cultural Reassertions and Feminisms in International Perspective*, ed. Valentine M. Moghadam, 391–407. Boulder, CO: Westview Press.

Hoodfar, Homa
    1988   "Household Budgeting and Financial Management in a Lower-Income Cairo Neighborhood." In *A Home Divided: Women and Income in the Third World*, ed. Daisy Dwyer and Judith Bruce, 120–42. Palo Alto, CA: Stanford University Press.
    1991   "Return to the Veil: Personal Strategy and Public Participation in Egypt." In *Working Women: International Perspectives on Labour and Gender Ideology*, ed. Nanneke Redclift and M. Thea Sinclair, 104–24. New York: Routledge.

Ibrahim, Barbara Lethem
    1985a   "Cairo's Factory Women." In *Women and the Family in the Middle East: New Voices of Change*, ed. Elizabeth Warnock Fernea, 293–99. Austin: University of Texas Press.
    1985b   "Family Strategies: A Perspective on Women's Entry to the Labor Force in Egypt." In *Arab Society: Social Science Perspectives*, ed. Nicholas S. Hopkins and Saad Eddin Ibrahim, 257–68. Cairo: American University in Cairo Press.

Ibrahim, Saad Eddin
    1982   "Social Mobility and Income Distribution in Egypt, 1952–1977." In *The Political Economy of Income Distribution in Egypt*, ed. Gouda Abdel Khalek and Robert Tignor, 375–434. New York: Holmes and Meier.
    1985   "Urbanization in the Arab World: The Need for an Urban Strategy." In *Arab Society: Social Science Perspectives*, ed. Nicholas S. Hopkins and Saad Eddin Ibrahim, 123–47. Cairo: American University in Cairo Press.

Inhorn, Marcia C.
    1994   *Quest for Conception: Gender, Infertility, and Egyptian Medical Traditions*. Philadelphia: University of Pennsylvania Press.
    1996   "Population, Poverty, and Gender Politics: Motherhood Pressures and Marital Crises in Poor Urban Egyptian Women's Lives." In *Middle East Cities in Crisis: Population, Poverty, and Politics*, ed. Michael E. Bonine. Gainesville: University Press of Florida, forthcoming.
    n.d.a   "Sex, Medicine, and Infertility in Egypt: Doctors in Denial, Patients in Predicaments." Unpublished manuscript.
    n.d.b   " 'The Worms Are Weak': Patriarchy, Procreative Ideology, and the Paradoxes of Male Infertility in Urban Egypt." Unpublished manuscript.

Inhorn, Marcia C., and Kimberly A. Buss
    1993   "Infertility, Infection, and Iatrogenesis in Egypt: The Anthropological Epidemiology of Blocked Tubes." *Medical Anthropology* 15:1–28.
    1994   "Ethnography, Epidemiology, and Infertility in Egypt." *Social Science and Medicine* 39:671–86.

Irigaray, Luce
    1985 *This Sex Which Is Not One*. Translated by Catherine Porter. Ithaca, NY:
            Cornell University Press.
Jaggar, Alison M.
    1983 *Feminist Politics and Human Nature*. Totowa, NJ: Rowman & Allanheld.
Jemai, Hedi
    1993 "Women and Development in the Arab World." Paper presented at the
            Arab Population Conference, Amman, Jordan, April 4–6.
Jones, Kathleen B.
    1988 "On Authority: Or, Why Women Are Not Entitled to Speak." In *Femi-
            nism and Foucault: Reflections on Resistance*, ed. Irene Diamond and Lee
            Quinby, 119–33. Boston, MA: Northeastern University Press.
Jordan, Brigitte
    1987 "Crosscultural Theories of Conception, Gestation, and the Newborn: The
            Achievement of Personhood." Unpublished manuscript.
Joseph, Suad
    1986 "Study of Middle Eastern Women: Investments, Passions, and Problems."
            International Journal of Middle East Studies 18:501–48.
    1993 "Connectivity and Patriarchy Among Urban Working-Class Arab Fami-
            lies in Lebanon." *Ethos* 21:452–84.
    1994 "Brother/Sister Relationships: Connectivity, Love, and Power in the Re-
            production of Patriarchy in Lebanon." *American Ethnologist* 21:50–73.
Jowkar, Forouz
    1986 "Honor and Shame: A Feminist View from Within." *Feminist Issues* 6:45–
            65.
Kandiyoti, Deniz
    1988 "Bargaining with Patriarchy." *Gender and Society* 2:274–90.
    1991 "Islam and Patriarchy: A Comparative Perspective." In *Women in Middle
            Eastern History: Shifting Boundaries in Sex and Gender*, ed. Nikki R. Ked-
            die and Beth Baron, 23–42. New Haven, CT: Yale University Press.
Keddie, Nikki R.
    1979 "Problems in the Study of Middle Eastern Women." *International Journal
            of Middle East Studies* 10:225–40.
Keller, Catherine
    1986 *From a Broken Web: Separation, Sexism, and Self*. Boston, MA: Beacon
            Press.
Kennedy, Mark C.
    1991 "Dilemmas in Middle Eastern Social Sciences: Contours of the Problem
            of the Relevance of Western Paradigms as Guides to Research, Policy and
            Practice." In *The Contemporary Study of the Arab World*, ed. Earl L. Sullivan
            and Jacqueline S. Ismael, 65–80. Edmonton: University of Alberta Press.
Khattab, Hind A., and Syeda Greiss el-Daeiff
    1984 "Female Education in Egypt: Changing Attitudes over a Span of 100
            Years." In *Muslim Women*, ed. Freda Hussain, 169–97. New York: St.
            Martin's Press.

Kiray, Mubeccel
　　1976　"The New Role of Mothers: Changing Intra-Familial Relationships in a Small Town in Turkey." In *Mediterranean Family Structures*, ed. J. G. Peristiany, 261–71. Cambridge: Cambridge University Press.
Kleinman, Arthur M.
　　1992　"Local Moral Worlds of Suffering: An Interpersonal Focus for Ethnographies of Illness Experience." *Qualitative Health Research* 2:127–34.
Lane, Sandra D., and Beth Osborn Daponte
　　1994　"Gender-Linked Health Risks in Egypt." Paper presented at the 93rd Annual Meeting of the American Anthropological Association, Atlanta, Georgia, December 3.
Lane, Sandra D., and Afaf I. Meleis
　　1991　"Roles, Work, Health Perceptions and Health Resources of Women: A Study in an Egyptian Delta Hamlet." *Social Science and Medicine* 33:1197–1208.
Lane, Sandra D., and Robert A. Rubinstein
　　1991　"The Use of *Fatwas* in the Production of Reproductive Health Policy in Egypt." Paper presented at the 90th Annual Meeting of the American Anthropological Association, Chicago, November 23.
LaTowsky, Robert J.
　　1984　"Egyptian Labor Abroad: Mass Participation and Modest Returns." *MERIP Reports* 14:11–18.
LeFebvre, Henri
　　1971　*Everyday Life in the Modern World*. Translated by Sacha Rabinovich. New York: Harper and Row.
Lerner, Gerda
　　1986　*The Creation of Patriarchy*. New York: Oxford University Press.
MacLeod, Arlene Elowe
　　1991　*Accommodating Protest: Working Women, the New Veiling, and Change in Cairo*. New York: Columbia University Press.
Maloney, Clarence
　　1976a　"Introduction." In *The Evil Eye*, ed. Clarence Maloney, v–xvi. New York: Columbia University Press.
　　———, ed.
　　1976b　*The Evil Eye*. New York: Columbia University Press.
Marshall, Susan E.
　　1984　"Politics and Female Status in North Africa: A Reconsideration of Development Theory." *Economic Development and Cultural Change* 32:499–524.
Marsot, Afaf Lutfi al-Sayyid
　　1978　"The Revolutionary Gentlewoman in Egypt." In *Women in the Muslim World*, ed. Lois Beck and Nikki Keddie, 261–75. Cambridge, MA: Harvard University Press.
Mernissi, Fatima
　　1985　*Beyond the Veil: Male-Female Dynamics in Muslim Society*. London: Al Saqi Books.

1989   *Doing Daily Battle: Interviews with Moroccan Women*. Translated by Mary Jo Lakeland. New Brunswick, NJ: Rutgers University Press.

Mitchell, Tim

1991   "America's Egypt: Discourse of the Development Industry." *Middle East Report* 21(2):18–36.

Moghadam, Valentine M.

1993   *Modernizing Women: Gender and Social Change in the Middle East*. Boulder, CO: Lynne Rienner.

1994   "Introduction: Women and Identity Politics in Theoretical and Comparative Perspective." In *Identity Politics and Women: Cultural Reassertions and Feminisms in International Perspective*, ed. Valentine M. Moghadam, 3–26. Boulder, CO: Westview Press.

Mohsen, Safia K.

1985   "New Images, Old Reflections: Working Middle-Class Women in Egypt." In *Women and the Family in the Middle East: New Voices of Change*, ed. Elizabeth Warnock Fernea, 56–71. Austin: University of Texas Press.

Moore, Henrietta L.

1988   *Feminism and Anthropology*. Cambridge, England: Polity Press.

Morsy, Soheir A.

1978a   "Sex Differences and Folk Illness in an Egyptian Village." In *Women in the Muslim World*, ed. Lois Beck and Nikki Keddie, 599–616. Cambridge, MA: Harvard University Press.

1978b   "Sex Roles, Power, and Illness in an Egyptian Village." *American Ethnologist* 5:137–50.

1980   "Body Concepts and Health Care: Illustrations from an Egyptian Village." *Human Organization* 39:92–96.

1990   "Rural Women, Work and Gender Ideology: A Study in Egyptian Political Economic Transformation." In *Women in Arab Society: Work Patterns and Gender Relations in Egypt, Jordan and Sudan*, by Seteney Shami, Lucine Taminian, Soheir A. Morsy, Zeinab B. El Bakri, and El-Wathig M. Khameir, 97–159. Paris: Berg/UNESCO.

Morsy, Soheir, Cynthia Nelson, Reem Saad, and Hania Sholkamy

1991   "Anthropology and the Call for Indigenization of Social Science in the Arab World." In *The Contemporary Study of the Arab World*, ed. Earl L. Sullivan and Jacqueline S. Ismael, 81–111. Edmonton: University of Alberta Press.

Musallam, B. F.

1983   *Sex and Society in Islam: Birth Control Before the Nineteenth Century*. Cambridge: Cambridge University Press.

Nader, Laura

1989   "Orientalism, Occidentalism and the Control of Women." *Cultural Dynamics* 2:323–55.

Nadim, Nawal Al-Messiri

1985   "Family Relationships in a 'Harah' in Cairo." In *Arab Society: Social Science Perspectives*, ed. Nicholas S. Hopkins and Saad Eddin Ibrahim, 212–22. Cairo: American University in Cairo Press.

Nelson, Cynthia
 1974   "Public and Private Politics: Women in the Middle Eastern World."
        American Ethnologist 1:551–63.
 1976   "Social Change and Sexual Identity in Contemporary Egypt." In *Responses
        to Change: Society, Culture, and Personality*, ed. George A. DeVos, 323–41.
        New York: D. Van Nostrand.
 1991   "Old Wine, New Bottles: Reflections and Projections Concerning Re-
        search on Women in Middle Eastern Studies." In *The Contemporary Study
        of the Arab World*, ed. Earl L. Sullivan and Jacqueline S. Ismael, 127–52.
        Edmonton: University of Alberta Press.
Oakley, Ann
 1974   *Woman's Work: The Housewife, Past and Present*. New York: Pantheon.
Obermeyer, Carla Makhlouf
 1992   "Islam, Women, and Politics: The Demography of Arab Countries." *Popu-
        lation and Development Review* 18:33–60.
Omran, Abdel Rahim
 1992   *Family Planning in the Legacy of Islam*. London: Routledge.
Omran, Abdel R., and Farzaneh Roudi
 1993   "The Middle East Population Puzzle." *Population Bulletin* 48(1)1–40.
Ortner, Sherry B.
 1974   "Is Female to Male as Nature Is to Culture?" In *Woman, Culture, and
        Society*, ed. Michelle Zimbalist Rosaldo and Louise Lamphere, 67–87.
        Stanford, CA: Stanford University Press.
 1978   "The Virgin and the State." *Feminist Studies* 4:19–33.
Philipp, Thomas
 1978   "Feminism and Nationalist Politics in Egypt." In *Women in the Muslim
        World*, ed. Lois Beck and Nikki Keddie, 277–94. Cambridge, MA: Har-
        vard University Press.
Population Reference Bureau
 1993   *World Population Data Sheet of the Population Reference Bureau, Inc.: Demo-
        graphic Data and Estimates for the Countries and Regions of the World*. Wash-
        ington, DC: Population Reference Bureau.
Rassam, Amal
 1987   "Towards a Theoretical Framework for the Study of Women in the Arab
        World." In *Social Science Research and Women in the Arab World*, ed.
        UNESCO, 122–38. London: Frances Pinter.
Rich, Adrienne
 1976   *Of Woman Born: Motherhood as Experience and Institution*. New York:
        W. W. Norton.
Rosaldo, Michelle Zimbalist
 1974   "Women, Culture, and Society: A Theoretical Overview." In *Woman, Cul-
        ture, and Society*, ed. Michelle Zimbalist Rosaldo and Louise Lamphere,
        17–42. Stanford, CA: Stanford University Press.
Rosen, Lawrence
 1978   "The Negotiation of Reality: Male-Female Relations in Sefrou, Morocco."
        In *Women in the Muslim World*, ed. Lois Beck and Nikki Keddie, 561–84.
        Cambridge, MA: Harvard University Press.

Rowland, Robyn
   1992   *Living Laboratories: Women and Reproductive Technology*. London: Lime
          Tree.
Rugh, Andrea B.
   1982   Foreword to *Khul-Khaal: Five Egyptian Women Tell Their Stories*, by Nayra
          Atiya, vii–xxii. Syracuse, NY: Syracuse University Press.
   1984   *Family in Contemporary Egypt*. Syracuse, NY: Syracuse University Press.
   1985   "Women and Work: Strategies and Choices in a Lower-Class Quarter of
          Cairo." In *Women and the Family in the Middle East: New Voices of Change*,
          ed. Elizabeth Warnock Fernea, 273–88. Austin: University of Texas Press.
Sabbah, Fatna A.
   1984   *Woman in the Muslim Unconscious*. New York: Pergamon Press.
Sacks, Karen Brodkin
   1989   "Toward a Unified Theory of Class, Race, and Gender." *American Eth-
          nologist* 16:534–50.
Schiffer, Robert L.
   1988   "The Exploding City." *Populi* 15:49–54.
Schleifer, Aliah
   1986   *Motherhood in Islam*. Cambridge, England: Islamic Academy.
Schur, Edwin M.
   1984   *Labeling Women Deviant: Gender, Stigma, and Social Control*. Philadelphia,
          PA: Temple University Press.
Scott, James C.
   1985   *Weapons of the Weak: Everyday Forms of Peasant Resistance*. New Haven,
          CT: Yale University Press.
Serour, G. I., M. El Ghar, and R. T. Mansour
   1991   "Infertility: A Health Problem in Muslim World." *Population Sciences* 10:
          41–58.
Sharabi, Hisham
   1988   *Neopatriarchy: A Theory of Distorted Change in Arab Society*. New York:
          Oxford.
Smock, Audrey Chapman, and Nadia Haggag Youssef
   1977   "Egypt: From Seclusion to Limited Participation." In *Women: Roles and
          Status in Eight Countries*, ed. Janet Zollinger Giele and Audrey Chapman
          Smock, 34–79. New York: John Wiley.
Sonbol, Amira el Azhary
   1992   "Adoption in Islamic Society: A Historical Survey." Paper presented at
          the 26th Annual Meeting of the Middle East Studies Association, Port-
          land, Oregon.
Spivak, Gayatri Chakravorty
   1988   "Can the Subaltern Speak?" In *Marxism and the Interpretation of Culture*,
          ed. Cary Nelson and Lawrence Grossberg, 271–313. Urbana: University
          of Illinois Press.
Spooner, Brian
   1976   "The Evil Eye in the Middle East." In *The Evil Eye*, ed. Clarence Maloney,
          76–84. New York: Columbia University Press.

Stokes, C. Shannon, Wayne A. Schutjer, and John R. Poindexter
   1983   "A Note on Desired Family Size and Contraceptive Use in Rural Egypt."
           Journal of Biosocial Science 15:59–65.
Stowasser, Barbara F.
   1987   *The Islamic Impulse*. London: Croom Helm.
   1993   "Women's Issues in Modern Islamic Thought." In *Arab Women: Old
           Boundaries, New Frontiers*, ed. Judith E. Tucker, 3–28. Bloomington: Indi-
           ana University Press.
Strathern, Marilyn
   1987   "An Awkward Relationship: The Case of Feminism and Anthropology."
           Signs: Journal of Women in Culture and Society 12:276–92.
Stycos, J. Mayone, Hussein Abdel Aziz Sayed, Roger Avery, and Samuel Fridman
   1988   *Community Development and Family Planning: An Egyptian Experiment*.
           Boulder, CO: Westview Press.
Sullivan, Earl L.
   1981   "Women and Work in Egypt." *Cairo Papers in Social Science* 4:1–44.
Sullivan, Earl L., and Jacqueline S. Ismael
   1991a   "Introduction: Critical Perspectives on Arab Studies." In *The Contempo-
           rary Study of the Arab World*, ed. Earl L. Sullivan and Jacqueline S. Ismael,
           1–32. Edmonton: University of Alberta Press.
   ———, eds.
   1991b   *The Contemporary Study of the Arab World*. Edmonton: University of
           Alberta Press.
Taylor, Elizabeth
   1984   "Egyptian Migration and Peasant Wives." *MERIP Reports* 14(5):3–10.
Tillion, Germaine
   1983   *The Republic of Cousins*. London: Al-Saqi Books.
Tong, Rosemarie
   1989   *Feminist Thought: A Comprehensive Introduction*. Boulder, CO: Westview
           Press.
Toth, James
   1991   "Pride, Purdah, or Paychecks: What Maintains the Gender Division of
           Labor in Rural Egypt?" *International Journal of Middle East Studies* 23:
           213–36.
Tucker, Judith E.
   1985   *Women in Nineteenth-Century Egypt*. Cambridge: Cambridge University
           Press.
   1993   "Introduction." In *Arab Women: Old Boundaries, New Frontiers*, ed. Judith
           E. Tucker, vii–xviii. Bloomington: Indiana University Press.
Turner, Bryan S.
   1987   *Medical Power and Social Knowledge*. London: Sage.
Turner, Victor W.
   1974   *Dramas, Fields and Metaphors*. Ithaca, NY: Cornell University Press.
UNICEF
   1985   *Child Care in Islam*. Cairo: UNICEF.

Valsiner, Joan

1989   *Human Development and Culture*. New York: Lexington Books.

van Spijk, Marileen van der Most, Hoda Youssef Fahmy, and Sonja Zimmerman

1982   *Remember to Be Firm: Life Histories of Three Egyptian Women*. Leiden: Research Centre for Women and Development, State University of Leiden.

Warren, Kay B., and Susan C. Bourque

1991   "Women, Technology and International Development Ideologies: Analyzing Feminist Voices." In *Gender at the Crossroads of Knowledge: Feminist Anthropology in the Postmodern Era*, ed. Micaela di Leonardo, 278–311. Berkeley: University of California Press.

Watson, Helen

1992   *Women in the City of the Dead*. London: Hurst.

Weeks, John R.

1988   "The Demography of Islamic Nations." *Population Bulletin* 43(4):1–54.

White, Elizabeth H.

1978   "Legal Reform as an Indicator of Women's Status in Muslim Nations." In *Women in the Muslim World*, ed. Lois Beck and Nikki Keddie, 52–68. Cambridge, MA: Harvard University Press.

Wikan, Unni

1980   *Life Among the Poor in Cairo*. London: Tavistock.

Williams, John Alden

1980   "Veiling in Egypt as a Political and Social Phenomenon." In *Islam and Development: Religion and Sociopolitical Change*, ed. John L. Esposito, 71–85. Syracuse, NY: Syracuse University Press.

Wrong, Dennis H.

n.d.   "Some Problems in Defining Social Power." Unpublished manuscript.

Yanagisako, Sylvia Junko, and Jane Fishburne Collier

1987   "Toward a Unified Analysis of Gender and Kinship." In *Gender and Kinship*, ed. Jane Fishburne Collier and Sylvia Junko Yanagisako, 14–50. Stanford, CA: Stanford University Press.

Yassin, Shadia A. T.

1985   "A Comparative Study of the Personality Traits of Infertile and Fertile Egyptian Females." Master's thesis. High Institute of Nursing, Alexandria University, Alexandria, Egypt.

Young, Iris

1981   "Beyond the Unhappy Marriage: A Critique of the Dual Systems Theory." In *Women and Revolution: A Discussion of the Unhappy Marriage of Marxism and Feminism*, ed. Lydia Sargent, 43–69. Boston, MA: South End Press.

Youssef, Nadia H.

1978   "The Status and Fertility Patterns of Muslim Women." In *Women in the Muslim World*, ed. Lois Beck and Nikki Keddie, 69–99. Cambridge, MA: Harvard University Press.

Zuhur, Sherifa

1992   *Revealing Reveiling: Islamist Gender Ideology in Contemporary Egypt*. Albany: State University of New York Press.

Index

This book has been set in Carter & Cone Galliard. Galliard was designed for Mergenthaler in 1978 by Matthew Carter. Galliard retains many of the features of a sixteenth-century typeface cut by Robert Granjon but has some modifications that give it a more contemporary look.

Printed on acid-free paper.